The Enlightenment

The Enlightenment

HISTORY, DOCUMENTS, AND KEY QUESTIONS

William E. Burns

Crossroads in World History

An Imprint of ABC-CLIO, LLC
Santa Barbara, California • Denver, Colorado

Library of Congress Cataloging-in-Publication Data

Names: Burns, William E., 1959- author.
Title: The Enlightenment : history, documents, and key questions / William E. Burns.
Description: Santa Barbara, California : ABC-CLIO, LLC, 2016. | Series: Crossroads in world history | Includes bibliographical references and index.
Identifiers: LCCN 2015028980| ISBN 9781610698450 (acid-free paper) | ISBN 9781610698467 (ebook)
Subjects: LCSH: Enlightenment. | Enlightenment—Sources. | Enlightenment— Examinations, questions, etc. | Europe—Civilization—18th century. | Europe— Intellectual life—18th century. | Europe—Colonies—Civilization—18th century.
Classification: LCC CB411 .B87 2016 | DDC 909.7—dc23 LC record available at http://lccn.loc.gov/2015028980

ISBN: 978-1-61069-845-0
EISBN: 978-1-61069-846-7

20 19 18 17 16   1 2 3 4 5

This book is also available on the World Wide Web as an eBook.
Visit www.abc-clio.com for details.

ABC-CLIO
An Imprint of ABC-CLIO, LLC

ABC-CLIO, LLC
130 Cremona Drive, P.O. Box 1911
Santa Barbara, California 93116-1911

This book is printed on acid-free paper ∞
Manufactured in the United States of America

Dedicated to Leisha and Crystal

Contents

Alphabetical List of Entries

Topical List of Entries

ATTITUDES TOWARD OTHER CIVILIZATIONS AND CULTURES

Enlightenment Views of Africa and Africans
Enlightenment Views of Asian Civilizations
Enlightenment Views of Jews and Judaism
Enlightenment Views of Muslims and Islam
Enlightenment Views of Native Americans

BIOGRAPHIES

Alembert, Jean Le Rond d'
Beccaria, Cesare
Catherine II, "the Great," of Russia
Châtelet, Émilie du
Condorcet, Marie-Jean-Antoine-Nicolas Caritat, Marquis de
Diderot, Denis
Franklin, Benjamin
Frederick II, "the Great," of Prussia
Gibbon, Edward
Holbach, Paul Heinrich Dietrich, Baron d'
Hume, David
Joseph II, of Austria
Kant, Immanuel
Leibniz, Gottfried Wilhelm
Lessing, Gotthold Ephraim

Locke, John
Mendelssohn, Moses
Montesquieu, Charles-Louis de Secondat, Baron de
Newton, Isaac
Paine, Thomas
Pombal, Sebastião José de Carvalho e Melo, 1st Marquis of
Priestley, Joseph
Rousseau, Jean-Jacques
Smith, Adam
Spinoza, Baruch
Voltaire

EVENTS

American Revolution and Founding
Calas Case
French Revolution
Lisbon Earthquake

INSTITUTIONS

Academies and Learned Societies
Freemasonry
Jesuits
Salons

REGIONAL AND ETHNIC ENLIGHTENMENTS

England, the Enlightenment in
France, the Enlightenment in
Germany, the Enlightenment in
Italy, the Enlightenment in
Jewish Enlightenment
Scotland, the Enlightenment in

TEXTS

Bible, the
Books, Publishing, and Censorship
Encyclopédie

THEMES

Art and Architecture
Colonialism
Economics
Education
Gender
Literature
Nature
Political Philosophy
Religion
Science
Sex
Slavery
Theater

How to Use This Book

Throughout the course of history various events have forever changed the world. Some—such as the assassination of Julius Caesar—happened centuries ago and took place quickly. Others—such as the rise of Christianity or the Enlightenment—occurred over an extended period and reshaped worldviews. These pivotal events—or crossroads—were departures from the established social order and pointed to new directions and opportunities. The paths leading to these crossroads in world history often were circuitous, and the routes which branched off from them led to developments both anticipated and unexpected. This series helps readers to understand the causes and consequences of these historical turning points.

Each book in this series explores particular crossroads in world history. Some of these events are from the ancient world and continue to reverberate today through our various political, cultural, and social institutions. Others are from the modern era and have markedly changed society through their immediacy and the force of technology. The books help readers to discover what happened, and to understand the causes and effects linked to each event.

Each volume in the series begins with a time line charting the essential elements of the event in capsule form. An overview essay comes next, providing a narrative history of what occurred. This is followed by approximately 50 alphabetically arranged reference entries describing people, places, themes, movements, and other topics central to an understanding of the historical crossroad. These entries provide essential information about their topics and close with cross references and suggestions for further reading. A selection of 10 to 15 primary source documents follows the reference entries. Each document is accompanied by an introductory paragraph discussing the background and significance of the text. Due to their critical nature, the events covered in these volumes have generated a wide range of opinions and arguments. A section of original essays presents responses to key questions concerning the events, with each writer offering a different perspective on a particular topic. An annotated bibliography of print and electronic resources concludes the volume. Users can locate specific information through an alphabetical list of entries and a list of entries grouped in topical categories, as well as through a detailed index.

The various elements of each book are designed to work together to promote greater understanding of a crossroad in world history. The timeline and introductory essay overview the event, the reference entries offer easy access to essential information about key topics, the primary source documents give firsthand accounts of the historical event, and the original argumentative essays encourage readers to consider different views related to the events and to appreciate the complex nature of world history. Through its combination of background material, primary source documents, and argumentative essays, the series helps provide insight into historical causation as for those learning about the pivotal events that changed the course of history.

Preface

The 18th century in Europe and its colonies saw a revolution of the mind. In sphere after sphere of thought, traditional authorities and customs—often but not always religious—were challenged in the name of reason. We call this revolution "the Enlightenment." In many areas, the Enlightenment marks the beginning of a distinctly modern era, leading to the creation of an industrial capitalist economy, religious pluralism, and new, more democratic and less tradition-bound politics arising after the American Revolution and the French Revolution.

A clo look, however, shows that the unity of the Enlightenment gives way to its diversity. The Enlightenment was French salons, English academies; and Scottish and German universities. It included Protestants, Catholics, Jews, atheists, Deists, and skeptics; men and women; aristocrats; middle-class people; and even a few upwardly mobile members of the working class. Revolutionaries such as Thomas Jefferson, Benjamin Franklin, and Maximilien Robespierre were part of the Enlightenment, and so were "enlightened despots"—authoritarian rulers such as the Marquis of Pombal in Portugal, Frederick II in Prussia, and Catherine the Great in Russia. Some hoped to use Enlightenment thought to reform Christian institutions and beliefs, others hoped to destroy them. Enlightenment thinkers rejected many aspects of tradition, but did not always agree on what should replace them. The leading thinkers themselves vigorously opposed one another on many topics.

Even the modernity of the Enlightenment can be questioned. Numerous institutions that we now would call archaic—ranging from chattel slavery in the Americas to the domination that men exerted over women in virtually every area of European life—were not effectively challenged during the

Enlightenment. Despite Enlightenment pleas against entrenched privilege, many Enlightenment figures benefited from the patronage of aristocrats and monarchs, or even were aristocrats themselves, enjoying the privileges which European society continued to offer to men of their class.

This book is an introduction to many of the themes, topics, and current debates in the exceptionally vigorous field of Enlightenment studies. After providing a time line and historical overview to set the stage, the heart of the book is an alphabetically arranged series of articles on major Enlightenment topics. Articles presented include individuals such as Voltaire, national Enlightenments such as the German, events such as the French Revolution, and areas of Enlightenment thought such as political philosophy. Each section includes a short list of further readings that can be used to continue to explore the topic presented. Primary source documents enable readers to come to grips with major thinkers and ideas directly. Essays for both sides of three of the central questions of the Enlightenment—its feminism, secularity, and democracy—reveal some of the key arguments of modern Enlightenment scholarship. An annotated bibliography and list of Web resources help guide readers in their further studies of the Enlightenment.

Timeline

1748   Publication of Montesquieu's *The Spirit of the Laws*; publication of Hume's *Philosophical Essays Concerning Human Understanding*.

1750   Publication of Jean-Jacques Rousseau's *Discourse on the Arts and Sciences*; accession of Portuguese King Joseph I, followed by the coming to power of the "Enlightened" Marquis of Pombal.

1751   Publication of the first volume of the *Encyclopédie* with Jean Le Rond d'Alembert's *Preliminary Discourse*, Benjamin Franklin's *Experiments and Observations on Electricity*, and Voltaire's *Century of Louis XIV*.

1754   Publication of the first volume of Hume's *History of England*. The complete set is published in 1762; Frederick II abolishes torture in Prussian law; fighting between Britain and France in North America begins the Seven Years War.

1755   Destructive earthquake and tidal wave in Lisbon kills more than 10,000 people. Calamity raises interest in earthquakes and helps call philosophical and religious optimism into question; Rousseau publishes *Discourse on Inequality*; successful premiere of Gotthold Ephraim Lessing's "bourgeois" play, *Miss Sara Sampson*.

1756   Seven Years War spreads to Europe.

1758   Halley's Comet returns as predicted; Pombal's expulsion of the Jesuits from Portugal begins the process that leads to the suppression of the Jesuits.

1759   Publication of Voltaire's *Candide*, the Marquise du Châtelet's French translation of Newton's *Mathematical Principles of Natural Philosophy*, and Adam Smith's *Theory of Moral Sentiments*.

1761   First transit of Venus across the face of the sun leads to worldwide scientific activity; Rousseau publishes the novel *Julie*.

1762   Catherine II seizes throne of Russia; Rousseau publishes *The Social Contract* and *Emile*; Protestant Jean Calas executed in Toulouse on charges of having murdered his son.

1763   Seven Years War ends in conclusive British victory and a return to the status quo in Central Europe.

1764   Publication of Cesare Beccaria's *On Crimes and Punishments*; suppression of the Jesuits in France.

1765   Calas's sentence overturned.

1766   Publication of Lessing's aesthetic treatise *Laocoon*.

1768   Founding of the American Philosophical Society in Philadelphia, the first successful American learned society; publication of Joseph Priestley's *An Essay on the First Principles of Government*.

1769   Second transit of Venus with more observations; Benjamin Franklin elected president of the American Philosophical Society, a position he holds until his death.

1770   Raynal and Diderot's *Philosophical and Political History of the Establishments and Trade of Europeans in the Two Indies* denounces colonialism; anonymous publication of Baron Holbach's *System of Nature*.

1773   Dissolution of the Jesuits; Pugachev peasant uprising in Russia and its bloody suppression leads to end of liberal, "Enlightened" period of Catherine II's reign.

1774   Priestley discovers "dephlogisticated air," later known as "oxygen."

1775   American Revolution begins.

1776   Publication of the last volume of the *Encyclopédie*, Adam Smith's *The Wealth of Nations*, and the first three volumes of Edward Gibbon's *Decline and Fall of the Roman Empire*; founding of the Masonic Lodge of the Nine Sisters in Paris, which will include Franklin and Voltaire among its members; American Declaration of Independence; Benjamin Franklin sent to Paris as emissary from the American rebels; founding of the Bavarian Illuminati.

1777   Death of Joseph I of Portugal followed by Pombal's fall and exile.

1778   Premiere of Lessing's play, *Nathan the Wise*, whose principal character, a wise and tolerant Jew, is modeled on Lessing's friend Moses Mendelssohn.

1779   Posthumous publication of Hume's *Dialogues Concerning Natural Religion*.

1780   Death of Habsburg Austrian Empress Maria Theresa leads to the taking of power by her son, the Enlightened reformer Joseph II.

1781   Joseph II's Edict of Toleration increases religious freedom in the Habsburg lands for most Protestants and Orthodox Christians and to a lesser extent, Jews; Joseph also emancipates serfs in Austria and Bohemia; publication of Kant's *Critique of Pure Reason*.

1782   Publication of Rousseau's *Confessions*.

1783   First balloon ascensions; Moses Mendelssohn publishes *Jerusalem*, American Revolution ends with the Peace of Paris.

1785   Publication of Kant's *Groundwork of the Metaphysics of Morals*.

1786   Death of Frederick II of Prussia (his nephew and successor, Frederick William II, will oppose the Enlightenment); publication of Kant's *Metaphysical Foundations of Natural Science*.

1787   Convention in Philadelphia with Franklin's participation writes the American Constitution; French Royal decree establishes toleration for Protestants.

1788   Publication of Kant's *Critique of Practical Reason*; founding of the Society of the Friends of the Blacks, an "Enlightened" French antislavery group.

1789   French Revolution begins; *Declaration of the Rights of Man.*

1790   Death of Joseph II; French National Assembly sets forth plan for new, "objective" measurements eventually leading to the metric system.

1791   Priestley's house and laboratory in Birmingham attacked by a conservative mob; French National Assembly brings Voltaire's remains to Paris to be reburied in the Pantheon.

1792   Beginning of the measurements to establish the metric system.

1793   Publication of Kant's *Religion within the Limits of Reason Alone* inspires the Prussian government to ban his publishing on religious subjects.

1794   Priestley immigrates to America; Condorcet kills himself to avoid execution by French revolutionary government; Jean-Jacques Rousseau reburied in the Pantheon.

1795   Publication of Condorcet's *Sketch of the Progress of the Human Mind.*

1796   Death of Catherine II.

1798   Passage of the Alien and Sedition Acts in the United States of America, limiting freedom of the press.

Historical Overview

The Enlightenment was an intellectual movement extending from the late 17th century to the late 18th century. It was dedicated to challenging many aspects of European society—from religious intolerance to the domination of society and politics by aristocrats and monarchs. Thinkers of the Enlightenment viewed themselves as champions of reason and empiricism, questioning the beliefs and institutions that could not be justified by these principles.

During the Enlightenment period Christianity continued to dominate Europe. Regardless of which government was in power, it proclaimed that its power came from God. The government also restricted political participation to professed Christians—usually of one particular church. In many European countries, including France, to follow a form of Christianity other than that which dominated the government was illegal (although these laws were falling into disuse in many places). The only substantial non-Christian minority west of Russia and north of the Muslim-ruled territories of the declining Ottoman Empire in the Balkans—the Jewish community—faced many restrictions in most parts of Europe and was debarred from institutional political power in all of Europe.

Many areas of life that now are governed by secular law (such as marriage) fell under the jurisdiction of churches rather than governments, and each church had its own set of laws and courts. Education systems—particularly universities—were dominated by churches and staffed largely by clerics, who also were well-represented in elite intellectual institutions such as the French Academy. Churches—particularly in Catholic countries—were holders of extensive property, in land, money, and movable goods, much of which was exempt from taxes. The Enlightenment overthrew very little of this system, but it challenged nearly all of it. Religious toleration—for which England and the Dutch Republic were held out as models—was a *sine qua non* of Enlightenment thought, and clerical power was viewed with suspicion, even by those Enlightenment thinkers who were Christians, or even clerics, themselves.

Eighteenth-century European countries, with a few scattered exceptions such as the Dutch Republic and Switzerland, were ruled by monarchs whose power was treated as sacrosanct and unquestionable. Political power in most continental European countries was restricted to an elite group and based on hereditary nobility and wealth. The circulation of political information was tightly controlled by active state censorship that supplemented that of the church. Although not all Enlightened thinkers opposed monarchy on principle or supported more democratic forms of government, many found the conservative and repressive governments of kings to be unappealing and supported a freer circulation of political information.

Aristocratic power was social as well as political. Titled aristocrats expected—and demanded—deference from "lesser folk," including members of the middle class and many of the Enlightenment philosophers themselves, although a few Enlightenment thinkers came from an aristocratic background. Aristocrats in many countries had legal privileges, tax exemptions, and a monopoly on many prestigious positions—ranging from the officer corps of most European armies to the higher ranks of the Catholic Church. Enlightenment thinkers questioned why merely being born the son of an aristocratic father entitled a person to such honors.

Not all structures of privilege and tradition in European life were being questioned during the Enlightenment. All of the most prominent intellectual leaders of the Enlightenment were male, and they were comfortable with male privilege over women. Many were distrustful of democracy, fearing that the common people—at least until they were properly educated—were too superstitious and irrational to be entrusted with power. Although many Enlightenment thinkers questioned slavery and admired other cultures such as that of China, some accepted the idea of a racial hierarchy with white Europeans at the top. Some Enlightened thinkers also were hostile to the Jewish minority.

ORIGINS OF THE ENLIGHTENMENT

The roots of the Enlightenment are found in the 17th century, particularly in the Scientific Revolution, the development of radical religion, and the English Revolutions. Science, particularly as embodied in the mathematical physics of Enlightenment hero Isaac Newton, provided a model of reason and the advance of knowledge through cooperative endeavor. This model influenced many other areas. The progress of science, and the fact that scientists could disagree about fundamental issues without engaging in violent conflict, frequently were juxtaposed to the fruitlessness and pointless violence of religious conflict. Many Enlightenment leaders were scientists themselves or were passionate followers of science. The radical Deism of excommunicated Jew, Baruch Spinoza, challenged authority and tradition in Church, Synagogue, and State in favor of a reliance on reason. Spinoza's intellectual descendants later opposed religious and political hierarchy—some even described Jesus as one of the "Three Impostors" alongside Moses and Muhammad. The English revolutions of 1642–1649 and 1688–1689 provided a model of relatively liberal parliamentary government and religious tolerance in opposition to the intolerant monarchical absolutism still practiced on most of the European continent. "Anglophilia"—the admiration of things English—was a characteristic of much of the Enlightenment, particularly in its early stages.

THE ENLIGHTENMENT BEGINS

The Enlightenment is not the type of movement that can be said to have begun on an exact date. The writings of Baruch Spinoza in the mid-17th century put forth many radical ideas such as the attack on organized religion that would later be part of Enlightenment thinking. By the 1690s a movement to challenge existing authorities in church and state in the name of reason is evident. In England, a semi-underground movement of "Deists" denied Christianity, but supported the belief in an all-powerful God. Slightly different groups were the "Socinians" and "Arians," who accepted much of Christianity, but not the divinity of Christ. The Arians' membership included Isaac Newton.

The political and epistemological thinking of John Locke, a supporter of the English Revolution of 1688, had great influence on the Enlightenment. In politics, Locke emphasized the derivation of power from the consent of the governed, and in epistemology, he was a believer in empiricism—the derivation of knowledge from the senses, rather than from inborn "innate ideas." Locke was a Christian rather than a Deist, but he was a firm supporter of religious toleration (except for Catholics, whom he viewed as agents of a foreign power, and atheists, who Locke thought could not be trusted due to their lack of belief in a supernatural authority). In France, a growing—if largely clandestine—opposition to the authoritarian Catholicism of King Louis XIV increasingly looked to the values of reason and toleration. The French Protestants, or "Huguenots," who had been expelled from France by Louis XIV, also frequently spread Enlightened ideas from their new homes in the Dutch Republic and Britain.

An important means for the transmission of these new ideas was the Free-mason movement, which began in Britain in the 17th century and spread to the European continent in the 18th century. By emphasizing brotherhood across the lines of religious sect and class (but not gender), the Masons promoted the idea of a more egalitarian and enlightened society.

ENLIGHTENMENT AS A CAUSE

The Enlightenment still was marginal in the early 18th century, and Enlightened writers had to fight hard to overcome established authorities in church and state, who relied on the weapons of censorship and arbitrary imprisonment. In some countries, such as Spain and Portugal, the strength of traditional authorities was such that the Enlightenment barely penetrated them until the end of the century. The key battlefield of the early 18th century was France, a Catholic country but one where modern ideas could be expressed much more easily.

No one more embodied the fighting spirit of the French Enlightenment than the writer and Deist Voltaire, for whom Enlightenment was a larger cause that led him to fight for many and diverse smaller causes. His *Letters from England* attempted to win the French to the twin English improvements of Newtonian physics and religious toleration. (In France, the pre-Newtonian physics of René Descartes still dominated scientific thinking.) Back in France, Voltaire continued the struggle for Newtonian physics, along with his romantic partner, Émilie le Tonnelier de Breteuil, Marquise Du Châtelet-Lomont, who translated Newton's *Mathematical Principles of Natural Philosophy* into French. Voltaire also fought for the clearing of Jean Calas, a French Protestant unjustly executed for murdering his son to prevent him from converting to Catholicism as well as other victims of intolerance, and for the alleviation of the harsh and unfair French system of justice generally.

THE SPREAD AND ESTABLISHMENT OF
THE ENLIGHTENMENT

In the mid-18th century, the Enlightenment began to consolidate itself as a force on the European landscape. Voltaire was admitted to the French Academy, the bastion of "official" French culture, in 1746. The most massive textual embodiment of the Enlightenment's midcentury confidence was the *Encyclopédie*, which began as a translation of a recent English encyclopedia into French and expanded into a vast compendium of knowledge, drawing in such Enlightenment writers as Denis Diderot and Jean Le Rond D'Alembert, who served as editors, and Voltaire and the great political theorist Charles

Louis de Secondat de Montesquieu (among many others), who wrote individual entries. For those who could not or did not wish to acquire the entire, 35-volume *Encyclopédie* or even an abridgement, Voltaire summed up much of its skeptical message in his *Philosophical Dictionary* (1764)—which can be considered a portable *Encyclopédie*.

The mid-century Enlightenment also spread to new territories. Scotland—which at the beginning of the century was considered to be an intellectual backwater—was becoming one of Europe's intellectual leaders. Scottish Enlightenment thinkers, frequently associated with Scottish universities, often were particularly interested in the development of society. The greatest of these Scottish Enlightenment intellectuals, David Hume, was too religiously dangerous to win a university position but was an exceptionally bold thinker—not just regarding religious topics but on epistemology, society, and history as well. Another Enlightened Scotsman, Adam Smith, was the founder of modern economics. The Scottish church became divided between elite liberal, or "Moderate," and populist conservative factions. One of the greatest of Scottish Enlightened historians, William Robertson, also served as Moderator or head of the Church of Scotland and as head of the Moderate faction. The skeptical English writer Edward Gibbon drew on the French and Scottish Enlightenments to write *The Decline and Fall of the Roman Empire*, the greatest historical work produced by an Enlightenment author.

Germany too was moving in the direction of Enlightenment. Like Scotland, its Enlightenment movement was far more closely connected to its universities than were the Enlightenments of France and England. Although the traditional religious establishment fought hard to control German universities, the general direction—at least in Protestant Germany—was towards Enlightenment. Germany's greatest Enlightened thinker was the philosopher Immanuel Kant, a university professor and a supporter of the application of reason to religion. Connected with the German Enlightenment was the "Haskalah," or Jewish Enlightenment, which challenged the authority of the rabbis who had been the intellectual as well as social, political, and religious leaders of the Jewish community for many centuries. Moses Mendelssohn, Haskalah's leader, was a friend of Kant's who used the tools of Enlightened reason to defend traditional Judaism from Christian attack. Italy also was becoming more Enlightened through the influence of French culture and the waning of the power of the Inquisition. One important Italian Enlightenment figure was the reformer of the criminal law, Cesare Beccaria, whose call for the elimination of torture from the legal process was influential from Russia to the new United States.

As the Enlightenment grew it encompassed more diverse perspectives. Jean-Jacques Rousseau, emerging into prominence around 1750, supported many aspects of the Enlightenment, including toleration and responsible government, but was far less optimistic about the progress of reason and science than were most Enlightenment philosophers. Rousseau's writings emphasized the passions and the importance of living true to the heart in a way that differed from the usual Enlightenment emphasis on reason and observations, and his ideas contributed to the later romantic movement, which in many ways (but not all) was a rejection of the Enlightenment.

ENLIGHTENED ABSOLUTISM

Although many champions of Enlightenment admired English parliamentarianism, they were willing to support monarchical reformers who used, or seemed to be using, absolutism to advance Enlightened programs and ideals. Sebastião de Carvalho, the Marquis of Pombal, in Portugal; Frederick the Great in Prussia; and Catherine the Great in Russia, all attracted support from Enlightened thinkers who saw them as advancing the cause of reason and humanity. Frederick and Catherine in particular patronized Enlightenment thinkers, inviting them to their courts and corresponding with them, while carrying out aspects of the Enlightenment program such as abolishing torture, promoting religious toleration, and liberating some (but by no means all) of their serfs. These relationships were often short-lived, however, as the Enlightenment philosophers decided that the rulers were using them and that royal despotism was not really compatible with the advance of Enlightenment. The practical requirements of ruling in an age of nearly constant war also made rulers think that Enlightenment idealism was not a workable approach to government. The relationship of Frederick the Great—known for his love of French culture, his extreme skepticism of religion, and his unscrupulous and militaristic foreign policy—and Voltaire was particularly tempestuous.

One area in which Enlightenment philosophers found themselves allied with absolutist governments was the 1773 suppression of the Jesuits, a Roman Catholic religious order frequently identified as the leading intellectual opponents of the Enlightenment in Catholic Europe. The movement to abolish them as a politically subversive organization was begun by Pombal, and quickly spread to France, Spain, and Europe's other Catholic monarchies, along with their colonies. Enlightenment thinkers—who mostly hated the Jesuits despite or because of the fact that many of them were educated in the excellent Jesuit schools—cheered on the suppression, although the governments that carried it out were driven by political concerns rather than Enlightened ideals.

ENLIGHTENMENT IN THE AGE OF REVOLUTION

The late 1770s were marked by a changing of the guard in the Enlightenment leadership, as many of the foremost champions of the movement died within a few years of each other—Hume in 1776, and Voltaire and Rousseau in 1778. An even more dramatic change was the American Revolution, carried out in part by men such as Benjamin Franklin and Thomas Jefferson who were members of the Enlightened community. Franklin had long been an Enlightenment hero, both for his scientific achievements and for his image as a plain, unpretentious thinker—conforming to European stereotypes of the simplicity and honesty of Americans. Franklin's term as the Revolution's ambassador in Paris is particularly noteworthy for how he deployed his position as an Enlightened sage to benefit the revolutionary cause. He was succeeded in Paris by another Enlightened American, Thomas Jefferson. A more radically democratic supporter of the American Revolution was the English pamphleteer, Thomas Paine.

The political thinking of the American revolutionaries themselves drew on Enlightened thinkers such as John Locke and the Baron de Montesquieu, who helped shape the American constitution—one of the most enduring legacies of the Enlightenment. The new nation's lack of an official or "established" church or hereditary titles—including king—was a fulfillment of the Enlightenment program far more radical than anything European nations had even tried to achieve.

The independent American republic partially displaced Great Britain, discredited by its harsh policies towards the Americans, its failure to crush the Revolution, and growing awareness of the corruption of the British Parliament, as the object of Enlightened admiration. Only the most radical thinkers, however, considered establishing anything similar to the United States in Europe itself. Abortive revolutions in Geneva and the Dutch Republic in the 1780s proved the difficulty of revolutionary political change. Enlightened British thinkers began a campaign lasting for decades for a reform of the British Parliamentary system, increasingly viewed as archaic, into something more representative of the British people, but they were initially ineffective against powerful entrenched interests.

Far more radical and successful was the French Revolution of 1789. The weakness of the late 18th-century French state and the growing mobilization of the discontented opened the door for many aspects of the Enlightenment program. The early and more moderate phases of the Revolution saw changes such as the "Declaration of the Rights of Man" which enshrined toleration of diverse ideas including religious ideas and the abolition of noble privilege. The privileges of the Church also came under attack, and the monarchy was dissolved in favor of a republic.

THE END OF THE ENLIGHTENMENT

Despite initial successes, the Enlightenment as a movement faltered and splintered in the era of the French Revolution. The radicalism of the period when France was ruled by a group of politicians called the "Jacobins" and the repressive terror that the Jacobins inflicted on their numerous enemies ("Reign of Terror," from September 5, 1793, to July 28, 1794, also known as "The Terror") went far beyond the changes envisioned by Enlightened thinkers. The "Rights of Man" largely were forgotten in the savage political and military struggles of the time. "De-Christianization" and the establishment of a Deist "Cult of the Supreme Being," the most radical attack on European Christianity since the Roman Empire, proved a complete failure. One of the last champions of the French Enlightenment, the Marquis de Condorcet, killed himself to avoid being executed as a traitor by the revolutionaries themselves. Ironically, his last (and posthumously published) work was a *Sketch of the Progress of the Human Mind.*

Conditions outside of France were not much better. The conservative reaction against the Revolution in many European countries saw a crackdown on radical or even reformist ideas. In Prussia, the government forbade Kant from writing about religion, afraid of the spread of subversive concepts such as a religion of reason. In England, a conservative "Church and King" mob sacked the home and laboratory of the Enlightened scientist and Unitarian minister Joseph Priestley, and the hostility he faced eventually forced him to move to the United States. The policies of the Holy Roman Emperor Joseph II, often seen as the last of the Enlightened absolutists, were viewed as a failure and were largely abandoned after his death in 1690. Even the United States, considered by many like Priestley as a haven of freedom, passed the repressive Alien and Sedition Acts in 1798. Much of Europe's intellectual energy, whether on the right or the left, was moving into Romanticism and religious revival and away from the Enlightenment emphasis on reason.

THE LEGACY OF THE ENLIGHTENMENT

The legacy of the Enlightenment as a movement can be seen in 19th-century liberalism, with its secularism, opposition to inherited privilege, and suspicion of democracy. In a larger sense, the legacy of the Enlightenment is the belief in the power of human reason and the hope for human progress.

The Enlightenment: A to Z

ACADEMIES AND LEARNED SOCIETIES Much of the intellectual activity of the Enlightenment was centered on academies and learned societies, particularly in France and England, where universities did not occupy the central intellectual position they held in Germany and Scotland. Learned societies could include both state-sponsored groups and informal gatherings that met regularly.

The premier humanistic learned society of the 18th century was the French Academy, the "Forty Immortals" (so-called because the membership was fixed at 40) founded by Cardinal Richelieu in 1635. The Academy was entrusted with the maintenance of the purity of the French language. The first edition of its *Dictionary of the French Academy* appeared in 1794, and several other editions appeared throughout the 18th century. Entrance into the academy was the highest honor a French male intellectual could receive from the state, and Voltaire's admission in 1746 was considered a major victory for the Enlightenment as well as for Voltaire personally. Another group ostensibly devoted to linguistic concerns and one of the oldest learned societies in Europe was the Della Crusca Academy in Tuscany, founded in 1583. The Della Crusca's interests broadened from the Italian language to archeology, local history, and agricultural improvement in the 18th century.

A rising force from the late 17th century was the association dedicated to the sciences. The two most important were the Royal Academy of Sciences in Paris and the Royal Society in London, both state-sponsored groups founded in the 1660s. The Royal Society was an unpaid group whose members ("Fellows") included many scientific amateurs as well as leading scientists. By contrast, the Royal Academy was a smaller, more professional group. The leading academicians were paid. Most state-sponsored scientific societies founded in the 18th century followed the model of the Royal Academy rather than the Royal Society. Other leading scientific societies following the Royal Academy model included the Berlin Academy founded in 1700, the Imperial Academy of Sciences in St. Petersburg founded in 1725, and the Swedish Academy of Sciences in Stockholm founded in 1739. Eighteenth-century scientific societies had many interconnections. They corresponded with each other, exchanged publications, and sometimes arranged joint endeavors, such as the worldwide astronomical observations of the transits of Venus across the face of the sun in 1761 and 1769.

In the 18th century, academies spread from their origin in Europe's capital cities to provincial cities, offering a venue for Enlightened and other intellectual activities in other locales. Provincial academies also played an active role in intellectual life, particularly in France. Jean-Jacques Rousseau's *Discourse on the Arts and Sciences* was produced in response to a prize offered by the Academy of Dijon (founded in 1725) on the question of whether progress in the arts and sciences purified morality. In the late 18th century, the north of England—remote from England's intellectual centers of London, Oxford, and Cambridge, all located in the south—saw a flowering of local societies, founded on a voluntary rather than state-sponsored basis. Local societies included the Lunar Society of Birmingham founded in the 1760s, the Manchester Literary and Philosophical Society founded in 1781, and the Derby Philosophical Society founded in 1783. Provincial societies in Italy and Germany frequently were associated with universities, such as the Bologna Academy of Sciences founded in 1714 or the Göttingen Academy of Sciences founded in 1751.

The second half of the 18th century saw academies spread to the colonial world. The first enduring scientific society in the American colonies of Great Britain—the American Philosophical Society—was founded in 1768, and its first president was Benjamin Franklin. The American Academy of Arts and Sciences was founded by the Massachusetts legislature in 1780, and its founders included many leaders of the American Revolution who had remained in Massachusetts, including John Adams (1735–1826), Samuel Adams (1722–1803), and John Hancock (1737–1793). The eminent philologist Sir William Jones (1746–1794) founded the Asiatick Society of Bengal in 1784 to study the culture and natural world of India. The Circle of Philadelphes founded in 1785 in the French Caribbean colony of Saint-Domingue (modern Haiti) was oriented towards social and administrative reform. It was torn apart by divisions over slavery and racial hierarchy.

Academies and societies devoted to economic improvement were a rising force in the 18th century. London's Society for the Encouragement of Arts,

Manufacture, and Commerce was founded in 1754, and its prestige came to rival that of the Royal Society itself. (In the 18th century, the term "arts" principally referred to technologies.) Members included such luminaries of the Enlightenment as Benjamin Franklin and Adam Smith. The Society of Arts, as it was called, offered lucrative and prestigious prizes for technical innovations. The Hamburg Patriotic Society, founded in 1765, was dedicated to the application of scientific ideas to economic development and the relief of the poor. Another type of economic society was the agricultural society, which spread throughout much of Europe in the 18th century. Agricultural societies brought together enlightened landowners with the aim of improving production and the return on land investments. Some were voluntary and others, such as the Royal Society of Agriculture founded in Paris in 1761, were state supported.

Membership in academies was an important source of prestige and intellectual authority. Some academies, such as the Royal Academy of Sciences, paid their members, although many others, particularly in the English-speaking world, did not. (Despite its royal charter and its flaunting of the royal connections in its name, the Royal Society was not state funded and did not pay its fellows.) For writers, listing memberships in prestigious societies on the title-pages of one's books was a common practice. Prestige could flow the other direction as well; leading intellectuals could attain many academy memberships, as academies sought to associate themselves with the great thinkers of the period.

Like universities, academies were male institutions that contributed to the male dominance of intellectual life. There were a few exceptions, mostly in Italy and led by the Bologna Academy of Science which admitted Bologna university professor Laura Bassi (1711–1778) and a few other women, including the French physicist the Marquise du Châtelet. The most spectacular exception, however, occurred in Russia in 1782, when Catherine the Great appointed her friend, Princess Ekaterina Dashkova (1743–1810), as head of the Imperial Academy of Sciences. Two years later Dashkova was appointed head of a newly created Russian Academy devoted to the Russian language and based on the model of the French Academy. Dashkova was a leader of the Russian Enlightenment who had traveled in Europe and was the friend and correspondent of several Enlightenment thinkers including Voltaire, Franklin, and Denis Diderot. Although Dashkova was admitted as a foreign member of several societies, including the Swedish Academy of Sciences and the American Philosophical Society, this did not open doors for women's participation in academies. Particularly in France, however, the world of the academies was closely connected with the female-dominated world of the salons, as entrée into the leading salons of Paris was considered a key stepping-stone into the academies.

The world of the academies was dealt a significant blow by the French Revolution, which in 1793 saw the (temporary) abolition of the central Parisian Academies as well as the numerous academies in the French provinces—all banned as elitist or "aristocratic" institutions, although informal gatherings of like-minded individuals partially filled the gap. The demands of the subsequent French Revolutionary and Napoleonic wars also saw the temporary or permanent closure of many academies and societies in Continental Europe, including Bologna, as well as the diminishing of contacts and collaboration between Continental and British academies.

See also: Alembert, Jean Le Rond d'; Newton, Isaac; Science.

Further Reading

Cochrane, Eric, *Tradition and Enlightenment in the Tuscan Academies 1690–1800* (Chicago: University of Chicago Press, 1961).

Hahn, Roger, *The Anatomy of a Scientific Institution: The Paris Academy of Sciences, 1666–1803* (Berkeley and Los Angeles: University of California Press, 1977).

McClellan, James E., III, *Science Reorganized: Scientific Societies in the Eighteenth Century* (New York: Columbia University Press, 1985).

Paul, Charles B., *Science and Immortality: The Éloges of the Paris Academy of Sciences (1699–1791)* (Berkeley and Los Angeles: University of California Press, 1980).

ALEMBERT, JEAN LE ROND D' (1717–1783)   Jean Le Rond d'Alembert's brilliance helped him emerge from a troubled background as an illegitimate and abandoned child in Paris to become one of the leading scientists and philosophers of the French Enlightenment. (He was named "Jean Le Rond" for the church where he had been abandoned a few days after his birth.)

D'Alembert's fame came principally from his contributions to mathematics and physics. For d'Alembert, physics was a mathematical science that worked by making deductions from first principles, not an experimental one that worked by observing phenomena and creating experiments. Although there is no evidence that d'Alembert ever performed an experiment, he was the rising star of French physics in the 1730s and 1740s, publishing papers and getting into nasty feuds with other scientists. Like many French philosophers and scientists, he was an admirer and correspondent of Frederick the Great of Prussia, who invited d'Alembert to be president of the Berlin Academy in 1752. D'Alembert, however, hated the very idea of living outside the Parisian salon world and graciously declined, although he advised Frederick on the management of the Academy and exerted a great deal of indirect influence. He would decline other invitations from Prussia and Russia in the following decades.

Outside science, d'Alembert was active along with his friend and ally Denis Diderot in the editing of the *Encyclopédie*, for which he wrote the famous "Preliminary Discourse"—a classic statement of the Enlightenment program first published separately in 1751—as well as many articles. (His article on "Geneva" led to a controversy with Jean-Jacques Rousseau, a native of the city, who attacked d'Alembert's argument that the authorities of Geneva should allow a theater there.) The "Preliminary Discourse" made a great sensation, and the adulation he received began to turn d'Alembert's attention from mathematics to literature. He already was a lion of the salons due to his personal charm and delightful conversation. D'Alembert's move in 1764 from the salon of the Marquise de Deffand (1679–1780) to that established by her younger contemporary, Julie-Jeanne-Éléanore de Lespinasse (1732–1776), was a major shock to the Parisian elite. Lespinasse and d'Alembert were close friends, and he nursed her through her final illness.

As a philosopher, d'Alembert hoped that natural science would furnish a basis for the reorganization of all knowledge. He shared his friend Voltaire's hatred of organized religion, along with a common dismay at the rise of materialism. D'Alembert's dislike of materialism contributed to his decision to quit the editorship of the *Encyclopédie* in 1759, leaving it to the increasingly materialistic Diderot.

By 1764, d'Alembert had abandoned original mathematics after a severe illness. He spent most of his labors advancing the Enlightenment cause—and his own career—in the Parisian intellectual world. He was admitted to the French Academy in 1754, and became its perpetual secretary in 1772. D'Alembert achieved the rare "triple" of being a member of the three leading academies in France—the Royal Academy of Sciences, the French Academy, and the historically oriented Academy of Inscriptions. His power in Parisian intellectual life and his dominant influence over the Berlin Academy made him an important patron of younger scientists and writers including the Marquis de Condorcet and the mathematicians Joseph-Louis Lagrange (1736–1813) and Pierre-Simon Laplace (1749–1827). On October 29, 1783, d'Alembert died in Paris of a bladder disease.

See also: Academies and Learned Societies; *Encyclopédie*; France, the Enlightenment in; Salons; Science; Theater.

Further Reading

Hankins, Thomas, *Jean d'Alembert: Science and the Enlightenment* (Oxford: Oxford University Press, 1990).

AMERICAN REVOLUTION AND FOUNDING   The American Revolution and the protracted process of the founding of the United States of America, the first post-colonial state in the Americas, drew heavily on Enlightenment ideas and culture. Scholars debate as to which elements of the Enlightenment had the greatest influence on America's founders, with some arguing for the influence of John Locke and some for the Scottish Enlightenment. The American rebels made a deliberate appeal to European opinion in the 1776 Declaration of Independence and the cause of the Revolution was taken up by much of the Enlightened population of Europe. Many revolutionary leaders, particularly Benjamin Franklin, Thomas Paine, and Thomas Jefferson, were part of the Enlightened world themselves. Franklin's position as an Enlightenment hero in Europe (and particularly France)—earned decades before the Revolution—was a priceless asset to the revolutionary cause, particularly after his appointment as the ambassador of the Continental Congress to France in 1778. Paine was one of the Revolution's most able pamphleteers. The Declaration of Independence, principally authored by Jefferson, employed many Enlightened concepts, such as the natural rights belonging to man.

In Europe, Denis Diderot was a very early advocate of the revolutionary cause, whose *The Revolution in English America* came out in 1775, before the Declaration of Independence. More practical assistance was provided by spy and gunrunner Pierre Caron de Beaumarchais (1732–1799) and the soldier Marquis de Lafayette (1757–1834). (The Enlightened Anne-Robert-Jacques Turgot, a leader in the French government in 1776, admired the ideals of the Revolution but opposed French support for the revolutionaries on the grounds that France could not afford it.) The major "Enlightened despots" of the era, Frederick II of Prussia and Catherine II of Russia, were sympathetic to the rebels, although neither would go to war with Great Britain to support the cause. Another Enlightened monarch, Charles III of Spain (1716–1788) did support the rebels by joining the war, although this was due to his desire to regain territory lost to Britain in the Seven Years War rather than his sympathy toward the cause of rebellion, which might threaten Spain's own vast American empire.

The influence of the Enlightenment did not cease with the American victory in the Revolution, but continued into the period of the creation of the Articles of Confederation and the Constitution, and the founding of American political institutions. Revolutionary leader and political theorist John Adams (1735–1826) requested that the French philosopher Gabriel Bonnot de Mably (1709–1785) convey his thoughts on the constitution of the new nation. Mably's *Observations on the Government and Laws of the United States of America* (1784) was one of the earliest European commentaries on the new nation and suggested that the states had not entirely purged themselves of a tendency towards aristocracy. Adams's own *Defence of the Constitutions of Government of the United States of America* (1787–88) was partially addressed to European criticism of American federalism. The Marquis de Condorcet, a firm supporter of the Revolution, became an honorary citizen of New Haven, Connecticut. Condorcet's *Four Letters from a Bourgeois of Newhaven to a Citizen of Virginia* (1788) was one of the few Enlightenment works to advocate full political and legal equality for women and helped earn Condorcet the contempt of Adams.

The extensive debate on the adoption of the Constitution is best known from the *Federalist Papers* by Alexander Hamilton (1755–1804), James Madison (1751–1836), and John Jay (1745–1829), which drew on Enlightenment political concepts. The separation of powers between executive, legislative, and judicial in the Constitution owes much to Montesquieu. The refusal to adopt an official religion or to require religious affiliation for government positions—one of the most radical innovations of the founders—was fully in harmony with the Enlightenment dislike of religious establishments. The American victory caused America to replace Great Britain as a model for government in the eyes of many of Europe's Enlightened, and the American leader George Washington (1732–1799) became an object of widespread admiration, even in Great Britain. Washington's voluntary relinquishment of power and retirement to his country estate after his second presidential term attracted particular notice as an example of a man who had overcome ambition.

See also: Colonialism; Franklin, Benjamin; Paine, Thomas; Political Philosophy; Slavery.

Further Reading
Staloff, Darren, *Hamilton, Adams, Jefferson: The Politics of Enlightenment and the American Founding* (New York: Hill and Wang, 2005).
Wills, Garry, *Cincinnatus: George Washington and the Enlightenment* (Garden City, NY: Doubleday, 1984).
Wood, Gordon S., *The Radicalism of the American Revolution* (New York: Vintage, 1993).

ART AND ARCHITECTURE Eighteenth-century Europe was marked by a profusion of artistic styles, from the sometimes bizarrely ornate rococo to the austere and rule-governed neoclassical. None of these styles was a quasi-official "Enlightenment style," and Enlightened thinkers had a range of artistic tastes. A few generalizations can be made, however. Enlightened anti-clericals tended to favor secular art and architecture over that devoted to religious topics or uses, and with a few exceptions the 18th century was not an age of great religious art. Classical and Renaissance art and architecture was preferred to that of the Middle Ages—which, like many medieval things, was denigrated by the Enlightened. "Gothic" was a term of abuse, linking the glories of medieval architecture with the barbarians who had destroyed the Roman Empire. In this the canons of Enlightened taste were in continuity with those of the 16th and 17th centuries. In architecture, the popular "Palladian" style, associated with the Renaissance architect Andrea Palladio (1508–1580), presented itself as a revival of classical Greek and Roman architecture. Eighteenth-century Palladian buildings embodied the Enlightenment values of reason and nature. Palladian architecture was particularly influential in the early American Republic, which harkened back to classical traditions.

An influential champion of the classical style was the German, Johann Joachim Winckelmann (1717–1768). Winkelmann viewed ancient Greek art as having reached a pinnacle that had never been exceeded. He converted to Catholicism to explore the classical heritage of Italy and the Vatican collections, becoming the head librarian and curator at the Papal capital. His *History of the Art of Antiquity* (1764), originally written in German, was translated into French, English, and Italian and put forth a neoclassical ideal that emphasized simplicity and calm, in opposition to Baroque styles that emphasized passion.

Some painters and other artists, such as Sir Joshua Reynolds (1723–1792) in England, were part of the community of Enlightened intellectuals. Membership in the Enlightened community was one way that artists, like other creative workers, could raise themselves from the status of artisans. The French neoclassical sculptor Jean-Antoine Houdon (1741–1828) was particularly identified with the Enlightenment, creating portraits of such Enlightenment luminaries as Voltaire, Jean-Jacques Rousseau, Catherine the Great of Russia, and George Washington, among many others. The most influential French Enlightenment art critic was Denis Diderot, who wrote a series of reviews of the "Salons," biennial exhibitions of French paintings. He placed himself in the tradition of the ancients who valued the "realistic" imitation of nature in the hopes that the evocation of nature would instruct the viewer or spectator in morality. Diderot was a great admirer of the French painter Jean-Baptiste Greuze (1725–1805), whose "moral paintings" emphasized the virtue of the patriarchal rural family in implied opposition to the corruption of the aristocracy and the city.

The French artistic tradition was highly influential—perhaps dominant—in Germany, particularly during the early part of the century. The German aristocracy's support of French-style neoclassicism was frustrating for many German artists. The Enlightenment monarch Frederick the Great of Prussia was no exception and was notorious for his contempt for German culture and even the German language. (Music—an art in which Germans were second to none in the era of Johann Sebastian Bach (1685–1750) and Wolfgang Amadeus Mozart (1756–1791)—was an exception.)

See also: Diderot, Denis; Lessing, Gotthold Ephraim; Literature.

Further Reading

Etlin, Richard A., *Symbolic Space: French Enlightenment Architecture and Its Legacy* (Chicago: University of Chicago Press, 1994).
Kennedy, Roger G., *Orders from France: The Americans and the French in a Revolutionary World, 1780–1820* (New York: Knopf, 1989).
Metropolitan Museum of Art, *Europe in the Age of Enlightenment and Revolution* (New York: The Museum, 1987).

BECCARIA, CESARE (1738–1794)   Cesare Beccaria was born on March 15, 1738, to an aristocratic Italian family in Milan. Milan was the capital of the Duchy of Lombardy then ruled by the Austrian Habsburgs. Beccaria became one of the most important legal writers of the Enlightenment. He was educated at a Jesuit institution, but educated himself by reading works of Enlightenment writers including Diderot, Hume, Montesquieu, and Rousseau.

The result of Beccaria's reading and his observations of the courts in his own country was his work, *On Crimes and Punishments* (1764). Beccaria argued for rationalizing legal procedure with greater attention to fairness for the accused, an end to secret trials, and the abolition of torture and capital punishment. Influenced by Montesquieu, he characterized legal punishment as a deterrent aimed at the improvement of society rather than as vengeance for crime. Beccaria's social theory was influenced by Rousseau and the idea of the social contract by which persons give up freedom in exchange for social order. Punishments are a necessary evil in maintaining this order. A punishment more severe than is necessary to serve the public good is evil and should be abolished. When meted out, however, punishment should follow the commission of the crime closely to enhance deterrence. One of Beccaria's arguments against capital punishment was that it failed to deter, and that perpetual slavery for those convicted of major crimes would be more effective. Laws must be clearly written, be known to all citizens, and allow no room for arbitrary actions by judges. They also must apply equally to all.

On Crimes and Punishments made a great sensation, being translated into French and English and attracting praise from leaders of the Enlightenment. Voltaire, a long-time campaigner for legal reform, was a particularly strong admirer and wrote a short commentary applying Beccaria's ideas to France.

(Beccaria's brief visit to Paris, however, proved a disaster due to his shyness.) More importantly for Beccaria's project, it also attracted praise from European sovereigns. Although more lip service was paid to legal reform than actual action devoted to it, Beccaria influenced the King of Sweden, Gustavus III (r. 1771–1792), to abolish torture in his kingdom by royal decree in 1772, and impacted the early efforts at legal reform in Russia by Catherine the Great. There also were some reforms in Beccaria's own country of Italy. Beccaria influenced the American founders and subsequent legal reformers, such as the English Utilitarian Jeremy Bentham (1748–1832). Beccaria never published anything else comparable to *On Crimes and Punishments*. He became a civil servant in the Duchy of Lombardy and died on November 28, 1794, in Milan.

See also: Italy, the Enlightenment in; Political Philosophy.

Further Reading
Bessier, John D., *The Birth of American Law: An Italian Philosopher and the American Revolution* (Durham: Carolina Academic Press, 2014).

BIBLE, THE　　The Bible remained by far the most important Christian text and a cultural touchstone—even for non-believers—throughout the Enlightenment. Although the belief in the Bible's divine inspiration remained dogma throughout most sects of Christianity, its authority was increasingly questioned by Enlightenment skeptics and by scholars. The most radical critic of the Bible in the 17th century, and one of the most influential in the Enlightenment, was Baruch Spinoza. Like all traditionally educated Jewish boys of ability, Spinoza was very well versed in the Hebrew Bible. He used his knowledge to put forth the first entirely secular reading of Scripture as a historical document. For Spinoza and his intellectual heirs, the Bible contained much valuable teaching and historical information but was not divinely inspired. Few followed in Spinoza's footsteps in the 17th century, and those who did usually were not the most advanced scholars, who worked in universities where conformity to church doctrine was expected.

One Deist influenced by Spinozism was the Englishman John Toland (1670–1722). Toland took advantage of the growing knowledge of early Christian writings to question the canonization of the Bible—the establishment of which texts were part of the Bible and which other ancient religious texts were not. He pointed out that the Church Fathers themselves did not agree on a single canon of scripture.

Spinozism raised the stakes of Biblical scholarship, which now not only was concerned with differences between Catholics and Protestants (as in the

16th and early 17th centuries), but with the defense of Christianity as a whole. Among the foremost Catholic Biblical scholars of the early Enlightenment was the French Oratorian priest, Richard Simon (1638–1712). Simon's historical studies of the Bible were partly meant as a Catholic counter to the Protestant belief in the Bible as the sole religious authority, but also were meant as a response to Spinoza's skepticism. Simon established the principle that although the Bible was divinely inspired in its original form, its copyists were not divinely protected from error. Despite his mission of supporting Catholic orthodoxy, Simon's studies aroused so much concern that his *Critical History of the Old Testament* (1678; English translation published in 1682) was confiscated and destroyed by the French government and he was expelled from the Oratorians in 1678. Simon influenced Isaac Newton's reading of the Bible, which accepted its divine inspiration but claimed that its real religious truth had been obscured. An accurate reading, Newton believed, would endorse his own anti-Trinitarian approach to Christianity. Newton spent much of his last decades trying to understand Biblical chronology and the prophecies of the last days, a dedication which would puzzle and bemuse many of his secularist Enlightenment admirers.

The most aggressively anti-Christian writers of the Enlightenment, such as Voltaire, were not biblical scholars but relied on their culture's familiarity with the Bible to read it against the grain, as Voltaire read and explicated the stories of the ancient Jews as showing not their special relationship with God but their barbarism and cruelty, sometimes bending the truth to do so. For much of his ammunition Voltaire relied on the work of the French Benedictine monk Antoine Calmet (1672–1757), a devout Catholic whose popular *Historical, Critical, Chronological, Geographical and Literal Dictionary of the Bible* (1722) was translated into several European languages. Voltaire's friend and intellectual ally, the Marquise du Châtelet, also was highly critical of the Bible, although her criticisms circulated only in manuscript form. David Hume attacked the miracle stories associated with Jesus in the gospels, often adduced by Christian apologists as the strongest evidence for Christianity. Edward Gibbon, although never explicitly denying the divinity of Christ, linked the stories of Jesus and his miracles in the New Testament to other ancient stories of pagan wonderworkers in Gibbon's *The Decline and Fall of the Roman Empire* (1776–1788), implying that Jesus was no more the son of God than the pagans were. The second part of Thomas Paine's *The Age of Reason* (1795) also included a detailed criticism of the Bible. Paine's friend, Thomas Jefferson (1743–1826), spent many hours in the study of the gospels, trying to separate Jesus's authentic message—which he saw as principally ethical—from the supernatural distortions including miracle stories and the Resurrection that Jefferson believed to have been introduced by others.

See also: Châtelet, Émilie du; Enlightenment Views of Jews and Judaism; Gibbon, Edward; Newton, Isaac; Paine, Thomas; Religion; Spinoza, Baruch; Voltaire.

Further Reading

Breuer, Edward, *The Limits of Enlightenment: Jews, Germans, and the Eighteenth-Century Study of Scripture* (Cambridge, MA: Harvard University Press, 1996).
Frampton, Travis L., *Spinoza and the Rise of Historical Criticism of the Bible* (New York: T & T Clark, 2006).
Sheehan, Jonathan, *The Enlightenment Bible: Translation, Scholarship, Culture* (Princeton and Oxford: Princeton University Press, 2005).

BOOKS, PUBLISHING, AND CENSORSHIP   The 18th century was a century of expansion in the European book trade. Factors driving this expansion included the growing literacy rate, the decline of censorship regimes, and the weakening of the guilds of printers and booksellers that had been gatekeepers in the 17th century. Copyright in published books usually was held by the publisher. In Britain, a series of legal battles resulted in an improvement of the position of authors and booksellers in relation to publishers. The distinction between publisher and book wholesaler was weak, and many publishers offered books from other publishers through a process of exchanging part of their stock of printed books for part of a rival's stock. A few prestigious books were published by "subscription," readers and libraries financed the publication in return for a copy or copies of the publication (the "crowdfunding" model that has been revived by Kickstarter).

Most European countries in the 18th century had active censorship, principally oriented toward controlling religious and political discourse. Censors examined texts before they were published, banned the publication of texts viewed as too dangerous, and recommended texts' expurgation. A work did not have to be submitted to the censors to be affected by censorship; many books were not submitted simply because the authors and publishers knew that there was no chance that censors would allow them to be published. Censorship could be exercised by both state and church bodies. The Catholic Church's censorship also was expressed through the "Index of Forbidden Books," a list of books that Catholics were forbidden to own or read, although the influence of the "Index" was declining in the 18th century. (In Catholic states with functioning Inquisitions—that is, most Mediterranean Catholic states other than France—the Inquisition also played a role in approving books for publication.) Censorship was a major problem for many Enlightenment writers, forcing them into adopting a variety of subterfuges to publish their controversial works including circulation in manuscript, anonymous publication, pseudonyms, and the publication of books with misleading information on the place and time of publication.

Censorship regimes varied greatly between European countries. Censorship in England had been abolished with the expiration of the Licensing Act in 1695, but this did not result in the modern concept of freedom of the press. Although work did not have to be submitted to a censor before publication, printers and writers could be prosecuted after the publication of works deemed blasphemous, libelous, or subversive. Reporting on the proceedings of Parliament also was illegal. Nonetheless, Britain's freedom of the press was one of the broadest in Europe—a marvel to visiting French people, including Voltaire. Another country with a traditionally free press was the Dutch Republic; its largest city, Amsterdam, was a center of illicit publishing in French, much of it carried out by the French Protestant diaspora. French books published in London, Amsterdam, or the French-speaking city-state of Geneva between France and Switzerland frequently were smuggled into France and included many of the greatest classics of the Enlightenment. (Geneva was not a paradise of liberalism for publishers, however; Jean-Jacques Rousseau's *The Social Contract*, which was partly inspired by Genevan political debates, was publicly burned there.)

The effects of the French censorship on Enlightenment writers were mitigated from 1750 to 1763, when censorship was run by Chretien Guillame des Malesherbes (1721–1794). Malesherbes was a sympathizer of the Enlightenment and allowed many controversial books to pass into print. The presence of strong French-language presses outside France, in Geneva, Amsterdam, and London also provided a way for French writers to see their controversial works in print and even smuggled into France in large quantities. The concentration of French censors on works of the Enlightenment had the paradoxical result that all books under censorship, including pornography, were referred to as "philosophical books." This connection was exploited by the anonymous author of a classic work of 18th-century pornography, *Thérèse Philosophe* [1748], which combined an explicit account of the sexual education of the heroine with materialist and anticlerical philosophy.

There was a developed industry in France of smuggling "philosophical books" with techniques including the mixing of the pages of permitted books with banned books, a practice known as "marriage" or "larding." (Books usually were shipped unbound, thus the books could be separated before being bound.) Risks were great; convicted smugglers of banned books could be sentenced to serve on the galleys. Due to the danger of printing, importing, smuggling, and selling them, "philosophical books" sold at a premium over books that had been approved by the censors. Even owning the "wrong" books could be risky—part of the prosecution's case against the young French nobleman the Chevalier de la Barre, who was convicted of blasphemy, was his possession of Voltaire's *Philosophical Dictionary*. Particularly horrifying to the philosophes was that Barre's conviction was upheld by the Parlement of Paris, the supreme court of appeal for most of France, sitting in the very center of Enlightenment. In 1766, after being tortured, Barre was beheaded and his body was committed to the flames—after which the executioner threw in a copy of the *Philosophical Dictionary*.

Germany also was an active center of buying and selling books, hosting two of the greatest book markets in Europe, the annual Frankfurt and Leipzig book fairs. The market for books aimed at a German readership and published in German was growing during the Enlightenment, particularly after 1760. German Enlightenment readers formed clubs, such as Berlin's "Wednesday Society," to buy and discuss new books or to subscribe to the growing number of magazines that ran book reviews to help Germans keep up with the flood of new material. Germany's decentralization, with its many different sovereignties, worked in favor of the ability to publish and read. Prussia, the largest state in Germany, had a notoriously disorganized censorship, with individual censors displaying a great deal of variation. Frederick the Great attempted to remedy this situation in 1740 by centralizing censorship in the Berlin Academy, but this plan failed partially due to the reluctance of the Academicians to take on the thankless task.

The Enlightenment-influenced founders of the United States of America went beyond the British and Dutch examples in the First Amendment to the Constitution, which guarantees freedom of the press. This provision, however, like others in the first ten amendments or "Bill of Rights," did not initially apply to the states, but only to the federal government. Many states retained blasphemy laws that could punish anti-religious publications. The Sedition Act of 1798—part of a package of repressive measures passed by President John Adams's government partly due to hostility toward revolutionary France—also substantially limited freedom of the press in the United States. (The law was never repealed and thus remains on the statute books, but is now considered a "dead letter.") The reaction against the French Revolution also led to stricter censorship in Russia, which in 1793 went from a loose overseeing of the press to an institutionalized censorship.

See also: American Revolution and Founding; Bible, The; *Encyclopédie*.

Further Reading

Darnton, Robert, *The Forbidden Best-Sellers of Pre-Revolutionary France* (New York and London: Norton, 1996).

Darnton, Robert, *The Literary Underground of the Old Regime* (Cambridge, MA: Harvard University Press, 1982).

Sher, Richard B., *The Enlightenment and the Book: Scottish Authors and Their Publishers in Eighteenth-Century Britain, Ireland, and America* (Chicago: University of Chicago Press, 2010).

CALAS CASE   The Calas case, a *cause celebre* of the French Enlightenment, began in 1761 when Marc-Antoine Calas, the son of a French Protestant family of Toulouse, committed suicide. Many French Catholics despised Protestants, whose minority religion had been technically illegal since 1685. Marc-Antoine's father, Jean Calas, was charged with having murdered his son to prevent the youth from converting to Catholicism. Local Catholic priests whipped up hatred against the Calas family. Marc-Antoine received a public funeral attended by dozens of Catholic clergy. Jean Calas was tried by the Parlement (law court) of Toulouse, refusing to confess even under extreme torture. He was convicted on flimsy evidence including hearsay, and executed by public strangulation on March 10, 1762. Other members of the Calas family were banished and their property confiscated. The Calas trial arguably followed the official procedures governing French criminal trials, but it also was unjust. The leaders of the Parlement were less directly swayed by the hysteria worked up by Catholic preachers than by the hope that a single execution would avert the prospect of mass anti-Protestant violence. The possibility of a Protestant revolt at a time when France was at war with Protestant Britain was another factor. A previous war against Britain—the War of the Spanish Succession—had seen the diversion of French forces to deal with a revolt by the Protestant Camisards from 1702 to 1710.

Shortly after Calas's execution Voltaire learned of the case. Always alert for the damage wrought by religious intolerance, Voltaire concluded that in this case it had either led a father to murder his son or allowed for the assembled majesty of French law to torture and murder an innocent man. Further study of the case led him to the conclusion that Jean Calas had been wrongly executed. Voltaire championed his rehabilitation, aiding the Calas family financially, and pouring forth a torrent of writings on the case. He also used his connections at the French court to have the case revived. Calas's sentence was overturned by a specially appointed panel of judges in 1765, and the Calas family was paid compensation and allowed to return to Toulouse. This was one of several cases of religious persecution and judicial tyranny that attracted the attention of Voltaire and other French Enlightenment leaders at this time. The campaign against intolerance and the injustice of French criminal procedures continued after Voltaire's death. In 1787, French Protestants were granted civic rights.

See also: France, the Enlightenment in; Religion; Voltaire.

Further Reading

Bien, David D., *The Calas Affair: Persecution, Toleration, and Heresy in Eighteenth-Century Toulouse* (Westwood, CT: Greenwood, 1979).

CATHERINE II, "THE GREAT," OF RUSSIA (1729–1796)   The German princess Sophie of Anhalt-Zerbst was born in Stettin, Prussia (now the Polish city of Szczecin) on May 2, 1729. In 1745, she married the future Czar of Russia Peter III (1728–1762), receiving the name Catherine upon her entrance into the Russian Orthodox Church. She became empress of Russia after engineering the overthrow of her husband in 1762, following his six-month reign. (Peter was also of German origin—although his mother was Russian—and he and Catherine were second cousins.) The overthrow was followed a few days later by Peter's death under suspicious circumstances, and pretenders claiming to be Peter would plague Catherine's reign.

Catherine had an ambiguous relationship with the European Enlightenment. A great reader, she was familiar with works by Voltaire, Montesquieu, and Beccaria among others. Her reign began with some abortive projects, inspired by Montesquieu and Beccaria, to liberalize Russia, granting more personal freedom to oppressed serfs and promoting equality before the law with the creation of a conference to reform Russian law, which dated to the mid-17th century, in a more Enlightened fashion. Her 1767 *Instructions to the Legislative Commission for Composing a New Code of Laws* was aimed at a European audience and was translated into a number of European languages including French, English, and Latin. They drew on Enlightenment sources including Montesquieu, Beccaria, and the *Encyclopédie*. Although many in Europe viewed the government of Russia as a despotism—the last and worst of Montesquieu's three forms of government—Catherine insisted it was a constitutional absolutism in the European mainstream. She endorsed Enlightenment ideas such as the abolition of judicial torture. She presented Russian monarchy in the *Instructions* in largely secular terms. The Legislative Commission itself, however, accomplished little.

Catherine's reign would be marked by an emphasis on education, an area in which Russia was considerably behind most European countries. She introduced education for women into Russia, founding the Smolny Institute for Noble Girls in St. Petersburg in1764, and the Novodevichy Institute for Girls of the Third Estate in Moscow. In the early part of her reign Catherine also remodeled the education of the cadets of the Russian military along more general and Enlightened lines rather than strict military professionalism.

The suppression of the massive peasant and Cossack rebellion of the pretender to the throne, Yemelyan Ivanovich Pugachev (c. 1742–1775), in 1773 and 1774 marked the end of this period of liberal reform, although far more had been planned and announced than actually had been accomplished. In the reaction against the rebellion and driven by the need to win the support of the Russian aristocracy, Catherine tightened the grip of the nobility on the peasantry, even extending serfdom into some areas of the Empire where peasants had previously been free. Her policies on the toleration of Jews, Muslims, Roman Catholics, and other religious minorities also were inconsistent. She continued to present herself as a "philosopher-empress," however, to some members of the European Enlightenment who had little awareness of conditions in Russia—nearly universally considered a backward and savage kingdom. Denis Diderot was particularly fulsome in his flattery of Catherine, and even visited Russia from 1773 to 1774. Catherine supported Diderot by buying his library, to be delivered after his death. (Catherine also acquired Voltaire's library from his heirs.)

Even after her turn towards conservatism, Catherine continued to promote Enlightenment culture among her kingdom's elite. She was a great collector of art and a voluminous writer—the author of memoirs, fiction, and several plays and opera libretti in Russian that actually were performed. She also founded an opera house in the Winter Palace in 1763 and the Hermitage Theater in St. Petersburg in 1785. She introduced smallpox inoculation to Russia, including using matter from her own pustules to inoculate her courtiers. Catherine patronized the Imperial Academy of Sciences of St. Petersburg, Russia's leading scientific body, breaking with the tradition and culture of European science by appointing a woman—her friend Princess Ekaterina Dashkova (1743–1810)—as its head in 1782. Catherine encouraged printing (although not freedom of the press) and the translation of European books into Russian. Despite her interest in western culture and her own non-Russian origin, however, Catherine rebuked Russians who went too far in aping foreign manners.

Catherine's plays served her cultural agenda by attacking both Russian backwardness and such western exports as Freemasonry, which she found subversive and thus began to crack down on after 1785. Her foreign policy was expansionist in the Russian tradition—mainly at the expense of the declining Ottoman Empire and Poland, which disappeared in 1795 after a series of partitions divided it between Russia, Prussia, and Austria. She moved further in the direction of conservatism after the French Revolution of 1789, installing strict censorship in 1793. Catherine died of a stroke on November 17, 1796, at Tsarskoye Selo.

See also: Gender; Political Philosophy.

Further Reading

Alexander, John T., *Catherine the Great: Life and Legend* (New York: Oxford University Press, 1989).

De Madariaga, Isabel, *Catherine the Great: A Short History* (New Haven: Yale University Press, 1990).

Le Donne, John P., *Ruling Russia: Politics and Administration in the Age of Absolutism* (Princeton: Princeton University Press, 1984).

Woronzoff-Dashkoff, Alexander, *Dashkova: A Life of Influence and Exile* (Philadelphia: American Philosophical Society, 2008).

CHÂTELET, ÉMILIE DU (1706–1749)   Émilie du Châtelet was born in Paris on December 17, 1706. From an aristocratic family, du Châtelet was exposed to French intellectual culture in her mother's salon. She showed an early interest in English thought, translating Bernard de Mandeville's controversial *Fable of the Bees* (1714) which advocated self-interest and even vice as the basis for prosperity. She learned advanced mathematics and Newtonian physics from two of France's leading Newtonian scientists, Pierre-Louis Moreau de Maupertuis (1698–1759) and Alexis Clairaut. By the early 1730s, she was settled in Paris where she frequented salons and—with the acquiescence of her tolerant husband—began a series of affairs with leading thinkers, including Voltaire, whom she met in 1733.

Voltaire drafted du Châtelet, whose mathematical skills far exceeded his own, into his campaign for the replacement of Cartesian physics in France with the physics of Isaac Newton. They operated from Cirey, a rural estate, where they carried on experiments and worked on their writings. Du Châtelet's assistance was vital to Voltaire in writing his Newtonian textbook, *Elements of the Philosophy of Newton* (1738).

Du Châtelet's first published work, the anonymous *Institutes of Physics* (1740), combined Newtonian and Cartesian ideas with some of those of Newton's rival Leibniz, such as *vis viva*, living force. There was little awareness of Leibniz's physics in France at the time, and du Châtelet's work was one of its first expressions in French. (Voltaire was horrified at her respect for Leibniz—whom he loathed—and her preference for Leibniz over Newton in some instances.) The work's anonymity was considered appropriate for the work of a woman, although the author's identity quickly became generally known.

The work led to two controversies. Swiss mathematician and Leibnizian physicist Johann Samuel Konig (1712–1757), one of du Châtelet's tutors, claimed that it was derivative of his own work, an argument which appealed to the widespread belief in the intellectual inferiority of women. The Cartesian Dortous de Mairan (1678–1771), the Secretary of the Royal Academy of

Sciences, challenged du Châtelet over the formula for momentum. Her other significant work in physics was a French edition of Newton's *Mathematical Principles of Natural Philosophy* (1687), drawing on a number of editions, commentaries, and popularizations of Newton. It was not a mere translation, but included a commentary incorporating work done on mathematical physics since Newton's time. It was completed in 1749 but not published until 1759, and remains the only French translation of Newton's masterpiece. Du Châtelet also wrote a highly skeptical critique of the Bible, attacking the veracity of the prophecies of the Old Testament and the miracles of Jesus. It was not published but circulated in manuscript.

Although du Châtelet was excluded from the Royal Academy of Sciences, France's leading scientific organization, because she was a woman, she was admitted to the Bologna Academy of Sciences, one of the few European academies to admit women, an achievement in which she took great pride. Du Châtelet died in childbirth on September 10, 1749, at Luneville in the French province of Lorraine.

See also: Gender; Science; Voltaire.

Further Reading

Bodanis, David, *Passionate Minds: Emilie du Chatelet, Voltaire, and the Great Love Affair of the Enlightenment* (New York: Three Rivers Press, 2006).
Sutton, Geoffrey V., *Science for a Polite Society: Gender, Culture, and the Demonstration of Enlightenment* (Boulder, CO: Westview Press, 1995).
Zinsser, Judith P., *Emilie du Chatelet: Daring Genius of the Enlightenment* (New York: Penguin, 2006).

COLONIALISM   The Age of Enlightenment followed 200 years of European colonialism after the voyages of Christopher Columbus and Vasco da Gama at the end of the 15th century. The 18th century itself saw a series of wars that involved European colonies on a worldwide scale, and the first successful anti-colonial settler revolution, the American Revolution.

Colonial empires in the 18th century included the Spanish Empire, covering a gigantic area of the Americas from Patagonia to what is now Northern California. Britain possessed another large empire, one which, unlike the Spanish, was growing rapidly during the 18th century. France was an imperial power, but in the great imperial clashes of the 18th century, particularly the Seven Years War (1754–1763), France lost huge parts of its empire, including possessions in continental North America and India. Unlike these predominantly seaborne empires, the Russian Empire was expanding by land into the far reaches of Siberia and, by the end of the century, across the Bering Strait into Alaska. Not only European empires were growing; the empire of the Great Qing centered in China was expanding into Tibet and Central Asia.

There was no unified Enlightenment position on colonialism. Enlightenment thinker John Locke, himself a participant in the establishment of South Carolina as a British colony, often was interpreted as justifying colonialism in North America. Lockeans argued that land belonged to those who could make the best use of it, and that European-style intensive agriculture was a better use than that of Native Americans. One of the most powerful indictments of colonialism was the Abbe Raynal's *Philosophical and Political History of the Establishments and Trade of Europeans in the Two Indies* (1770), much of which was actually written by Denis Diderot. Raynal and Diderot attacked the savagery, exploitation, and greed which had marked European conquests in Africa, Asia, and the Americas.

One area enduring "first contact" with Europeans during the Enlightenment was the South Pacific. French and English voyagers, most famously the French Captain Louis-Antoine de Bougainville (1729–1811) and the English Captain James Cook (1728–1779), voyaged and "discovered" numerous islands and societies. These societies became of interest to many of the Enlightened, as they seemed to be inhabited by "natural" people. Denis Diderot in *Supplement to the Voyage of Bougainville* (1772) used fictionalized Tahitians to promote his vision of an ideal sexual morality and to contrast it with the hypocritical and life-denying morality of Diderot's contemporaries in France.

The most common and successful anticolonial use of Enlightenment ideology was not by indigenous people suffering colonization but by European settlers and their descendants seeking independence from their colonizing power. The best-known and most influential example of this phenomenon is the American Revolution and the founding of the United States, which drew on Enlightenment ideals of human rights and self-government. The position of Native Americans, by contrast, did not improve and actually degenerated in the period. Enlightenment intellectuals in Spanish America, sometimes inspired by the example of the United States, also were likely to be interested in independence or at least increased self-government, as became manifest in the Latin American revolutions of the early 19th century.

See also: American Revolution and Founding; Enlightenment Views of Africa and Africans; Enlightenment Views of Asian Civilizations; Enlightenment Views of Native Americans; Political Philosophy; Slavery.

Further Reading
Agnani, Sunil M., *Hating Empire Properly: The Two Indies and the Limits of Enlightenment Anticolonialism* (New York: Fordham University Press, 2013).

Muthu, Sankar, *Enlightenment Against Empire* (Princeton: Princeton University Press, 2003).

Whelan, Frederick G., *Enlightenment Political Thought and Non-Western Societies: Sultans and Savages* (New York: Routledge, 2009).

CONDORCET, MARIE-JEAN-ANTOINE-NICOLAS CARITAT, MARQUIS DE (1743–1794)

The Marquis de Condorcet was born on September 17, 1743, to a family of poor nobles in the city of Ribemont, France. He became a minor mathematician but an outstanding scientific statesman and a prophet of the application of mathematics to politics. His *Essay on the Application of the Analysis of Probability to Decisions Made on a Plurality of Votes* (1785), the first mathematical treatment of voting, is famous for "Condorcet's paradox," of how purely majoritarian voting must fail to represent people's true choices. Condorcet promoted liberal rather than authoritarian scientific politics. Informed by science, average citizens could make correct decisions.

Condorcet was a prodigy, one of the youngest contributors to the *Encyclopédie*. He was admitted to the Royal Academy of Sciences in 1769 on the strength of his early mathematical work. He became Secretary to the Academy in 1775. The secretary had the responsibility of writing the eloges (eulogies), of deceased members, a task Condorcet handled with such polish as to win admittance to the French Academy in 1782. He was excited by the American Revolution and was a strong supporter. Condorcet's support was recognized in America, where he was named an honorary citizen of New Haven, Connecticut. He also was a member of the anti-slavery group, the Society of the Friends of the Blacks.

Condorcet's politics were growing increasingly radical. (He was the only French Enlightenment leader to openly support the full social and political equality of women.) A supporter of the French Revolution in its early stages, Condorcet tried to secure the role of the scientific community and the Royal Academy in the new France, ultimately failing to save the Academy from abolition by the revolutionary government. He worked on a draft constitution that never went into effect. In October 1793, the victorious Jacobin party issued a warrant for the arrest of Condorcet, a member of the rival Girondin faction. Condorcet spent several months in hiding, writing his most famous work, *Sketch for a History of the Progress of the Human Mind* (1795), a classic statement of Enlightenment belief in the possibility of human advance through science and knowledge. After his arrest and imprisonment by the Jacobins, Condorcet on March 28, 1794, killed himself to avoid execution.

See also: Academies and Learned Societies; France, the Enlightenment in; French Revolution; Gender; Political Philosophy.

Further Reading

Baker, Keith, *Condorcet: From Natural Philosophy to Social Mathematics* (Chicago: University of Chicago Press, 1975).

Paul, Charles B., *Science and Immortality: The Éloges of the Paris Academy of Sciences (1699–1791)* (Berkeley and Los Angeles: University of California Press, 1980).

Rothschild, Emma, *Economic Sentiments: Adam Smith, Condorcet, and the Enlightenment* (Cambridge, MA: Harvard University Press, 2001).

DIDEROT, DENIS (1713–1784)   Denis Diderot was born on October 5, 1713, in Langres, France. He became one of the most influential French Enlightenment thinkers, particularly in his role as editor and coordinator of the *Encyclopédie*, the massive reference work which took up most of his energies from the publication of its first volume in 1751 to its last in 1765. In addition to editing the *Encyclopédie* and numerous writings on philosophy and science, Diderot was a novelist and art critic. A committed Parisian who rarely ventured far from the city, he also was a star of the salons and, like many other philosophes, was a voluminous correspondent. He engaged in numerous affairs and two long-term relationships with women.

The son of a cutler, Diderot originally was intended by his family to enter the Church. He was one of the few leaders of the French Enlightenment to attend a university and he even took a degree in theology at the Sorbonne, but he loathed religion in general and Christianity in particular. For Diderot, human desire was the ultimate arbiter of good and evil, or beauty and ugliness, and these designations had no reality transcending humanity. Diderot was a materialist influenced by Spinoza who denied any separate "spiritual" reality, and he eventually became an atheist. Humans were material beings, with no "cosmic destiny" or "free will," and as material beings they needed to follow their natural biological and social instincts. Religion restrained humans' natural desires, including sexual desires and was, at best, suspect; at worst it was destructive to natural human happiness. Diderot's posthumously published novel *The Nun* was a denunciation of the convent system along with sexual repression, and contains one of the most explicit depictions of lesbianism in 18th-century literature, treating it as a product of the convent's repression of natural sexuality. His most sexually explicit novel was *The Indiscreet Jewels* (1748), about the owner of a magic item that enables women's vaginas, or "jewels," to talk. So controversial and obscene was the work that it was a factor in Diderot's four-month confinement to the Bastille, the notorious prison in Paris, in 1749. This was not the first run-in Diderot would have with censorship; his first published book, *Philosophical Thoughts* (1746), had been sentenced to be burned by the public hangman.

In 1746, Diderot, already an experienced translator of English works into French, became involved in a project to translate an English encyclopedia. This project eventually developed into the *Encyclopédie*, not a translation but a massive compendium of knowledge according to the French Enlightenment. The project took up an enormous amount of his time and brought him into contact with most of the leading thinkers in France, as well as a vast number of second- and third-rate ones who wrote articles for him. His partner was Jean Le Rond d'Alembert, but Diderot did most of the work, particularly after d'Alembert withdrew from the project in 1759. The finished project reflects Diderot more than any other individual.

Diderot's politics were varied and inconsistent. He distrusted many of the authoritarian monarchies of 18th-century Europe, including the "enlightened despotism" of Prussia's Frederick the Great, but publicly flattered the mistress of Louis XV (of France), Madame du Pompadour (1721–1764), and Catherine the Great of Russia—even visiting Russia for a short time. (Catherine enjoyed her conversations with Diderot, but found his ideas unrealistic.) At different times he supported and opposed the hereditary law courts of France, the parlements, identifying them either as reactionaries defending their unearned privileges or as champions of the liberty of the French people against the monarchy. He also deplored European colonialism, and secretly collaborated with another French writer, Abbé Raynal, on *Philosophical and Political History of the Establishments and Trade of Europeans in the Two Indies* (1770) a passionate denunciation of the evils of imperialism. He was an early champion of the American Revolution in *The Revolution in English America* (1775). In France, much of Diderot's work circulated clandestinely in manuscript to avoid further trouble with the law. Several of Diderot's most important books were published only after his death.

Although Diderot was a materialist and a determinist, he did not believe in a "dead," clockwork universe governed solely by mechanical laws on the Newtonian model. His *Thoughts on the Interpretation of Nature* (1753) presented a theory of a self-acting, "alive" matter. Diderot integrated his "vitalistic" theory of matter with militant atheism in another dangerous work, *D'Alembert's Dream*, written in the late 1760s but not published until 1782. In the form of an imaginary dialogue with d'Alembert, *D'Alembert's Dream* attacked the idea that the universe had to be created by God by suggesting that matter not only acted by itself, but also organized itself. Diderot denied a rigid distinction between living and non-living matter, as well as between animals and humans.

Diderot also was among the most influential writers on art in the Enlightenment. In 1759, he began to review the biennial "Salons" or exhibitions of French painting. His appreciation of painting in part was based on the ability of the artist to imitate nature and promote good moral values. Diderot particularly admired Jean-Baptiste Greuze (1725–1805), whose rustic scenes combined wholesome domesticity with a sly eroticism. Diderot died in Paris on July 31, 1784.

See also: Art and Architecture; *Encyclopédie*; France, the Enlightenment in; Literature; Salons.

Further Reading

Agnani, Sunil M., *Hating Empire Properly: The Two Indies and the Limits of Enlightenment Anticolonialism* (New York: Fordham University Press, 2013).
Crocker, Lester G., *Diderot: Embattled Philosopher* (New York: Free Press, 1966).
Fowler, James (ed.), *New Essays on Diderot* (Cambridge: Cambridge University Press, 2011).
Goodden, Angelica, *Diderot and the Body* (Oxford: Legenda, 2001).

ECONOMICS   Although humans have been thinking about wealth and poverty for many centuries, the Enlightenment saw the birth of economics as an intellectual discipline. The general tendency before the Enlightenment was described—during the Enlightenment itself—as "mercantilism." Some economic historians question the usefulness of the term, but generally economic thought before the Enlightenment was characterized by an emphasis on precious metals as the embodiment of wealth and a belief in a strong state role in the economy. In Central Europe, this was called "cameralism" and justified a strong emphasis on economic discipline under overall guidance from the state.

The French school of "physiocrats" (they preferred the term "economists") tried to analyze the sources and extent of national wealth. They believed that the most important source of wealth was agriculture, and that "luxury"—by diverting resources away from the land—was an economic threat. The principal asset of a state was not gold, as earlier theorists had assumed, but productive land. Physiocrats and others also believed that a large and growing population made a country stronger. They shared the Newtonian belief that the universe was governed by laws, and believed that economic laws dictated the superiority of free trade over the economic controls that were common throughout Europe.

The prescriptions of the physiocrats, calling for free trade as well as equal taxation and the abolition of the complicated system of privileges and exemptions that distorted French finance, were a radical challenge to the existing order. The one attempt to put physiocracy into effect was the establishment of a free market in grain—a policy put into temporary, but disastrous, effect in 1774 and 1775 by the physiocrat-influenced government minister Anne-Robert-Jacques Turgot (1727–1781). (Diderot was so impressed by the failure of Turgot's policies that he broke with the consensus of most of the Enlightened to denounce free trade.) The economic literature produced in the mid-18th century usually took the form of advice to potential reforming rulers, rather than advocating revolutionary political change as the route to economic improvement. Despite the physiocratic interest in working with existing authorities, much of their program would be put in practice only after the French Revolution.

The ideas of the physiocrats were reflected in the economic articles in the *Encyclopédie* and influenced the most important economist of the Enlightenment, the Scotsman Adam Smith. The publication of Smith's *The Wealth of Nations* in 1776 often is considered the founding moment of "free market" economics. Smith's suspicion of the regulation of trade and economic activity, however, did not make him an innovator. The mainstream of Enlightenment economic theory before Smith generally looked askance on attempts to regulate or fix markets, whether they were carried out by the state or by quasi-official organizations such as guilds, organizations of workers, and business owners in particular industries. The French Revolution's abolition of guilds was part of an attempt to implement Enlightenment ideals. Smith's powerful synthesis raised the level of the debate, however, and also began to move it away from the physiocratic obsession with agriculture by focusing more of his argument on commerce and manufacturing processes. Although Smith did not directly influence the American Revolution, his criticism of an overly regulated economy had parallels in the complaints of the American colonists about the regulation of their economies for the benefit of Great Britain.

The biggest economic change in the late 18th century, the Industrial Revolution beginning in northern England, largely eluded the notice of Enlightenment writers on economics. Even Smith focused on non-industrial methods of production when discussing manufacturing.

See also: Political Philosophy; Smith, Adam.

Further Reading

Hirschman, Albert O., *The Passions and the Interests: Political Arguments for Capitalism before its Triumph,* new ed. (Princeton: Princeton University Press, 2013).

Rothschild, Emma, *Economic Sentiments: Adam Smith, Condorcet, and the Enlightenment* (Cambridge, MA: Harvard University Press, 2001).

Sakamoto, Tatsuya, and Hideo Tanaka (eds.), *The Rise of Political Economy in the Scottish Enlightenment* (London and New York: Routledge, 2003).

EDUCATION   At the beginning of the Enlightenment, European educational systems largely were in the hands of churches. The inculcation of correct religious beliefs was considered an important responsibility of educators. The 18th century saw a move towards a more secular and state-controlled system of education, one which many Enlightenment figures supported or advanced. Enlightenment philosophers believed that education should focus on subjects of practical use rather than religious dogma. The Breton magistrate Louis-Rene de Caradeuc de la Chalotais's (1701–1785) *Essay on National Education* (1763) attracted wide European interest. La Chalotais argued for a basically secular system of education in which religion would play little role and the primary determinant of what was taught was what was useful to the state.

One of the most influential Enlightenment thinkers in the philosophy of education was John Locke. Locke's belief that the mind was shaped by its perceptions of the external world rather than being born with innate ideas made education central to human development. Jean-Jacques Rousseau was another influential thinker in the field, although the type of education that he prescribed for the hero of his novel *Emile, or a Treatise on Education* (1762) was more admired than emulated. Rousseau advocated that the training of the sentiments—the "heart"—should precede the training of the mind.

The idea of compulsory education across all classes and genders remained controversial for much of the 18th century. Generally, Protestant states were more oriented to compulsory education and an ideal of universal literacy due to the Protestant emphasis on Bible reading. Leaders in the field included Scotland, Sweden, and Frederick the Great's Prussia. In Lutheran Germany, the Pietist movement strongly emphasized education and teacher training. England was a laggard among Protestant societies with a relatively low level of elementary education and literacy.

Like other activities in the Enlightenment, education was strongly gendered. Primary education frequently was offered to both boys and girls (Locke had advocated this), but higher education was almost entirely a male monopoly. This was less true in Catholic societies, where there was a tradition of convents as educational centers. Catherine the Great of Russia established institutions for the education of upper- and middle-class girls, although given the vast size of Russia these institutions had little effect.

The expulsion and suppression of the Jesuits in the third quarter of the 18th century was a crisis for education in Catholic societies on both sides of the Atlantic. The Jesuits played such a central role in schooling that their disappearance left a yawning gap—a gap that many Enlightened reformers saw as an opportunity. The vacuum created usually was filled by secular governments, rather than the Jesuit schools being transferred to another religious order. The order's expulsion from Portugal in 1759 as part of a drive toward Enlightenment centralization was followed by an increase in technical education. Although the effect largely was limited to the big urban schools, the expulsion of the Jesuits from France in 1764 was followed by an increase in the time devoted to mathematics and experimental physics in the schools the Jesuits had left.

See also: Jesuits; Political Philosophy; Religion.

Further Reading

Chisick, Harvey, *The Limits of Reform in the Enlightenment: Attitudes towards the Education of the Lower Classes in Eighteenth-Century France* (Princeton: Princeton University Press, 1981).

Hilton, Mary, and Jill Shefrin (eds.), *Educating the Child in Enlightenment Britain: Beliefs, Cultures, Practices* (Farnham, England and Burlington, VT: Ashgate, 2009).

Palmer, Robert, *The Improvement of Humanity: Education and the French Revolution* (Princeton: Princeton University Press, 1985).

ENCYCLOPÉDIE   The French Enlightenment was embodied textually in the *Encyclopédie*, an encyclopedia which appeared in France between 1751 and 1765 under the editorship of two prominent philosophes, Denis Diderot and Jean Le Rond d'Alembert. Originally planned as a French translation and expansion of Ephraim Chambers's two-volume English *Cyclopedia* (1728), it ballooned to 35 volumes of text, plates, supplements, and index, and nearly 72,000 entries. It drew on the resources of more than 100 contributors, including such leaders of the French Enlightenment as Montesquieu, Voltaire, Jean-Jacques Rousseau, Anne-Robert-Jacques Turgot (1727–1781), the Marquis of Condorcet, and the Baron d'Holbach. The workhorse of the project—writing more articles than any other contributor—was Diderot's friend, the Chevalier Louis de Jaucourt (1704–1779), who wrote approximately 18,000 articles. D'Alembert contributed a celebrated prefatory discourse, expounding an arrangement of the arts and sciences based on a threefold distinction between the sciences of reason, memory, and imagination, a classification scheme ultimately deriving from the English philosopher Francis Bacon (1561–1626). Bacon was a hero to many in the Enlightenment for his empiricism and emphasis on collaborative approaches to knowledge. The presentation of knowledge in the *Encyclopédie* marginalized theology, which often had been given pride of place in previous compilations.

The editors had great difficulty getting the book out, due to both its size and troubles with the French government over its content. D'Alembert quit in 1759, the same year that the French government formally banned the *Encyclopédie*, leaving Diderot to finish the work with the collusion of some government ministers. Despite the support it received from some members of the government, the perception of the work as politically and religiously dangerous persisted long after its publication. Like other "philosophical books" the *Encyclopédie* had to be published outside France and smuggled into the country.

The editors and many of the contributors conceived of the *Encyclopédie* not as a mere reference book but as a contribution to the progress of human society. Although the principal audience of the *Encyclopédie* was French, its mission of Enlightenment was universal and its spread was facilitated by the wide knowledge of French in European society. The contributors were of varying political and religious opinions–some were quite conservative—but the dominant voice of the *Encyclopédie* was opposed to the existing order in Church and State. In religion, it was anticlerical, strongly in favor of religious toleration, and in places anti-Christian, Deistic, and even atheistic.

The general political attitude of the *Encyclopédie* emphasized that governments and rulers should be evaluated by the degree to which they provide a better life for the common people. Although some monarchs are praised, the important criteria by which they are judged is not glory in war or religious devotion, but justice and concern for their subjects. Aristocrats frequently are contrasted unfavorably with the common people, as in the article "People." Well-being was defined largely in economic terms—in addition to its famous articles on the crafts practiced in the 18th century, the *Encyclopédie* contains more extensive and systematic treatment of economics and finance than previous encyclopedias. Not only did economic wealth contribute to human well-being, so did freedom. Some articles in the *Encyclopédie*, including several by Jaucourt, denounced contemporary slavery, although others accepted it as a fact of life. Cross-references were used to make political points—at the end of a short article on France which emphasized the country's flaws, for example, readers were directed to articles on "Taxes" and "Toleration," leading them to conclude that high taxes and lack of religious toleration were harming the country. The article on "Cannibalism," written by Diderot, cross-referenced "Eucharist," mocking the Catholic doctrine of transubstantiation, the belief that the bread and wine of the Mass literally are transformed into the body and blood of Christ.

See also: Alembert, Jean Le Rond d'; Books, Publishing, and Censorship; Diderot, Denis; France, the Enlightenment in.

Further Reading

Darnton, Robert, *The Business of Enlightenment: A Publishing History of the Encyclo-pédie, 1775–1800* (Cambridge, MA: Belknap Press of Harvard University Press, 1979).

Kafker, Frank A., in collaboration with Serena L. Kafker, *The Encyclopedists as Individuals: A Biographical Dictionary of the Authors of the Encyclopedie; Studies in Voltaire and the Eighteenth Century* 257 (Oxford: Voltaire Foundation, 1988).

ENGLAND, THE ENLIGHTENMENT IN   Many of the most characteristic elements of the Enlightenment originated in England, including Newtonian physics, John Locke's approach to political theory and epistemology, Grand Lodge Freemasonry, and limited constitutional monarchy. For a long time, however, historians debated whether there was an "English Enlightenment." Few English writers—and most of those quite marginal—displayed the hostility to religion and tradition characteristic of the French Enlightenment. Some of the most important thinkers of 18th-century England, such as the author Samuel Johnson (1709–1784) and the founder of Methodism, John Wesley (1703–1791), were opponents rather than representatives of the Enlightenment. Although the Enlightenment did not always take center stage in the intellectual and cultural history of 18th-century England, however, it definitely was a strong presence.

English intellectuals operated with certain advantages that others lacked. In 1695, the Licensing Act—which had established censorship in England—expired, and Parliament never renewed it. English writers still could be persecuted for what they published (and at the end of the Enlightenment the reaction to the French Revolution actually made publishing more dangerous), but they no longer had to receive permission for publication. Although the Church of England remained a force to be reckoned with, it lacked the institutional power and cultural hegemony wielded by the French Catholic Church or even the Scottish Presbyterian Church. Not only were Deist and anti-Christian positions aired with relative openness, the Church also coexisted with other religious bodies, including a marginalized Roman Catholicism as well as several "Dissenting" Protestant churches, including Congregationalists, Presbyterians, Baptists, and Quakers and a small but active Jewish community. The Church of England's inability to repress dissent might have been one reason that—with the exception of Edward Gibbon—the English Enlightenment produced few outspoken opponents of Christianity. (Church opposition to the secular account of the rise of Christianity in Gibbon's *The Decline and Fall of the Roman Empire* was strong, but the Church could not block its publication.)

Several champions of the English Enlightenment were Dissenting ministers, including Joseph Priestley and Richard Price (1723–1791), who were among the most prominent English intellectuals of the late Enlightenment. (The difference between the English and French Enlightenments can be seen in the shock of many Parisian intellectuals, who admired Priestley as a scientist, when finding out that he was a sincere Christian.) Even Price and Priestley targeted not the doctrine as much as the privileged position of the Church of England, which held a *de jure* monopoly on political power. This led them to support political reform, and, eventually, to sympathize with the French Revolution. The Church of England itself was an intellectually pluralistic institution, harboring several who took a skeptical and Enlightened—but not openly hostile—attitude towards Christianity. The clergyman and classical scholar Conyers Middleton (1683–1750) was skeptical towards many aspects of traditional Christianity, including the authority of the Bible, miracles (although like Gibbon he avoided direct attacks on the miracles ascribed to Jesus Christ himself), and prophecy.

In addition to being relatively religiously open, England was relatively politically open. Its parliamentary government incorporated the concept of a "loyal opposition," and under many circumstances criticism of the government, even pointed, personal criticism of leading politicians, was not considered criminal in itself. There were limits—writings aimed at the legitimacy of the British constitution or considered politically extreme in other ways could be prosecuted under the law of seditious libel, especially during the conservative backlash following the French Revolution—but in the early 18th century English freedom generally was considered a model by residents of continental countries, particularly France.

The English Enlightenment was less institutionally based than Enlightenments occurring elsewhere. England did not have the network of state-sponsored academies characteristic of France and other Continental European countries and, unlike Scotland and Germany, its universities were not intellectual leaders. (England had only two universities, Oxford and Cambridge, but Scotland—a much smaller country—had four, and Germany had dozens.) The gap was filled by Britain's major scientific society, the Royal Society, the technically oriented Society of Arts, and a variety of informal clubs and groups. Many of the informal groups that spread Enlightenment ideas and values in England were based outside of London, in the provinces and particularly in the north, where Dissent was strong. The influence of Scotland, with its innovative universities and lively Enlightenment, also was stronger in the north. There was a pronounced emphasis on the contributions of science and philosophy to economic development, as these areas also were cradles of the Industrial Revolution. The Lunar Society of Birmingham, which met from the 1760s until the early 19th century, included a leading Enlightenment philosopher and scientist, Joseph Priestley; as well as the great engineer, James Watt (1736–1819), the inventor of the separate condenser for the steam engine; and the industrialists Matthew Boulton (1728–1809) and Josiah Wedgwood (1730–1795). Other informal groups in the north included the Derby Philosophical Society, led by the Enlightened physician and poet Erasmus Darwin (1731–1802) and the Manchester Literary and Philosophical Society.

See also: Gibbon, Edward; Locke, John; Newton, Isaac; Paine, Thomas; Priestley, Joseph.

Further Reading

Bulman, William J., *Anglican Enlightenment: Orientalism, Religion, and Politics in England and its Empire, 1648–1715* (Cambridge: Cambridge University Press, 2015).

Porter, Roy, *The Creation of the Modern World: The Untold Story of the British Enlightenment* (New York and London: W. W. Norton, 2000).

Porter, Roy, *Flesh in the Age of Reason: The Modern Foundations of Body and Soul* (New York and London: W. W. Norton, 2003).

Stewart, Larry, *The Rise of Public Science: Rhetoric, Technology, and Natural Philosophy in Newtonian Britain, 1660–1750* (Cambridge: Cambridge University Press, 1992).

Uglow, Jenny, *The Lunar Men: Five Friends whose Curiosity Changed the World* (New York: Farrar, Straus, and Giroux, 2002).

ENLIGHTENMENT VIEWS OF AFRICA AND AFRICANS Enlightenment philosophers often shared the derogatory view of the intellectual and moral capacities of African and African-descended peoples common among 18th-century whites. One notorious example is David Hume, who likened Africans who seemed to be educated in European literature and thought to trained parrots, repeating what they had learned without understanding it.

Much of the African continent was a "blank space on the map" to 18th-century Europeans, despite the growth of travel literature dealing with Africa. Outside of the coastal areas, the interior of Africa was largely unknown due to the difficulties of the terrain and the presence of numerous diseases with which Europeans had no experience. African states, although willing to trade with Europeans, also were interested in restricting European involvement in Africa to the coasts. European ignorance of Africa made it a good setting for imaginary or quasi-imaginary kingdoms in fiction, the most famous example being *The History of Rasselas, Prince of Abisinnia* (1759) by the anti-Enlightenment English writer Samuel Johnson (1709–1784). (Abisinnia is modern

Ethiopia, but Johnson's kingdom had little to do with the real Ethiopia.) Denis Diderot's semi-pornographic *The Indiscreet Jewels* (1748) was set in a fictitious African kingdom in the Congo, but was really a satire of Louis XV's France.

Contact between Europeans and Africans in Europe was growing in the 18th century, and a few Africans were accepted as members—albeit marginal members—of the intellectual community. Abram Petrovich Gannibal (1696–1781) was a Russian military engineer of Central African origin and an acquaintance of some Enlightenment leaders. (Gannibal was the great-grandfather of the Russian poet Alexander Pushkin (1799–1837), who wrote his biography.) Anton Wilhelm Amo (1703?–1759?) became the first African to be awarded a degree from a European university when he received his degree from the University of Halle in 1729. His dissertation was on the legal rights of Africans in Europe. Amo went on to earn a doctoral degree from the University of Wittenberg and then taught in a German university. The hostility he was subjected to, however, eventually led him to return to Africa.

Africans active in the English-speaking intellectual world included the letter-writer Ignatius Sancho (1729–1780), the autobiographer and abolitionist Olaudah Equiano (1745–1797), the abolitionist pamphleteer Qobna Ottobah Cugoano (1757–1791), and the American poet Phyllis Wheatley (1753–1784).

Much of the contact that Europeans had with Africans was through the slave trade, which was becoming controversial in the 18th century. Attitudes towards Africans did not always relate directly to attitudes towards slavery. Despite his belief in the inferiority of Africans, Hume opposed slavery, but the Enlightened American slave owner Thomas Jefferson (1743–1826) used the language of 18th-century science to assert that the inferiority of Africans justified their enslavement despite his own ambivalence towards the institution.

Emerging ideas of racial hierarchy in the Enlightenment generally put the dark-skinned peoples—and particularly Africans—at the bottom. The Khoikhoi people of the extreme African south, known as "Hottentots," were particularly disparaged, frequently viewed as the lowest rung of humanity (although, by the end of the century, Australian aborigines had come to challenge them for that unenviable distinction). The dominant framework for thinking about race in the late 18th century saw Africans as having "degenerated" from an original state that was more like that of Europeans due to the hot climate of Africa. A minority view saw Africans as having emerged from a different group than Europeans and being other "races" entirely—in effect being a separate species. The late 18th century saw a series of attempts to quantify racial differences, often based on measurements of skulls.

See also: Colonialism; Slavery.

Further Reading

Eze, Emmanuel Chukwudi, *Race and the Enlightenment: A Reader* (Cambridge, MA: Blackwell, 1997).

Jordan, Winthrop D., *White over Black: American Attitudes towards the Negro 1550–1812,* 2nd ed. (Chapel Hill: University of North Carolina Press, 2012).

Schiebinger, Londa, *Nature's Body: Gender in the Making of Modern Science* (Boston: Beacon, 1993).

ENLIGHTENMENT VIEWS OF ASIAN CIVILIZATIONS The 18th century was a time when Europe's connections with Asia were becoming closer and richer through trade, travel, and warfare. Knowledge of Asian societies was growing, and their ways posed many questions for enlightened thinkers. There was debate about the nature of Asian societies and polities. Montesquieu asserted that despotism—the worst form of government—was broadly characteristic of Asian societies, from Europe's neighbor the Ottoman Empire to Japan. Others argued that Asian societies were not despotic and that they had strong similarities to the limited monarchies of Europe.

China dominated European awareness of East Asia in the 18th century. Japan was the "closed country," its contact with the west was restricted to a few Dutch traders confined to an artificial island in the harbor of the port of Nagasaki. Korea was even more closed, limiting all foreign contact to intermittent contact with China. In the West, Korea was known as the "Hermit Kingdom." Relatively accessible China was popular among many of the Enlightened, particularly in France, as it seemed to be governed by philosophers rather than priests. This picture owed much to the Jesuit missionaries who had been active in China since the late 16th century and were the principal source of European knowledge of the country. The Jesuits emphasized Confucianism—a religion of the Chinese elite with a strong, "classical," written tradition—over the Buddhist and polytheist practices of the Chinese people. The first translation of Confucian classics into a European language, *Confucius, Philosopher of the Chinese* appeared in Latin under Jesuit auspices in 1687. The Jesuit authors proclaimed that the Confucian system represented a height of what human reason, unaided by divine revelation, could achieve. Dependence on the Jesuits for knowledge of China meant that enlightened thinkers, like other Europeans, were more aware of Confucianism than they were of the importance of Buddhism, Taoism, and the worship of gods in Chinese life.

Gottfried Wilhelm Leibniz had a strong interest in Chinese thought, and corresponded with Jesuits in China. He hoped that China could provide a model of toleration for religiously divided Europe. Such was Leibniz's admiration for the civility of Chinese culture that he hoped (in vain) for China to send missionaries to Europe. His intellectual follower, Christian Wolff (1679–1754), argued in a lecture at the University of Halle that Confucianism showed that human reason unaided by supernatural revelation could come up with a sound system of morality. This was so controversial that Wolff lost his position at Halle and was forced to leave Prussian territory under penalty of death. Europeans also knew China from the vogue for collecting and displaying Chinese porcelains and the mid-18th century craze for *chinoiserie*, the use of decorative motifs in the Chinese style.

Although none of the major thinkers of the Enlightenment ever made the long journey to China, there was personal contact with a few Chinese Christians that had come to Europe. Montesquieu conversed with a Chinese Christian named Arcadio Huang (1679–1716), who had done pioneering work on presenting the Chinese language in French and had become the librarian of the Chinese works in the collection of the French King. A broader range of Chinese literature extending beyond the classics became available to Europeans. Voltaire freely adapted a Chinese play, *The Orphan of Zhao*, into *The Orphan of China,* which premiered at the Comédie Française in 1755 and praised civilized Chinese values over the barbarity of the invading Tartars of Genghis Khan. The long Chinese annals stretching back thousands of years was also a weapon for European skeptics of the Biblical narrative of humanity's past, who pointed out that the Chinese historical records said nothing of a worldwide flood and other global events recounted in the Bible.

Not all understanding of China was positive. Although Confucianism was admired, Buddhism and Chinese popular religion frequently were scorned as superstitious. Westerners believed that their own science, mathematics, and music were demonstrably superior to that of the Chinese (and some Chinese agreed), and some painted a picture of the Chinese people as weak and subservient in comparison with the independent peoples of the west. The stereotype of Chinese men as "effeminate" in contrast with virile and warlike European men had a long history before the Enlightenment. China also was viewed negatively as a "stagnant" civilization, in which reverence for the past prevented progressive development. The growing influence of racial thinking in the late Enlightenment subordinated Chinese and other East Asian peoples to Europeans in European thinking, although East Asians were often allotted the second place in the racial hierarchy after white people.

Voltaire's attitude to China was ambivalent. He employed China as an example of how a civilization could grow and flourish without any significant influence from the monotheistic religions of the West. He also thought, however, that the Chinese had failed to develop anything like Western science or music.

By contrast with philosophical China, Hindu India often was portrayed as priest-ridden and its population excessively "superstitious" in its religion, plagued with "Brahmins" portrayed in anticlerical terms as parasites on society. The Enlightenment picture of the Brahmins was ambivalent, however. Brahmins could also be portrayed as wise and serene, for example, as in Voltaire's parable of the Good Brahmin. Politically, India—like China—often (but not always) was viewed as despotic. Generally, the active role in the construction of India despotism was ascribed to the Muslims and the "passive" role to the Hindus. Knowledge of Indian culture was expanding particularly rapidly at the end of the century, with the growing empire exerted by the English East India Company and the activities of the British philologist and company employee Sir William Jones (1746–1794) and the Asiatick Society of Bengal. Jones identified the commonalities between Indian and European languages, drawing the two cultures closer together and eventually leading to the creation of the category of "Indo-European."

Eighteenth-century Europeans had little awareness of Buddhism—a word that Buddhists themselves did not use. Edward Gibbon and other scholars thought that Buddha was the same figure as the god Odin who was worshipped by the early medieval Norse.

See also: Colonialism; Enlightenment Views of Muslims and Islam.

Further Reading

Ahmed, Siraj, *The Stillbirth of Capital: Enlightenment Writing and Colonial India* (Stanford: Stanford University Press, 2012).

Ching, Julia, and Willard G. Oxtoby (eds.), *Discovering China: European Interpretations in the Enlightenment* (Rochester, NY: University of Rochester Press, 1992).

Whelan, Frederick G., *Enlightenment Political Thought and Non-Western Societies: Sultans and Savages* (New York: Routledge, 2009).

ENLIGHTENMENT VIEWS OF JEWS AND JUDAISM   The Enlightenment inherited much of the hostility to Jews and Judaism that seemed a permanent feature of European life. Traditional condemnation of the Jews for not accepting Christianity—extending to the belief that Jews were responsible for the death of Jesus Christ—was not usually held by the Enlightened, but there were numerous other ways Enlightenment thinkers denigrated Jews and their religion. The hostility was accompanied by more favorable attitudes among some Enlightened thinkers, however, and Jews themselves could be followers or even widely admired leaders of the movement.

Ideas about Judaism were affected by ideas about religion in general. Those hostile to organized religion of any sort were naturally hostile to Judaism. Moses, along with Jesus and Muhammad, was identified by religious radicals as one of the "Three Impostors." One area where Enlightened anti-Semitism differed from traditional European anti-Semitism was that the Enlightened did not exempt the Jews of the Old Testament from criticism. The genocidal brutality towards the indigenous inhabitants of Canaan displayed in the early books of the Jewish Bible received particularly harsh criticism as did aspects of Jewish law, including circumcision and dietary restrictions, which seemed ridiculous in the eyes of people of the 18th century.

Hostility was not reserved for the ancient Jewish people and their religion and often also was directed to contemporary Jews. Stereotypes of Jews as greedy and dishonest were held by many leaders of the Enlightenment— Voltaire prominent among them—although the more extreme Christian stereotypes of the Jews as ritual murderers were scorned.

There also was a positive view of Jews, however, particularly among advocates of religious toleration who condemned the long history of European Christian discrimination and violence against the Jewish community. Montesquieu bitterly denounced the cruelty of anti-Semitic persecution. He then suggested that persecution had contributed to the development of society by forcing the Jews into commerce, a field in which they had made innovations that were beneficial to society as a whole. Even those who did not like Jews usually believed that their religion should be tolerated openly, if ridiculed privately. A few Jews, most notably Moses Mendelssohn of Berlin, were accepted as members of the Enlightened community. Mendelssohn argued that Judaism—which unlike its offshoots Christianity and Islam did not seek to make converts—actually was more compatible than was an Enlightened society based on religious toleration. This argument found some support among non-Jewish Enlightened thinkers as well.

Mendelssohn's Christian admirer—Gotthold Ephraim Lessing—used him as a model for the main character in his play, *Nathan the Wise* (1778), which strongly advocated mutual toleration among Jews, Christians, and Muslims. Jean-Jacques Rousseau—although he devoted little of his writings to Jewish topics—was a strong admirer of Moses as a lawgiver and the institutions he had bequeathed to the Jews that had preserved a strong Jewish sense of a collective identity separate from that of other peoples. Rousseau even admired Jewish institutions as superior in some ways (such as their emphasis on compassion) to the ancient societies of the Spartans and Romans that he otherwise held as exemplars.

The growing toleration of Judaism in "Enlightened" states was very different from admitting Jews as citizens fully equal to their Christian fellows. The identification of Christian affiliation with full membership in the polity was a very old one in the West, dating back to the late Roman Empire. The first western state to treat Jews as full citizens was the United States, inspired by the ideals of the Enlightenment. American leaders including George Washington distinguished the equal role Jews could play in the new American commonwealth from mere toleration. Revolutionary France was the first European state to admit Jews as full citizens, although revolutionaries generally had a dim view of traditional Jewish institutions, culture, and religion.

See also: Jewish Enlightenment; Mendelssohn, Moses; Religion; Spinoza, Baruch.

Further Reading

Bodeker, Hans Erich, Clorinda Donato, and Peter Hanns Reill (eds.), *Discourses of Tolerance and Intolerance in the European Enlightenment* (Toronto: University of Toronto Press, 2009).

Hertzberg, Arthur, *The French Enlightenment and the Jews: The Origins of Modern Anti-Semitism* (New York: Columbia University Press, 1990).

ENLIGHTENMENT VIEWS OF MUSLIMS AND ISLAM   For centuries, Europeans had had more exposure to Islam and more awareness of it than they had of any other "non-Western" religion or culture. Enlightenment views of Islam built on this long history, but also marked a partial break from the traditional hostility to the "faith of the Prophet" shown by Western Christians. As Europe's nearest Muslim neighbor, the Ottoman Empire, declined militarily—particularly following the Austrian Habsburg reconquest of Hungary in 1687—no Islamic power was a serious menace to European Christian civilization, a fact which worked for more balanced views of Islam and its adherents. The secularism and hostility to Christianity characteristic of some parts of the Enlightenment also enabled writers to break through the traditional hostility to Islam to treat it in innovative ways. There was a growing body of scholarship by historians and religious scholars studying Islamic history and texts with new translations of the Quran and other Islamic writings into European languages. The new circumstances, however, did not mean that Enlightenment writers always were favorable in their discussions of Islam.

Views of Islam and its founder were shaped by overall attitudes toward religion as well as feelings about Islam specifically. Radical opponents of religion linked Muhammad with Moses and Jesus as the "Three Imposters." Paradoxically, by implying that Muhammad was no worse than Jesus or Moses, these works actually might have raised the status of Islam. More positive views also existed. Some people, such as the French historian Comte Henri de

Boulainviller (1658–1722), author of *Life of Mohammed* (1728), were sympathetic toward Deism or Unitarian Christianity and hostile toward the doctrine of the Trinity. They saw the Prophet of Islam as a reformer of a corrupted Christianity, admiring Muhammad for emphasizing the unity of God against the Christian tendency to treat Jesus as a divine son of God rather than a wise man or a prophet. The most complex and balanced treatment of Muhammad in the European Enlightenment came from Edward Gibbon, whose discussion of the origin of Islam in *The Decline and Fall of the Roman Empire* (1776–1788) treated the prophet as an evolving figure from early religious visionary to mature statesman and warrior, rather than trying to reduce him to a simple type, whether fraud, fanatic, or sage.

Islam historically had been more tolerant than Christianity, which attracted some Enlightenment admiration. The medieval Muslim ruler Saladin (1137–1198)—who had defeated the Crusaders—was given positive treatment in Gotthold Ephraim Lessing's play *Nathan the Wise* (1778). The prominence of charitable institutions in Islamic societies also drew praise for the way in which Muslims practiced the religious duty of charity. Islamic countries, however, regardless of how tolerant or charitable their beliefs and practices, generally were not believed to have "Enlightened" governments and were not subject to the idealization that sometimes was granted to the Chinese government or to ancient non-Christian societies. The Islamic government that Europeans were most familiar with was that of the Ottoman Empire, and the Ottoman sultan was widely viewed as a despot, a view with roots going back for centuries. The aggressive wars that Russia (under Catherine the Great) fought against the Ottomans were supported by many of the Enlightened, who saw the wars as advancing a superior civilization. This view extended to other Muslim rulers, such as the rulers of Persia and India. Montesquieu in *The Spirit of the Laws* (1748) identified Islam as well-suited for despotic governments as Catholicism was for monarchies and Protestantism was for republics. Montesquieu's earlier work, *Persian Letters* (1721), however, used a philosophical Muslim visitor to France to mock what he saw as the follies of contemporary Christian civilization.

Muslim societies, along with other non-western societies, were also condemned for their customs regarding marriage and gender. Europeans condemned polygamy and the custom of the strict separation of women from men outside of their families. Lacking the civilizing influence of women, Muslim societies were condemned to cultural backwardness and despotism. Even Montesquieu's philosophical Persian was a tyrant over his harem.

See also: Enlightenment Views of Asian Civilizations; Gender; Montesquieu, Charles-Louis de Secondat, Baron de; Political Philosophy; Religion.

Further Reading

Bulman, William J., *Anglican Enlightenment: Orientalism, Religion, and Politics in England and its Empire, 1648–1715* (Cambridge: Cambridge University Press, 2015).

Elmarsafy, Ziad, *The Enlightenment Qur'an: The Politics of Translation and the Construction of Islam* (Oxford: Oneworld, 2009).

Gunny, Ahmad, *The Prophet Muhammad in French and English Literature, 1650 to the Present* (Markfield, UK: Islamic Foundation, 2010).

Whelan, Frederick G., *Enlightenment Political Thought and Non-Western Societies: Sultans and Savages* (New York: Routledge, 2009).

ENLIGHTENMENT VIEWS OF NATIVE AMERICANS   By the time of the Enlightenment, Europeans had been in contact with the indigenous people of America for centuries. Ideas about them varied from the belief that they were ignorant savages who should be displaced or killed by European settlers, to the less common belief that they were wise and that their societies were marked by a contempt for wealth and status that Europeans would do well to emulate. The French and Spanish, whose colonizing ventures in North America relied on cooperation with Native groups, generally were more positive toward Natives than were the British, whose colonizing strategy—with a few exceptions—relied on the exclusion of Native communities and the settlement of the land by European colonists and their slaves.

The dislike of Native Americans carried over into the Revolutionary movement. The Declaration of Independence, the product of Enlightened revolutionaries, refers to Natives allied with the British government as "merciless Indian savages." French writers, by contrast, were more likely to cast Natives as "noble savages" and as satirical commenters on the follies of European society, as in Voltaire's *The Innocent* (1767) which uses a fictional late 17th-century Huron visitor to France to mock Christianity and religious intolerance. Voltaire's novel *Candide* (1759) presents a Native American utopia in the form of the land of El Dorado.

The Native American frequently was portrayed in Enlightenment writing as living a simple life in a society that, unlike Europe's, was not dominated by social inequality and private property. Natives, like South Pacific islanders, stood for the ideal of "natural man" untouched by either the vices or the refinements of civilization. The common—though inaccurate—perception of North American Natives as being entirely hunter-gatherers rather than agriculturalists, however, was used to justify the taking of Native lands by settlers. In the minds of many Enlightenment leaders, particularly John Locke, settlers could use the land in more productive ways. Particularly for the Scottish Enlightenment, Natives also could serve as living examples of the early "hunting" stage of social development, before the rise of herding and agriculture, and thus frequently were linked to the early Greeks, Romans, and Germans whose societies had originated under similar circumstances.

The growth of racial thinking in the late Enlightenment led to a diminishment of the status of Native Americans. In the "debate over the New World" some European naturalists argued that humans, like other animals, tended to degenerate in the Americas. This applied to European colonists as well as Natives, but it more strongly emphasized Natives who had been residing in the Americas for many centuries. Europeans seized on the sparse facial hair of Native men to argue for their innate inferiority and degeneracy as compared to fully bearded Europeans, and claimed that Natives has a lower level of sexual desire than did Europeans.

See also: Colonialism; Locke, John; Nature; Political Philosophy; Sex.

Further Reading
Gerbi, Antonello, *The Dispute of the New World: History of a Polemic, 1750–1900,* translated by Jeremy Moyle (Pittsburgh: University of Pittsburgh Press, 1973).
Pagden, Anthony, *European Encounters with the New World: From Renaissance to Romanticism* (New Haven: Yale University Press, 1993).
Whelan, Frederick G., *Enlightenment Political Thought and Non-Western Societies: Sultans and Savages* (New York: Routledge, 2009).

FRANCE, THE ENLIGHTENMENT IN   French culture was at the heart of European civilization in the 18th century. French was the international language of the social elite, and the etiquette and customs of the French court and the Parisian upper classes were widely imitated. Persons from all over Europe as well as from the French provinces came to Paris to experience the glory of French civilization and the legendarily sophisticated society and beautiful women of the capital. France also could glory in having a set of Enlightenment thinkers and institutions that was second to none.

Despite the French achievement, however, the French Enlightenment was driven not by cultural chauvinism and complacency but by a struggle to make France better. In this struggle the enemy was the intellectual and political authority of the Catholic Church and the inefficiency and repressiveness of the French state, the French class system, and French culture. So universal was the consensus of the French Enlightenment that France needed reform, that the country never developed an "Enlightened conservatism" such as that of David Hume in Scotland. The struggle to transform France largely was carried on in the name of reason, and in it the French Enlightenment proudly incorporated influences from foreign cultures and countries. Foremost among these was England, which from France looked like a land of free speech and religious toleration. The publication of Voltaire's *Letters from England* in 1732 was not the beginning of French "Anglomania," but it was a high point.

French philosophes—led by Voltaire and Montesquieu—admired England for its "free institutions" (such as Parliament), the lack of censorship, and the ability of persons to worship as they pleased. Voltaire and his girlfriend and intellectual partner, the Marquise du Châtelet, worked tirelessly to introduce the physics of Isaac Newton to a France where the physical concepts of Rene Descartes (1596–1650) still held sway over much of science. Britain's success in its wars with France—including the major conflicts of the War of the Spanish Succession, the War of the Austrian Succession, and the Seven Years War—added to the prestige of Britain in France and the feeling among many French intellectuals that the British must be doing something right. By the late 18th century, however, England had been replaced as an object of admiration in the minds of many by the newly independent United States of America.

Foreign rulers—enlightened despots such as Frederick of Prussia and Catherine of Russia—also were admired, and implicitly or explicitly contrasted with the feckless rulers of Enlightenment France, Louis XV (r. 1715–1764) and Louis XVI (r. 1764–1792). Realizing the importance of France as an intellectual and cultural leader, Frederick, Catherine, and other European rulers cultivated relationships with French Enlightenment intellectuals through flattery and patronage. Madame du Pompadour [1721–1764], the mistress of Louis XV, who was a leading figure in the government for many years, was a friend and admirer of many of the Enlightenment leaders, however. Some praised her, although Pompadour also was blamed for French defeat in the Seven Years War. The brief ministry of the Enlightened statesman Anne-Robert-Jacques Turgot (1727–1781) at the beginning of the reign of Louis XVI also attracted Enlightened admiration, but Turgot's fall reinforced the disappointment which many felt with the French political system.

Despite their admiration of foreign cultures and rulers, and their grumbling at the inefficiencies and repressiveness of their own government, French people never lost sight of the glories and pleasures of French life. Even the "Anglomaniac" Voltaire believed that many aspects of English civilization were inferior to those of France and few French philosophes ever made England a home. Voltaire journeyed to Frederick's Berlin, and Diderot to Catherine's St. Petersburg, but both quickly lost their enthusiasm for these "enlightened despots" after a closer look and returned home. Foreigners shared this admiration for the French culture and way of life. The American Thomas Jefferson (1743–1826), ambassador to France from 1785 to 1789, said that every well-traveled man would prefer to live in his own country, but every man's second choice would be France.

French religious institutions in the 18th century still were shaped by Louis XIV's revocation of the Edict of Nantes in 1685. The revocation deprived French Protestants (or "Huguenots") of their tolerated position and made France officially intolerant of all religions other than Catholicism, the religion of the vast majority of the French people. The ban on non-Catholic religion had many loopholes in practice, but it was scorned universally by the philosophes. Not only did they condemn it as religiously intolerant, they also pointed out the Huguenot diaspora had taken its industry and skill and used them for the benefit of other European countries.

One particularly aggravating challenge that church and state posed to French philosophes was censorship. Censorship forced many of the most important French Enlightenment books either to remain in manuscript form or be published outside of France and smuggled into the country. French society, however, also offered a multitude of opportunities and venues for the circulation and promotion of Enlightenment ideas. The presence of a lively French-language press outside of France—in the Dutch Republic, in the French-speaking city-state of Geneva, and even in London, much of it run by French Protestant exiles and their descendants—meant that challenging Enlightenment books in French could be published outside of the country and then smuggled into it. The trade was so established that many respectable, middle-class French people made regular orders for illegal books just as they did for legal books. The French government also monitored the conversation of the French people, particularly in Paris, via a system employing hundreds of police spies. The spies reported on conversations in public houses and on the streets, and monitored even the humblest writers if their work was in any way "dangerous" to the French regime. Despite this fact, many pamphlets and broadsheets attacking the monarchy circulated freely in the last decades before the French Revolution.

As well as being repressive, French society and the French State also were viewed by Enlightened thinkers as being irrational. Centuries of inherited custom and privilege had produced a society both inefficient and inequitable. Although nobles in the 18th century had lost some of the unchallenged social preeminence they had possessed in earlier eras, they still held many privileges—including a virtual monopoly on the higher offices in church and state. The irrationality of French institutions also was clear in the presence of internal trade barriers between French provinces, which prevented the emergence of a national market for grain.

The one time before the Revolution when France could be said to have been governed in an enlightened way was the brief period under Louis XVI when Turgot was in power. Turgot was an ally of the physiocratic school of economics and one of the few Enlightenment intellectuals to hold power before the American and French revolutions. In the disputes between King Louis XV and the *parlements,* Turgot had taken the side of the king. Turgot also was a vehement supporter of the Calas family in its struggle to have the conviction of Jean Calas reversed. Turgot's interest in economics led him to the French physiocrats Francois Quesnay (1694–1774) and Jean-Claude Gournay (1712–1759). Turgot became identified as a champion of the Enlightenment party, and Enlightenment intellectuals worked to place him in power in the French government. His period in power saw attempts to establish a national market in grain—attempts that proved disastrous and were followed by court intrigues that saw Turgot driven from power.

One of the principal institutions of the French Enlightenment was the salon, a regular social gathering of intellectuals and conversationalists. The unmonitored and unregulated conversation of the salon made it a place for relative intellectual freedom. Nearly all salons were run by women, which is testimony to the role that intellectual women played in the French Enlightenment. This was noted and frequently praised by visitors from other countries.

Another institution central to French Enlightenment culture—but far more regulated than other institutions, and one that demonstrated that the relationship of the French State to the Enlightenment was ambiguous rather than forthrightly hostile—was the Academy. Academies were state-sponsored groups of men who were recognized for and, for the most prestigious positions at the most prestigious academies, were paid for their outstanding contributions. The three great academies—all founded in the 17th century, well before the Enlightenment—were based in Paris, the center of French intellectual life. They were the French Academy, which recognized achievements in literature and language, the Royal Academy of Sciences which was devoted to science, and the Academy of Inscriptions, which was devoted to classical knowledge. Admission to one of the national academies was both financially rewarding and the highest honor the French system could bestow on an intellectual. The campaign of the Enlightened to enter the national academies, originally dominated by conservatives, was long and painstaking. The country also had many provincial academies, bodies of somewhat lesser prestige but which offered an intellectual life to provincial towns and sometimes attracted attention from leading writers and philosophers, such as when Rousseau's *Discourse on the Arts and Sciences* was submitted to a contest at the Academy of Dijon.

See also: Academies and Learned Societies; Alembert, Jean Le Rond d'; Calas Case; Condorcet, Marie-Jean-Antoine-Nicolas Caritat, Marquis de; Diderot,

Denis; *Encyclopédie*; French Revolution; Holbach, Paul Heinrich Dietrich, Baron d'; Montesquieu, Charles-Louis de Secondat, Baron de; Rousseau, Jean-Jacques; Salons; Voltaire.

Further Reading

Gay, Peter, *The Party of Humanity: Essays in the French Enlightenment* (New York: Knopf, 1964).

Hesse, Carla, *The Other Enlightenment: How French Women Became Modern* (Princeton: Princeton University Press, 2009).

McManners, John, *Death and the Enlightenment: Changing Attitudes to Death among Christians and Unbelievers in Eighteenth-Century France* (Oxford: Oxford University Press, 1981).

Roche, Daniel, *France in the Enlightenment,* translated by Arthur Goldhammer (Cambridge, MA: Harvard University Press, 2000).

FRANKLIN, BENJAMIN (1705–1790) Benjamin Franklin, the first native of the American colonies to win European recognition as a philosopher and scientist, was born in Boston on January 17, 1706, the son of a tallow chandler and soap boiler. As a printer in Boston and Philadelphia, the young Franklin was a voluminous writer, spreading Enlightenment ideas of reason and toleration as well as hard work and sociability. Franklin was raised in a household of New England Puritans, but he did not publicly espouse a particular creed or attend a church regularly, and his religion appears to have been Deistic, particularly after he moved to Philadelphia in 1723 and went into business as a printer. One major vehicle for disseminating Franklin's ideas was *Poor Richard's Almanac,* a yearly publication appearing from 1732 to 1758. Upon retiring from his printing business in 1748, Franklin devoted more of his time to electrical science and politics.

Franklin's greatest contribution to science was the "one-fluid" theory of electricity, one of the liveliest topics in 18th-century science. Previous electrical theories had been based on "effluvia"—tiny electrical particles. Although he did not dispense totally with effluvia, Franklin identified electricity as a universal fluid, and distinguished between electrified states as "positive," or saturated with the electrical fluid, and "negative" or deficient in it. Although this theory was zealously contested for years, with many scientists in Europe advocating a "two-fluid" theory, Franklin also supported—although he did not originate—the idea that lightning was electricity. It is not clear whether he actually performed the famous experiment with a kite and a key. His invention of the lightning rod, however, had a huge cultural impact as an outstanding example of the practical benefits of science. The debate over whether it was permissible to use lightning rods pitted secularists against those ministers and others who believed it blasphemous to ward off "God's lightning" and was a classic quarrel of the Enlightenment. Franklin's theories eventually formed the basis of electrical science. *Experiments and Observations on Electricity, Made at Philadelphia in America, by Mr. Benjamin Franklin, and Communicated to Mr. P. Collinson of London, F.R.S.* (1751) was printed in London. It was translated into French, German, and Italian and made a great impression in Europe. Franklin became by far the best-known British American natural philosopher in Enlightened circles. In America, he became the first president of the American Philosophical Society, a position he held from its founding in 1768 until his death in 1790.

Franklin—who had spent some time in England as a young man—originally worked for closer relations between Britain and its American colonies. After the British bitterly disappointed him by not following his advice, however, Franklin became supportive of American independence. As the ambassador of the American rebels in Paris, he played a crucial role in the formation of the alliance with France and in garnering French financial support for the rebellion. Franklin presented himself as both a wise philosopher and as a simple, unpretentious man whose plain dress contrasted with the elaborate clothing of the French elite. His universal respect among "enlightened" French people helped raise the prestige of the American cause. In Paris, he was closely involved with leading Enlightenment institutions, including the salon of Madame Helvetius (1722–1800), the Royal Academy of Sciences, and the Masonic Lodge of the Nine Sisters (which he headed from 1779 to his departure from France in 1781. Upon his return to America after the Revolution, Franklin helped devise the new constitution and was one of the earliest prominent advocates of the abolition of slavery.

Franklin died of pleurisy on April 17, 1790, at his home in Philadelphia. He received a magnificent public funeral befitting the city's leading citizen, and the American Congress and the French National Assembly also paid tribute. Franklin's posthumously published autobiography was the first secular American autobiography, and provided an influential model for the "American dream" of self-advancement through hard work and study. His French contemporary Anne-Robert-Jacques Turgot (1727–1781) said of Franklin that he snatched the lightning from heaven and the scepter from tyrants.

See also: Academies and Learned Societies; American Revolution and Founding; Freemasonry; Science.

Further Reading

Dull, Jonathan R., *Benjamin Franklin and the American Revolution* (Lincoln, NE: University of Nebraska Press, 2010).

Morgan, Edmund S., *Benjamin Franklin* (New Haven: Yale University Press, 2002).

Schiffer, Michael Brian, *Draw the Lightning Down: Benjamin Franklin and Electrical Technology in the Age of Enlightenment* (Berkeley and Los Angeles: University of California Press, 2003).

FREDERICK II, "THE GREAT," OF PRUSSIA (1712–1786)   Frederick the Great, King of Prussia, was born on January 24, 1712, in Berlin, the capital of the Kingdom of Prussia. From an early age Frederick was attracted to French culture, despite the vehement opposition of his conservative and military-obsessed father, the "Soldier-King," Frederick William I (1688–1740). The relations between the father and son hit their lowest level in 1730, when Prince Frederick attempted to flee the country only to be brought back, imprisoned, and court-martialed. His best friend, Hans Hermann von Katte (1704–1730), was executed in front of him at his father's order.

On his succession to the throne in 1740 after his father's death, Frederick was determined to remold Prussia partially along Enlightened lines. He presented himself as the greatest champion of Enlightenment among European sovereigns, although the degree to which Enlightenment principles informed his government is another matter. Frederick's main interest in Enlightened government was efficiency. Prussia was far smaller than the principal Continental European powers, Austria, Russia, and France. To compete with them militarily, it was necessary that the Prussian government maximize the resources it had, with high and honestly collected taxes, efficient courts, responsible bureaucrats, and a nobility that served the state.

Strict administration had existed in Prussia long before the Enlightenment and was particularly associated with Frederick William I, but Frederick rationalized Prussian government further with the beginning of a long effort to codify Prussian civil law and numerous projects for economic development. Combined with Frederick's own military genius and eye for talent, and a healthy amount of luck, Prussian administration was effective enough for Prussia to become a great power of 18th-century Europe. Frederick's territorial acquisitions include the seizure of the Austrian province of Silesia in 1740 shortly after his accession, which led to the Europe-wide War of the Austrian Succession, and his leading role in the first partition of Poland in 1772. The most dangerous part of his reign was the Seven Years War (1756 to 1763), in which Prussia faced a coalition of the leading continental powers—France, Austria, Russia, and Sweden—with only Britain for an ally. Prussia and its ruler only narrowly survived.

King Frederick's commitment to the more idealistic side of the Enlightenment often was more rhetorical than real. He proclaimed his devotion to religious toleration, but in practice maintained many of the discriminatory laws against Jews (particularly those that transferred Jewish wealth to the Prussian treasury) and personally intervened to prevent the leading thinker of the Jewish Enlightenment—Prussian subject Moses Mendelssohn—from being admitted to the Berlin Academy. Areas in which Frederick did apply Enlightenment principles include the abolition of judicial torture in 1754, and the liberation of serfs on estates owned by the king (although Frederick was able to do little to improve the lot of the majority of serfs, who toiled on noble estates).

Frederick was a great builder. His most famous building is the small Rococo palace of Sanssouci ("without care") located in the town of Potsdam outside Berlin. His voluminous writings were mostly in French, and he paid little attention to the Enlightenment culture of Germany. He was friends with Voltaire, although the two had a falling out when Voltaire, after years of correspondence, actually visited Frederick in Berlin in 1750 and found Frederick's militaristic court and authoritarian personality rather disappointing. (Voltaire's Berlin experiences informed his satire of German life in the early chapters of his novel *Candide*.) Although Frederick and Voltaire later patched things up, their friendship never was entirely restored. Frederick also was a great admirer of Jean Le Rond d'Alembert, whom he invited several times to come to Prussia to head the Berlin Academy. D'Alembert refused, but Frenchmen still dominated the Academy. Frederick composed music and wrote several works, the most important of which are on topics of statecraft. Naturally, all of his writing for publication was in French. Many of Frederick's personal beliefs, such as the atheism he concealed from the public, were characteristic of the French Enlightenment and found little support in the German environment. Additionally, his court served as a refuge for philosophers and others who had become too controversial in their respective countries, such as the French materialist Julien Offroy de la Mettrie (1709–1751).

Frederick also was a composer and patron of musicians. Unlike his lack of interest in German literature, Frederick appreciated German musicians at a time when Germany led Europe in musical creativity. The *Musical Offering* of Johann Sebastian Bach (1685–1750) was inspired by a theme given by Frederick. King Frederick also was a leader in German Freemasonry.

Frederick the Great died at his palace in Potsdam on August 17, 1786. His wish to be buried at Sanssouci finally was fulfilled in 1991, on the 205th anniversary of his death.

See also: Freemasonry; Germany, the Enlightenment in; Political Philosophy.

Further Reading

Behrens, C. B. A., *Society, Government and the Enlightenment: The Experiences of Eighteenth-Century France and Prussia* (London: Thames and Hudson, 1985).

Fraser, David, *Frederick the Great: King of Prussia* (London and New York: A. Lane, 2000).

Gaines, James R. *Evening in the Palace of Reason: Bach Meets Frederick the Great in the Age of Enlightenment* (London and New York: Fourth Estate, 2005).

FREEMASONRY The secret society known as the "Freemasons" originated in Britain and spread to Europe and America in the early 18th century. The Freemasons were based on guilds of stoneworkers that had existed since the Middle Ages, but Freemasonry changed from occupational guilds to social organizations sometime in the 17th century. The organization's rise was intertwined with the Enlightenment. The leader of the Masonic movement in early 18th-century London was the Newtonian scientist and Church of England cleric, Jean Desaguliers (1683–1744). Much of the early leadership of the Grand Lodge of London—leadership that many European and American lodges acknowledged—was composed of members of the Royal Society, Britain's foremost scientific organization. Much of the mythology and rhetoric of early Masonry was congenial to Newtonian natural philosophy and natural theology, as it emphasized a "great architect" who had created the universe in a mathematical fashion. This conception of God appealed to many Deists. Freemasons also spoke of society as bound together by the "attraction" of its individual members, just as Newton's gravity held the universe together. The religious toleration practiced by lodges—some of which even admitted Jews—was also congenial to Enlightenment values, as was the egalitarianism practiced between Masons of different social classes. Many members, however, viewed Masons as a group to be superior to non-Masons (the "profane").

The Catholic Church saw Masonry as enough of a threat that in 1738 Catholics were barred from becoming Masons, and the ban was renewed in 1751. This ban was not completely effective, however, and served to create a strong identification between Freemasonry and liberal anticlericalism in the Catholic world. In the Protestant world, the royal families of the Enlightened states of Great Britain and Prussia were Masonic leaders. Catherine the Great of Russia suspected the subversive potential of Freemasonry and its links to her rival, Frederick II of Prussia, and cracked down on the lodges in Russia in 1785. Despite Freemasonry's connection with the British Royal Family, it also was popular among the leaders of the American Revolution—Benjamin Franklin, George Washington, and the Marquis de Lafayette (the leader of French aid to the rebels) all were Masons.

As Freemasonry spread and developed, it took many different forms and developed many subcultures. Some groups, particularly in the Germanic lands, moved away from the original emphasis on reason into occultism and mysticism. The most important in the history of the Enlightenment were the lodges founded as intellectual societies, notably Vienna's True Harmony Lodge, founded in 1781, and the famous Lodge of the Nine Sisters (the classical Greek Muses) in Paris. Members of the True Harmony lodge included the composer Wolfgang Amadeus Mozart (1756–1791), whose opera *The Magic Flute* is full of Masonic images and references. The Nine Sisters was founded in 1776 by the French astronomer and atheist Joseph-Jérôme Lefrançais de Laland (1732–1807), who served as its first master. Members included Benjamin Franklin—who also served as master during his time as ambassador of the American rebels to France—and Voltaire, who was admitted somewhat irregularly only a few weeks before his death. The group sponsored educational institutions. It was abolished in 1792, as the French revolutionary government held Masonry to be "aristocratic." The True Harmony Lodge had been suppressed earlier in 1786 in a Habsburg government crackdown on secret societies. More radically Enlightened, although less intellectually distinguished, than the Nine Sisters or True Harmony was a short-lived group founded in 1776 by the Ingolstadt church law professor Adam Weishaupt (1748–1830). Weishaupt's "Bavarian Illuminati" were inspired by the materialism of radical philosophes such as the Baron d'Holbach and opposition to the reactionary Bavarian government. The group was quickly suppressed, but is a favorite source of conspiracy theories up to the present day.

See also: American Revolution and Founding; Franklin, Benjamin; Frederick II, the Great, of Prussia; Voltaire.

Further Reading

Bullock, Steven C., *Revolutionary Brotherhood: Freemasonry and the Transformation of the American Social Order, 1730–1840* (Chapel Hill: Published for the Institute of Early American History and Culture by the University of North Carolina Press, 1996).

Jacob, Margaret C., *Living the Enlightenment: Freemasonry and Politics in Eighteenth-Century Europe* (New York: Oxford University Press, 1991).

Jacob, Margaret C., *The Radical Enlightenment: Pantheists, Freemasons, and Republicans* (London and Boston: Allen and Unwin, 1981).

FRENCH REVOLUTION   One of the most debated questions in the historiography of the Enlightenment is the relationship of the Enlightenment and the French Revolution (which began in 1789). Some historians—dating back to the Revolution itself—have seen it as a fulfillment of the "Enlightenment program" of a society governed by reason rather than superstition and tradition. Others, however, have seen the Revolution—particularly in its radical phases—as a repudiation of the Enlightenment or even as marking its termination. Conservative historians have linked the Enlightenment with the "Reign of Terror"—the most radical phase of the Revolution—to argue that the Enlightenment rests at the foundation of 20th-century totalitarianism, an interpretation particularly popular during the Cold War. Others have argued that the Enlightenment was fundamentally irrelevant to the revolution, which was driven by social and political conflicts and the financial and military failures of the French state.

Elements of the Enlightenment might have contributed to the outbreak of the Revolution. The Enlightenment ideal of a reasonable, accountable, effective government caused many French people to question their own rulers. France was marked by neither the openness of such Enlightenment-admired societies as Great Britain and the United States, nor by the efficiency and rationality of such "Enlightened despots" as Frederick of Prussia and Catherine of Russia. Although elements of the French government were moving in an Enlightened direction—Protestantism finally was legalized throughout the realm in 1787, an important victory for the Enlightened cause of religious toleration—many French people were frustrated at how slowly things were moving.

The revolutionaries, particularly in the early period, placed themselves in the tradition of philosophes such as Voltaire and Rousseau. The remains of Voltaire were brought back to Paris in 1791 to be reburied in the Pantheon, a place conceived as a shrine to the great citizens of France, and the occasion was marked by a national festival. Rousseau was interred there three years later. A central document of the early Revolution, the *Declaration of the Rights of Man* adopted by the National Assembly in 1789, endorsed many Enlightened principles such as the abolition of the unearned privileges of the aristocracy, and freedom of opinion, thought, and religion. Leaders of all sides in the Revolution and even many counter-revolutionaries were avid readers of Enlightenment literature, and no one side can be identified as the "Enlightenment" side.

The more radical phase of the revolution saw the rise of "Republicanism" after the deposition and execution of the king. Revolutionary republicanism often is seen as having been influenced by Rousseau, and particularly *The Social Contract* (1762). Rousseau was a particularly powerful influence on the Revolutionary leader Maximilien Robespierre (1758–1794), the leader of the Committee of Public Safety during the most radical phase of the Revolution. The Terror carried out by the Republican "Jacobin" faction under Robespierre's leadership, however, was an assault on the principles of free speech and free thought embodied in the *Declaration of the Rights of Man*. Enlightenment thinkers and institutions were not immune to the Terror or the Republican and Jacobin reform of French government. France's greatest chemist, Antoine-Laurent Lavoisier (1743–1794), was condemned and executed for his pre-revolutionary career as a tax farmer, and the Marquis de Condorcet committed suicide to avoid execution. The astronomer Jean-Sylvain Bailly (1736–1793) had a successful revolutionary career at first, reaching the high positions of president of the National Assembly and mayor of Paris, but like other leaders of the earlier phases of the Revolution he was guillotined during the Terror. Institutions central to the French Enlightenment, such as the French Academy, the Royal Academy of Sciences, and the Masonic Lodge of the Nine Sisters were abolished as "aristocratic"—catering to an elite and thus unsuitable for an egalitarian French Republic. Revolutionaries also were hostile to salon culture.

Non-French Enlightenment leaders who lived into the period of the Revolution had a mixed reaction to the French events. Thomas Paine and Joseph Priestley were supporters of the Revolution in its early stages. Paine was elected a foreign representative to the National Convention, and was imprisoned by the Jacobins. Edward Gibbon was an opponent. Immanuel Kant admired the Revolution from the safe distance of Königsberg.

Enemies of the French Revolution often identified it as a continuation of the Enlightenment challenge to what they saw as the divinely sanctioned order of Christian Europe. This connection goes as far back as one of the earliest books written against the Revolution, the Irish politician Edmund Burke's *Reflections on the Revolution in France* (1790).

See also: Condorcet, Marie-Jean-Antoine-Nicolas Caritat, Marquis de; France, the Enlightenment in; Paine, Thomas; Political Philosophy.

Further Reading

Israel, Jonathan, *Revolutionary Ideas: An Intellectual History of the French Revolution from the Rights of Man to Robespierre* (Princeton: Princeton University Press, 2014).

Kennedy, Emmet, *A Cultural History of the French Revolution* (New Haven: Yale University Press, 1989).

Plassart, Anna, *The Scottish Enlightenment and the French Revolution* (New York: Cambridge University Press, 2015).

GENDER The Europe of the Enlightenment was an intensely male-dominated, patriarchal society. With the occasional exception of ruling queens and regents in some countries, men monopolized political office. Men ruled the established churches of European countries, the dissenting churches, and the Jewish religious community. With a very few scattered exceptions, men maintained exclusive control of higher education and were the more literate of the two genders, publishing a vast majority of books and journalism. Men also controlled most of Europe's wealth.

The mainstream of the Enlightenment did not challenge male domination. It did, however, ideologically recast this dominance away from religious justifications of male superiority based on the Bible and Christian tradition, to arguments based on the innate natures of men and women. In line with Enlightenment materialism, women increasingly were viewed as shaped primarily by their female bodies rather than by a transcendent—and genderless—soul. As such, women were perceived primarily in terms of sexuality and reproduction. Female sexuality, much more than male sexuality, was viewed in a reproductive context. This tendency to conceive of opposing genders worked for the exclusion of women from intellectual life, as rationality was gendered viewed as an essentially masculine quality. Women were characterized not as beings whose reasoning power was inferior to men's, but as completely nonreasoning beings. This allowed fewer openings for the "exceptional" intellectual and scientific woman, who now was labeled "unnatural." Although not all male philosophers and scientists held such beliefs, they were held by such leading Enlightenment thinkers as Rousseau and Immanuel Kant. Maternal breast-feeding, seen as a fulfillment of female responsibility, also was a cause championed by many Enlightened men, although not all supporters viewed themselves as Enlightened.

This did not mean that women were not perceived as carrying out an important social role. Many Enlightenment thinkers believed that free association and conversation between men and women was essential to the progress of civilization, and that this was a central way in which European civilization was superior to other civilizations, such as China or the Islamic world, where women were secluded from contact with men outside of their immediate families. This ideal, which was particularly associated with the salon culture of France, still cast women primarily as supporters of men, rather than thinkers and doers in their own right, however.

Although women entering the community of Enlightened thinkers faced challenges that men did not, these challenges were not insurmountable. Some women participated as salon hostesses, a function that mainly—but not entirely—was carried out by women. Others participated in Enlightenment life as writers or researchers, such as the Marquise du Châtelet. A rare few, such as the Italian professor and academician Laura Bassi (1711–1778) or the Russian princess Ekaterina Dashkova (1743–1810), even made it into intellectual institutions. The emergence of modern feminism in the work of the Englishwoman Mary Wollstonecraft (1757–1797), particularly *A Vindication of the Rights of Woman* (1792), drew heavily from Enlightenment emphasis on the life of reason and the critique of traditional privilege. Wollstonecraft extended the Enlightenment assault on the unearned privileges of aristocrats and clerics to the far more pervasive privilege of men. Rousseau was a particularly prominent target of Wollstonecraft's feminism. Another late-Enlightenment feminist was the Marquis of Condorcet, who argued that women should be politically and socially equal to men, and also that women had not made equal intellectual contributions to men due to their lack of an equivalent education, not because of an innate lack of ability.

See also: Catherine II, "the Great," of Russia; Châtelet, Émile du; Education; Nature; Salons.

Further Reading

Hesse, Carla, *The Other Enlightenment: How French Women Became Modern* (Princeton: Princeton University Press, 2009).

Hufton, Olwen, *The Prospect Before Her: A History of Women in Western Europe, 1500–1800* (New York: Vintage, 1998).

O'Brien, Karen, *Women and Enlightenment in Eighteenth-Century Britain* (Cambridge: Cambridge University Press, 2009).

Steinbrugge, Lieselott, *The Moral Sex: Woman's Nature in the French Enlightenment,* translated by Pamela Selwyn (New York: Oxford University Press, 1995).

Sutton, Geoffrey V., *Science for a Polite Society: Gender, Culture, and the Demonstration of Enlightenment* (Boulder, Colorado: Westview Press, 1995).

GERMANY, THE ENLIGHTENMENT IN   Germany was not a united country in the Enlightenment era. It was part of a vast political entity known as the "Holy Roman Empire," which also included modern Austria, the Czech Republic, and other territories. The emperor—almost always a member of the Habsburg family—controlled his or her own hereditary territory (the Habsburg lands were in Austria, and they also were kings of Hungary, which lay outside the Empire). The rest of the Empire was made up of kingdoms, principalities, bishoprics, and free imperial cities, all of which had different histories and institutions. Many of these states went to war with each other in the 18th century. The Seven Years War (1756–1763) pitted Prussia, the largest kingdom within the Empire, against the Holy Roman Emperor Maria Theresa (1717–1780), her hereditary lands in Austria and elsewhere, and other German states such as Bavaria.

Germany also was religiously divided. The dominant churches were roughly Lutheran in the north and Catholic in the south, but the Lutheran churches themselves were divided between "orthodox" Lutherans and Pietists, who emphasized the religion of the heart over strict adherence to dogma. As a result of this fragmentation, Germany lacked a city that played the culturally central role of Paris, London, or Edinburgh. Germany, however, did have many active provincial capitals, the two most important being Berlin in the north, the capital of Prussia; and the Habsburg capital of Vienna in the south.

Relations between church and Enlightenment or state and Enlightenment varied enormously within the country. Germans frequently looked to foreign countries, particularly Britain and France, to furnish models for Enlightenment. Social divisions also affected the German Enlightenment. Divisions between the nobility and the prosperous middle class were greater in Germany than they were elsewhere in western Europe, particularly in the eastern part of Germany. Institutions such as the English Masonic lodges, coffeehouses, or the French salons—where members of different social classes could meet on a more or less equal basis—were relatively scarce.

Germany's political fragmentation benefited German intellectual life. Like Scotland, Germany was a land where universities played an enormous role in the Enlightenment. Because Germany was divided into so many political units, it had a very high density of universities; local governments wanted their own. Leading institutions were the University of Göttingen and the Pietist University of Halle, but the greatest philosopher of the German Enlightenment (some would say of the whole Enlightenment), Immanuel Kant, was a professor at the relatively remote University of Königsburg in East Prussia (now Kaliningrad in Russia.) Of course, like other Enlightenment societies, Germans had academies and societies as well as universities, many of them connected to the university.

The climate for Enlightenment in German states varied according to their political and religious regime. Many—particularly those in Catholic areas—had authoritarian states and churches which attempted to prevent new ideas from entering or spreading. Some authoritarians, however, such as Prussia's Frederick II or the Holy Roman Empire's Joseph II, supported the new ideas. Frederick provides a good example of how important a change in monarch could be for a German state. His father and predecessor on the throne, Frederick William I (r. 1713–1740), had been a religious conservative far more interested in building the Prussian army than in advancing the German intellect. (He referred to the academicians of the Berlin Academy as court buffoons.) Under Frederick William, Halle in 1723 expelled the leading German philosopher—Christian Wolff (1679–1754), a follower of Leibniz—for impiety. In 1740, after Frederick II became king, he quickly forced the university to take Wolff back; he also reformed and revitalized the Berlin Academy. Because Germany was divided into many small and medium-sized states, enlightened Germans could move from one area where authority was limiting their activity to another—hopefully more liberal—political unit. Wolff, upon his expulsion, had been able to relocate to the University of Marburg in Hesse. Frederick's capital, Berlin, lacked a university, so he had the chance to directly shape its intellectual culture rather than work through an established and independent institution.

Frederick's Berlin enlightenment was an imported French Enlightenment. When he refounded the Berlin Academy in 1744 (it had originally been founded in 1700) he dropped its existing emphasis on German studies and declared French its official language. Frederick lured a leading French scientist, Pierre-Louis Moreau de Maupertuis (1698–1759), from Paris to be president of the new Academy. Frederick admired and patronized French philosophes such as Voltaire (with whom his relationship was stormy), d'Alembert, and Condorcet, but had no interest in promoting German culture or the Enlightenment in the German language. That was done elsewhere, and often in a way that ostensibly rejected French influences. Many of the people who created the German-language Enlightenment, particularly in Protestant Germany, were influenced by Britain as much as or more than they were by France. When Lessing wished to break with the existing German theater—which mostly was based on imitating classical 17th-century French tragedy and took as its subjects royalty and aristocracy—he wrote a tragedy about a middle-class English woman entitled, "Miss Sara Sampson," which premiered in 1755.

One of the most important achievements of the German Enlightenment was the spread of philosophical, intellectual, and literary writing in German. Wolff was a leader in this field as one of the first German academic philosophers to write philosophy in German rather than Latin, addressing a broad audience rather than a narrow one composed of university scholars. Wolff was followed by the most important German philosopher of the period, Immanuel Kant.

Despite Wolff's reputation for impiety, the German Enlightenment was less anti-religious and anti-Christian than the French or even the Scottish. There were no prominent German champions of atheism or Deism, and Kant strongly rejected atheism and championed a philosophical Christianity emphasizing morality. There were a few radically Enlightened people in Germany, such as Adam Weishaupt (1748–1830), the founder of the quasi-Masonic Bavarian Illuminati, a group dedicated to radical reform in Germany, but one that collapsed shortly after its foundation.

The German Enlightenment was in decline by the end of the 18th century. The death of Frederick II in 1786 led to the succession of his nephew Frederick William II (r. 1786–1797). Frederick William II was not a supporter of the Enlightenment and had little interest in intellectual affairs. In Germany, as elsewhere, Enlightenment thought and freedom of thought generally came under greater suspicion after the French Revolution. The Prussian government in 1793 banned Kant from publishing on religious subjects. The younger generation in German culture was more interested in the nascent Romantic movement than in the tradition of the Enlightenment.

See also: Frederick II, "the Great," of Prussia; Joseph II of Austria; Kant, Immanuel; Leibniz, Gottfried Wilhelm; Lessing, Gotthold Ephraim; Mendelssohn, Moses.

Further Reading

Brunschwig, Henri, *Enlightenment and Romanticism in Eighteenth-Century Prussia,* translated by Frank Jellinek (Chicago and London: University of Chicago Press, 1974).

Reed, T. J., *Light in Germany: Scenes from an Unknown Enlightenment* (Chicago: University of Chicago Press, 2015).

Saine, Thomas P., *The Problem of Being Modern; or, The German Pursuit of Enlightenment from Leibniz to the French Revolution* (Detroit: Wayne State University Press, 1987).

Wilson, W. Daniel and Robert C. Holub (eds.), *Impure Reason: Dialectic of Enlightenment in Germany* (Detroit: Wayne State University Press, 1993).

GIBBON, EDWARD (1737–1794)   Edward Gibbon, the greatest historian of the Enlightenment, was born on April 27, 1737, in London. He is the author of *The Decline and Fall of the Roman Empire,* the first volume of which appeared in 1776 and the sixth and final in 1788. Although he was English, Gibbon was deeply influenced by the French and Scottish Enlightenments. He studied for a time in Lausanne, Switzerland, where his father sent him to study with a Protestant pastor after the young Gibbon had declared he intended to convert to Catholicism. Gibbon's Catholicism proved very short-lived, although it was replaced not by firm Protestantism, despite his claims at the time, but rather by skepticism with a Protestant veneer. Gibbon also took advantage of the time to become fluent enough in French to write in it (he would later claim that he even thought in French) and to become acquainted with French Enlightenment writers. An omnivorous reader, Gibbon later was influenced by Scottish Enlightenment writers as well, particularly the historians David Hume and William Robertson.

Gibbon when he was young decided that he wished to write a major work of history, and spent some time looking for a topic. He later claimed that in 1764, while visiting the ruins in Rome, he conceived the idea of writing about the fall of the empire. *The Decline and Fall of the Roman Empire* covers the period from the death of the Roman Emperor Marcus Aurelius in 180 CE to the final fall of Constantinople, the capital of the Byzantine or East Roman Empire, to the Ottoman Turks in 1453. Gibbon was the only Enlightenment historian to show much interest in Byzantine history. He gave multiple explanations for the fall of Rome, but the two main reasons were barbarian invasions and the rise of Christianity. Gibbon viewed Christianity—with its other-worldly emphasis—as distracting the Romans from dealing with the practical, real world problems their empire faced. Gibbon practiced the philosophical history of Enlightenment historians such as Voltaire and Hume, who sought to understand human societies and their changes rather than merely recount events. Unlike them, however, Gibbon combined philosophical with "erudite" history, based on a profound mastery of the sources and a wide reading in contemporary historians and antiquarians.

Gibbon's book was successful, but his treatment of Christianity was controversial. The famous 15th and 16th chapters of the *Decline and Fall* give a secular narrative of the rise of Christianity from the early post-Apostolic period. Gibbon was skeptical about the motives and virtues of the some of the early leaders of the church. Although Gibbon lacked the combativeness of Voltaire, and specifically recused himself as a historian from evaluating the specifically supernatural claims of Christianity, his secular analysis of the rise of the Church was far from flattering to Christians, ancient and modern. Although Gibbon never directly attacked Christianity, he mocked it in subtle ways—although not too subtly for his readers, Christian and non-Christian, to glean. His discussion of the early history of Christianity was by far the most controversial element of his work, provoking an enormous deluge of literature from outraged defenders of the faith. He deprecated religious intolerance, but Gibbon paradoxically seemed more sympathetic to the persecutors of Christianity than to the persecuted Christians, minimizing the tortures inflicted on Christians and treating the persecutions as an exception to polytheists' general practice of toleration. Gibbon also subtly made the point that contemporary Christian persecutors made many of the same arguments as ancient pagan persecutors. Indeed, ancient persecutors were more moderate in persecuting only the outward behavior of Christians, and having no concern with their inward beliefs. When Christians in power began to persecute heretics, Gibbon extended no such understanding to their brutal actions. Gibbon condemned many of the Christian saints of antiquity as fanatical zealots, and the Christian-turned-pagan emperor, Julian the Apostate (r. 361–363)—reviled by centuries of Christian historians—received Gibbon's praise. (Like Voltaire, whom he admired, Gibbon extended his dislike of Christians to a dislike of Jews as well.) Furthermore, in the famous conclusion to the work, the fall of the Roman Empire is described as the triumph of "barbarism and religion."

The Decline and Fall provoked some attacks, usually religiously motivated, on Gibbon's scholarship, which he handled without much difficulty. He responded to his critics in *A Vindication of Some Passages in the XVth and XVIth Chapters of the Decline and Fall of the Roman Empire* (1779). Despite his religious skepticism, Gibbon was more politically conservative than many leaders of the Enlightenment, and detested the French Revolution.

Gibbon served in Parliament without any distinction from 1774 to 1783. He then left England to live in the city of Lausanne in Switzerland. In addition to *The Decline and Fall of the Roman Empire*, Gibbon also wrote an autobiography that was only published after his death. Gibbon died on January 16, 1794, of an infection contracted after having surgery to relieve a swollen scrotum while on a visit to England.

See also: Bible, the; England, the Enlightenment in; Religion.

Further Reading

Craddock, Patricia B., *Edward Gibbon: Luminous Historian 1772–1794* (Baltimore: Johns Hopkins University Press, 1989).

Craddock, Patricia B., *Young Edward Gibbon: Gentleman of Letters* (Baltimore: Johns Hopkins University Press, 1982).

Pocock, J. G. A., *Barbarism and Religion*, 5 vols. (Cambridge and New York: Cambridge University Press, 1999–2010).

HOLBACH, PAUL HEINRICH DIETRICH, BARON D' (1723–1789)

Although he was a German nobleman, Baron Holbach spent his adult life in Paris, where he was a voluminous writer and translator, and one of the few men to host a Parisian salon. Born on an unknown date in the German town of Edesheim, Holbach was educated at the University of Leiden in the Dutch Republic. Holbach was an important intermediary in transmitting Protestant and especially German thought, particularly in the sciences, into France. He wrote several hundred articles on mineralogy and chemistry as well as other subjects for Diderot and d'Alembert's *Encyclopédie*, much of them adapted from German works. Holbach also read English, and translated several English anticlerical and anti-Christian books into French. He had inherited a fortune from his uncle and, unlike many of the writers of the Enlightenment period, he had no need to write for money.

Holbach was most notorious in his own time for being an atheist. Many philosophes opposed Christianity but most, including such radicals as Voltaire, stopped at Deism—believing in a God, even if not the Christian God. Holbach combined his atheism with materialism—the belief that the material universe was all that there is, and that the soul is an illusion. He was also a determinist in the tradition of Spinoza—all is predetermined, and freedom of the will is another illusion. In ethics, Holbach argued that people should do what pleases them, and argued against the personal and sexual repression he identified with Christianity and other religions. He set forth his ideas in books which had to be published anonymously and in many cases in Amsterdam, where the press was freer than in France. The books, like many other French Enlightenment books, then had to be smuggled into France.

Holbach's most celebrated atheistic book was *The System of Nature* (1770), which attracted pamphlets and treatises supposedly refuting its ideas from Voltaire and Frederick the Great of Prussia, among many others, both Enlightened and anti-Enlightened. Despite being banned by law and fiercely opposed by the Catholic Church, the book sold very well in France. Holbach's explicitly anti-Christian works, including *Critical History of Jesus Christ* (1770) also sold well, as did his political treatise *A System of Society* (1773). As a political observer, he was less impressed by the English system than were many of the French Enlightenment philosophers, viewing it as corrupt and dedicated to the protection of a privileged few. He also viewed the English obsession with trade and global commerce as a menace to the peace of the world.

Holbach influenced debate as a personality as well as a philosopher. His salon, which attracted many of the most eminent luminaries of the Enlightenment, had a reputation for intellectual radicalism (although many of the survivors of Holbach's circle would be on the conservative side during the French Revolution). Holbach's hedonistic ethics were more acceptable because he was widely admired as a generous and moral man, as well as pleasant company. Among his friends were Diderot, David Hume, and Jean-Jacques Rousseau (although Rousseau eventually quarreled with him as he did with Diderot and Hume, and even saw Holbach as the leader of a conspiracy against him). Holbach's wealth enabled him to preside over a rich and hospitable table, as well as affording him the leisure to write his books and translations. He died on January 21, 1789, in his beloved Paris during the last year that a life such as his was possible.

See also: Bible, the; France, the Enlightenment in; Religion; Salons.

Further Reading

Curran, Mark, *Atheism, Religion, and Enlightenment in Pre-Revolutionary Europe* (Woodbridge, Suffolk and Rochester, NY: Boydell Press, 2010).

Darnton, Robert, *The Forbidden Best-Sellers of Pre-Revolutionary France* (New York and London: Norton, 1996).

Kors, Alan Charles. *D'Holbach's Coterie: An Enlightenment in Paris* (Princeton: Princeton University Press, 1975).

HUME, DAVID (1711–1776)   A deeper thinker than Voltaire and a more accessible one than Immanuel Kant, the Scotsman David Hume is today best known as a philosopher, but also excelled as a historian and social analyst. Descended from a family of gentry and lawyers, Hume was born in Edinburgh on May 7, 1711. He attended the University of Edinburgh and originally intended to go into law himself. Instead Hume drifted from job to job in Britain and France and read intensively. Gradually, he lost his religious faith. His first book, the anonymous *Treatise of Human Nature*, published in two parts in 1739 and 1740, attracted little interest despite being now viewed as a philosophical masterpiece. The disappointed Hume concluded that the book was too difficult to be widely read, and his subsequent philosophical books, including *Essays, Moral and Political* (two vols., 1741 and 1742), *Philosophical Essays Concerning Human Understanding* (1748), and *An Enquiry into the Principles of Morals* (1751), were written in a more accessible style.

As a philosopher Hume was a skeptic, not just of religion (although that was what made the greatest impression on his contemporaries) but of many of the things taken for granted in ordinary life such as the idea that our sense perceptions are necessarily correlated with things that actually exist or that one event could "cause" another. Hume's philosophy was rooted in human nature rather than transcendent reality, regardless of whether transcendent reality was to be comprehended through faith or reason. Even if we cannot establish certain knowledge of objective nature through either senses or abstract reason, we are not obligated—in fact it is not even possible—to live in a constant state of skeptical doubt. Morality, too, is not based on divine commands or rational arguments, but in the pleasure or displeasure humans take in particular character traits.

Hume did not have much faith in reason, and famously stated in the *Treatise of Human Nature* that reason was "the slave of the passions." Religion itself, as he theorized in *Natural History of Religion* (1757), emerged in different human societies due to fear of the future and the unknown. His *Dialogues on Natural Religion* (1779) were a devastating attack on the idea that people could be led to belief in a providential God through reason alone. Hume's rejection of religion involved him in several controversies, and probably was the reason he never received a position at a Scottish university.

The work Hume was best-known for in his own lifetime was not his philosophy, but rather his six-volume history of England, published from 1754 to 1762. It quickly became the standard work, and enabled Hume to support himself by selling books on the market rather than through patronage. As a historian, Hume wrote in the tradition of "philosophical" historians, who placed more emphasis on the nature of human society and how it has changed than on the accumulation of accurate detail about the past. Hume's history was politically controversial because many found it too conservative. His approach to history and politics differed from that of Locke and others who based it on a social contract, which he found too abstract. Hume worked to debunk the "Whig" mythology of 17th-century English history as a struggle between virtuous parliaments and wicked, tyrannous Stuart kings. (The radical Whig Catherine Macaulay's eight-volume *History of England from the Accession of James I to the Revolution* [1763–1783] was widely treated as an answer to Hume's.) In keeping with his generally naturalistic approach, Hume placed greater weight on custom and tradition than on abstract rights. Conservatives in England and Scotland, however, could not fully embrace Hume's history due to its mockery of Christianity.

Hume was popular in the Parisian salons, which he enjoyed even though he was socially awkward in the polished society of the Parisian intellectual class. He regarded the conversation and society available in Paris as far superior to that in England, a country which he increasingly felt negatively about. Hume helped bring Jean-Jacques Rousseau to England, but the two had a bitter falling-out due to Rousseau's sensitivity and paranoia and Hume's obsession with protecting his reputation.

Hume died of colorectal cancer in Edinburgh on August 25, 1776. Hume's rejection of religion made his death particularly interesting. Many people—including the great English opponent of the Enlightenment, Samuel Johnson (1709–1784), who detested Hume—believed that no one could continue to be sincerely irreligious when faced with imminent death. Hume's serenity and acceptance of his own end was remarkable to believers and non-believers alike, although there is some evidence that in private he was not as composed as he appeared to visitors. His friend Adam Smith wrote a posthumous evaluation of Hume as the ideal of a wise and virtuous man, which shocked many who viewed religious skeptics as necessarily immoral. Hume remains a towering figure in the history of philosophy, often credited with the foundation of modern analytical philosophy.

See also: Religion; Scotland, the Enlightenment in; Smith, Adam.

Further Reading

Norton, David Fate, and Jacqueline Taylor (eds.), *The Cambridge Companion to Hume,* 2nd ed (Cambridge and New York: Cambridge University Press, 2009).

Mossner, Ernest Campbell, *The Life of David Hume,* 2nd ed. (Oxford: Oxford University Press, 2001).

Quinton, Anthony, *Hume* (New York: Routledge, 1999).

ITALY, THE ENLIGHTENMENT IN   Italy was politically divided in the 18th century: the Kingdom of the Two Sicilies with its capital at Naples in the South; the Papal States with their capital at Rome occupying a belt of territory in the center and north; and several smaller states in the northern region, including the Republics of Venice and Genoa, the Duchies of Tuscany and Milan, both ruled by the Austrian Habsburg family, and the Kingdom of Savoy. Division was not merely political; unlike Germans, Italians had little sense of a common "Italian" identity. Italy was not culturally isolated from the major centers of Enlightenment in Northern Europe; both French and English works were translated and widely available, despite the opposition of the Church, and many people from other European countries visited Italy and mingled with the Italian elite. Even Freemasonry flourished among some of the Italian elite.

Throughout Italy, the Enlightenment faced a powerful and repressive Catholic Church. The Inquisition, or "Holy Office," headquartered at Rome had jurisdiction over Italy. Basic premises widely accepted elsewhere—such as the Copernican idea that the earth revolves around the sun—were forbidden topics in Italy, although these prohibitions were irregularly enforced. Secular governments also were reactionary, and only Naples, Milan, Savoy, Tuscany, and the tiny state of Parma saw enlightened governments during the 18th century.

Naples, one of the largest cities in Europe, was the center of the Enlightenment in Southern Italy. The Neapolitan Enlightenment was particularly active under Charles III (r. 1734–1759), who with his minister, the Marchese de Tanucci (1698–1783), challenged the power of the Church and worked to advance intellectual and cultural life in the city through patronage and encouragement. Charles and Tanucci, who remained an important figure in the kingdom's government until 1776, worked to bring the country under a uniform law code, but this effort failed. Other legal reforms were more successful.

Florence, the capital of Tuscany and a city associated with thought and culture since the Middle Ages, was the most active center of Enlightenment in the North. The Academy of the Della Crusca—one of Europe's oldest academies, with roots going back to the 16th century—took an increasing interest in Enlightened thought and projects for social reform and agricultural improvement. Milan also was influenced by the Enlightenment, which fostered rule oriented to rational authority and economic development. Milan also produced one of the most influential Italian Enlightened reformers, the penologist Cesare Beccaria, who was read throughout Europe. Venice, by contrast, with its notoriously closed and oligarchic government, was less influenced by the Enlightenment although it remained a popular destination for tourists, particularly during the famous Carnival season.

The Enlightenment even affected the Papal States, particularly during the pontificate of Benedict XIV from 1740 to 1758. Benedict, the former Prospero Lorenzo Lambertini (1675–1758), carried out many similar measures as his secular Enlightened contemporary rulers, including founding academies and building infrastructure to encourage economic development, although he stopped well short of religious toleration. The Bologna Academy in the Papal States was remarkable in that it was one of the few European academies to admit women.

For many of the Enlightened outside Italy itself, it remained primarily the home of classical antiquity. Edward Gibbon, who had little regard for contemporary Italians, claimed that his experience of the city of Rome inspired him to write *The Decline and Fall of the Roman Empire.* The German aesthetic theorist Johann Joachim Winkelmann (1717–1768) was so awed by the remains of classical civilization that he converted from Lutheranism to Catholicism and moved to Rome, where he became head of antiquities and librarian at the Papal Court.

See also: Academies and Learned Societies; Art and Architecture; Beccaria, Cesare; Jesuits.

Further Reading

Cochrane, Eric, *Tradition and Enlightenment in the Tuscan Academies 1690–1800* (Chicago: University of Chicago Press, 1961).

Ferrone, Vincenzo, *The Intellectual Roots of the Italian Enlightenment: Newtonian Science, Religion, and Politics in the Early Eighteenth Century*, translated by Sue Brotherton (Atlantic Highlands: Humanities Press, 1995).

Venturi, Franco, *Italy and the Enlightenment: Studies in a Cosmopolitan Century*, translated by Susan Corsi (London: Longman, 1972).

JESUITS   The Society of Jesus (the Jesuits) is a Roman Catholic religious order founded in 1540. In many ways it was the greatest institutional enemy of the Enlightenment despite the fact that many Enlightenment leaders including two of its strongest anticlericals, Voltaire and Denis Diderot, had been educated at Jesuit institutions. The Jesuits were a self-consciously intellectual group, often regarded (not least by themselves) as the intellectual elite of the Catholic Church. They controlled many Catholic schools and universities, which made the group the target of some "reforming" Catholic groups, such as the French school of "Jansenist" Catholics, as well as of the Enlightened. In France, the Jesuit-run *Journal de Trevoux*, founded in 1701, was able to defend Catholic orthodoxy and take on Enlightenment thinkers on their own intellectual level. The Jesuits also were one of the principal sources for

European knowledge of the world outside Europe, and particularly of China, where a western Jesuit had headed the Emperor's Astronomical Bureau since the mid-17th century.

What led to the temporary abolition of the Jesuits, however, was not opposition from the Enlightenment philosophes or Jansenists but the concerns of European governments. The internationally minded order, with its wealth, power, and influence, was increasingly viewed as a menace by national leaders. The power of the Society in the European colonies of the Americas also was a matter of particular concern. The first country to expel and suppress the Jesuits was Portugal, under the leadership of the "Enlightened" statesman the Marquis of Pombal in 1759. In France, the bankruptcy of a branch of the Society in the colony of Martinique provided the opportunity for all of its French enemies to move against it, and the Society was suppressed in France and throughout the French Empire in 1764. The "Enlightened Despot" Charles III of Spain (r. 1759–1788) expelled the Jesuits from Spain and its empire in 1767. The smaller powers that were ruled by branches of the same Bourbon family that ruled France and Spain—the Kingdom of the Two Sicilies and Parma in Italy—followed by suppressing the Jesuits in their territories as well. The Habsburg rulers in Austria supported the Society.

The Society of Jesus was suppressed throughout the world by order of Pope Clement XIV (r. 1769–1774) in 1773 in the brief *Dominus ac Redemptor*. Pope Clement was under severe pressure of the Bourbon governments who had supported his candidacy under the assumption that he would suppress the Jesuits. The Society continued a semi-underground existence in some non-Catholic countries, notably Protestant Prussia and Orthodox Russia, both ruled by Enlightened monarchs who valued the Jesuit contribution to education. The Jesuits were restored by Papal authority in 1814, and continue to exist to the present day.

See also: Education; Religion.

Further Reading

Hellyer, Marcus, *Catholic Physics: Jesuit Natural Philosophy in Early Modern Germany* (Notre Dame: University of Notre Dame Press, 2005).

Northeast, Catherine M., *Parisian Jesuits and the Enlightenment, 1700–1762* (Oxford: Voltaire Foundation, 1991).

Whitehead, Maurice, *English Jesuit Education: Expulsion, Suppression, Survival, Restoration, 1762–1803* (Burlington VT: Ashgate, 2013).

JEWISH ENLIGHTENMENT   The Jewish Enlightenment, also known as the "Haskalah," had to face many challenges. The barriers European society presented to Jewish participation in elite intellectual culture were many—ranging from segregation into ghettoes in much of central and Eastern Europe to exclusion from most universities, academies, and scientific societies. In addition to facing the external barriers to full participation in the societies in which they lived erected by European Christians, enlightened Jews had to deal with the intellectual and cultural as well as institutional dominance of the conservative rabbinate in their own communities. The Jewish community itself, however, was becoming less culturally and geographically isolated. The "ghetto," the enclosed, all-Jewish area in which Jews were required to live under the jurisdiction of their communal institutions and rabbinical elite, was declining in many parts of Europe, particularly the West. The growing involvement of Enlightened states in Jewish communities also threatened the dominance of traditional Jewish elites, as the Jewish community as a whole was losing much of its traditional power of self-government. In England, where Jews had been expelled during the Middle Ages and officially were readmitted during the 17th century, there were no ghettoes at all.

Jewish awareness of and involvement in European science and culture increased during the 18th century. Barriers to Jewish participation in European cultural institutions were coming down, albeit slowly and unevenly. Jews were admitted into a few scientific societies—the first Jew, Isaac de Sequeira Samuda (1681–1729), was admitted to Britain's Royal Society in 1723. More middle- and upper-class Jews were receiving education in secular subjects, including science and the Greek and Roman classics. The number of universities accepting Jewish students increased, particularly in the Protestant world, although Catholic Padua, which had been admitting Jews into its medical school since the 16th century, remained dominant. Jewish and Christian enlightened intellectuals also socially interacted in Masonic lodges, particularly in England. Enlightened Jews also sought intellectual resources within their own tradition, in the work of the medieval Jewish rationalist philosopher Maimonides and others who had attempted to integrate Jewish and non-Jewish thinking.

Newtonianism was first absorbed into Jewish thought by Jewish intellectuals living in England. In addition to residing in Newton's homeland, Anglo-Jewish thinkers had the advantage of living in the society that posed the fewest barriers between Jewish and gentile society. After being expelled in the Middle Ages, Jews had been readmitted to Britain in the 1650s, and British Jews lacked the long-established ghettoes and separate legal systems that characterized many continental Jewish communities. Many Jewish writers were attracted to Newtonianism for reasons similar to those that attracted Christian writers—the adaptability of Newtonian ideas for natural theology. The first Jewish writer to incorporate Newtonianism into a Jewish natural theology in his writing was Rabbi David Nieto (1654–1728) of the Bevis Marks Synagogue in London. Probably the most important Jewish Newtonian was Mordecai Gumper Schnaber Levison (1741–1797), a cosmopolitan who lived in England, Sweden, and Germany and published in Hebrew, German, and English. The enormously prolific Levison wrote the first book in Hebrew fully expounding Newton's scientific theories as well as their relevance for Judaism, *A Dissertation upon the Law and Science* (1771).

Although the Anglo-Jewish community was among the first in bringing Enlightenment thought to the Jews, it was relatively small and somewhat marginal in the larger Jewish community. The leading Enlightenment Jewish community was the German community, which was home to Moses Mendelssohn, the most prominent Jew in the 18th century Republic of Letters. Mendelssohn provided an example of how an interest in enlightened philosophy was compatible with being a proud and observant Jew, and was a hero and role model for Enlightened Jews throughout Germany and Central Europe. Mendelssohn's Berlin was the capital of the Haskalah. In the face of the dislike of Judaism—if not outright anti-Semitism—displayed by many leaders of the Enlightenment, the Haskalah attempted to show the compatibility of Judaism and Enlightenment. The enlighteners also faced resistance from the traditional authorities in Jewish life, suspicious of interest in non-Jewish thought, and fearing that excessive interest in the non-Jewish world would distract from the study of the Torah. (A few Jewish Enlightenment figures even fulfilled the rabbis' worst fears by converting to Christianity.) The Jewish Enlightenment also vigorously opposed the rising Hasidic movement among Polish Jews which emphasized passionate devotion to God over knowledge of either Jewish or Enlightened texts. "Maskilim," Enlightened Jews, also sought to broaden Jewish exposure to Enlightened knowledge beyond the elite. They wrote textbooks in Hebrew on elementary science, mathematics, and other subjects for use in Jewish schools in Germany and Eastern Europe.

See also: Enlightenment Views of Jews and Judaism; Mendelssohn, Moses; Religion; Spinoza, Baruch.

Further Reading

Feiner, Shmuel, *The Jewish Enlightenment,* translated by Chaya Naor (Philadelphia: University of Pennsylvania Press, 2011).

Ruderman, David B., *Jewish Enlightenment in a New Key: Anglo-Jewry's Construction of Modern Jewish Thought* (Princeton and Oxford: Princeton University Press, 2000).

Sorkin, David, *Moses Mendelssohn and the Religious Enlightenment* (Berkeley: University of California Press, 1996).

JOSEPH II, OF AUSTRIA (1741–1790) Few 18th-century rulers were more devoted to the Enlightenment than was Joseph II, Holy Roman Emperor beginning in 1765 and King of Hungary beginning in 1780. Although nominally a co-ruler, Joseph was effectively excluded from power until the death of his mother, the Empress Maria Theresa, in 1780. Upon his mother's death, Joseph attempted to carry out an Enlightenment program in the lands of his Habsburg family including Austria, Hungary, and Bohemia. It included limited religious toleration, an attack on the extensive possessions of the Catholic Church, and improvement of the legal position of serfs and peasants. Municipal and provincial authorities were streamlined and standardized. Although there had been moves in these directions under Maria Theresa, Joseph pushed through far more radical changes. The program was influenced by Joseph's extensive reading in Enlightenment writers, particularly the French physiocrats, as well as the example of Frederick the Great's Prussia. All of these changes were subordinated to a vast centralization of the Habsburg realms under imperial leadership. Joseph's idea of reform had no democratic tendencies, but instead hoped that the emperor's rule would be strengthened against the church and nobility.

In 1781, Joseph promulgated an Edict of Toleration granting freedom of private worship for Greek Orthodox believers and members of the more widespread Protestant denominations, the Lutherans and Calvinists. The Edict also improved religious freedoms for Jews, although the smaller Protestant denominations as well as Deists were left out. The same year saw the beginnings of the abolition of serfdom and feudal dues. Reforms of the civil code saw a marginalization of the power of the church, and Joseph confiscated church wealth to found schools and hospitals, strongly promoting education in the Austrian lands. The censorship was abolished, and Joseph even allowed some free expression of criticism of the government.

Joseph's policies aroused strong opposition from the church and traditional elites, as well as disrupting traditional economies in the countryside. Despite Joseph's hope that rural emancipation would lead to greater revenues from agriculture, his finances were a mess. Peasants, encouraged by their new freedoms, sometimes rose in revolt against local landowners hoping for further improvements. Protestant, Catholic, and Jewish religious communities were disturbed by the possibilities that Joseph's more secular schools would destroy traditional religious learning. Joseph faced major uprisings in the southern Netherlands, then a Habsburg possession, and Hungary. His foreign policy, aimed at territorial expansion, also was unsuccessful, and much of his work of reform was undone after his death.

See also: Education; Germany, the Enlightenment in; Political Philosophy.

Further Reading

Beales, Derek, *Joseph II* (Cambridge: Cambridge University Press, 1987).

Bernard, Paul P., *Jesuits and Jacobins: Enlightenment and Enlightened Despotism in Austria* (Urbana: University of Illinois Press, 1971).

Blanning, T. C. W., *Joseph II* (London and New York: Longman, 1994).

Gates-Coon, Rebecca, *Charmed Circle: Joseph II and the "Five Princesses," 1765–1790* (West Lafayette, IN: Purdue University Press, 2015).

KANT, IMMANUEL (1724–1804)   Immanuel Kant was born on April 22, 1724, in the German city of Königsburg (presently the Russian city of Kaliningrad). Kant often is considered the Enlightenment's greatest philosopher, as well as one of the greatest in the history of philosophy. He spent his entire career at the University of Königsburg, being appointed to the chair of logic and metaphysics in 1770 and retiring in 1797. Kant was one of the few major thinkers of the Enlightenment who made his principal impact as a university professor. He was an extremely popular professor whose lectures were so crowded that people arrived hours early to get a seat.

In the struggles of the German university world, Kant, despite his Lutheran Pietist upbringing, was a champion of the more secularly minded and modern philosophical faculty against the conservative theological faculty. Much of his early intellectual effort dealt with the differences between the scientific and philosophical systems of Isaac Newton and Gottfried Wilhelm Leibniz, which Kant tried to reconcile by transcending both, rather than compromising between the two. Kant transcended the conflict between Newtonian absolute space and time and Leibniz's view of time and space as relations by identifying both space and time as mental categories.

Many of Kant's early writings treated scientific questions such as the origins of the solar system, but he is best known for his more philosophical writings beginning with the *Critique of Pure Reason* (1781). Kant credited David Hume with "awakening him from his dogmatic slumbers." He devoted himself to finding a way to know that would stand up to Humean skeptical scrutiny. Kant's philosophy of knowledge rested on a distinction between those truths known through perception (*a posteriori*), and those known prior to perception (*a priori*). We can never attain true knowledge of the "thing in itself" through perception. Kant's belief in the possibility of knowledge that existed prior to perception was a break with the Lockean tradition in Enlightenment psychology, which treated sense perception as the only source of knowledge. In the sciences, Kant distinguished between those based on *a priori* and *a posteriori* knowledge, doubting whether the latter truly deserved the name of science. To be a true science, a body of knowledge must be known aprioristically, with certainty, and as an ordered system, which usually meant a mathematical system. The best example of a true science was mathematical Newtonian physics, which Kant labored to show was aprioristic rather than based on observations. Other sciences, such as chemistry and psychology, were not true sciences—but that did not mean that they were not worth doing. Kant's work on the relations of science to philosophy was *Metaphysical Foundations of Natural Science* (1786).

Kant's religious views were controversial. During the conservative reaction to the French Revolution his *Religion within the Limits of Reason Alone* (1793) was radical enough for the Prussian government to order him to cease further publications on the subject. Kant attacked natural theology and the idea that God's existence was demonstrable from science. His philosophy often is seen as clearly distinguishing between science and religion without subordinating either to the other. He believed that Christianity was the "highest" and most valuable of the religions.

Kant asserted that it was possible for human beings to have knowledge of absolutes without assistance from divine revelations such as the Christian bible, although he doubted whether moral behavior was possible for pure atheists. His works dealing with morality, including *Groundwork of the Metaphysic of Morals* (1785) and *Critique of Practical Reason* (1788) set forth an influential moral theory based on the "categorical imperative." A simplified version of the categorical imperative is the idea that individual actions could be morally evaluated by considering the consequences if they became a general rule. Thus, stealing is wrong because, if everyone stole, life would become impossible. Moral actions only can be those carried out in conscious obedience to the moral law. "Good" actions carried out because that was the person's actual preference were not moral. Kant also wrote on aesthetics and politics. Kant died on February 12, 1804, in Konigsburg after a long illness. Kantianism became the dominant philosophy of German universities in the late 18th century, although it took longer to spread outside of Germany. Kant's philosophy often is considered—especially by Germans—to be the height and the culmination of the Enlightenment.

See also: Germany, the Enlightenment in.

Further Reading

Cassirer, Ernst, *The Philosophy of the Enlightenment*, translated by Fritz C. A. Koelln and James P. Pettegrove (Princeton: Princeton University Press, 1951).

Guyer, Paul, *The Cambridge Companion to Kant and Modern Philosophy* (Cambridge and New York: Cambridge University Press, 2006).

Kuehn, Manfred, *Kant: A Biography* (New York: Cambridge University Press, 2001).

Watkins, Eric (ed.), *Kant and the Sciences* (Oxford: Oxford University Press, 2001).

LEIBNIZ, GOTTFRIED WILHELM (1646–1715)   The German Protestant philosopher Gottfried Wilhelm Leibniz often is described as the last man knowledgeable in all branches of knowledge. Leibniz contributed to science, philosophy, language, history, religion, law, librarianship, and poetry. His father, a university professor, educated Leibniz by giving him the run of his library. Leibniz taught himself Latin at the age of seven or eight years. He attended the universities of Leipzig, Jena, and Altdorf, taking his doctorate from Altdorf. After an early visit to Paris, where he studied with the physicist and astronomer Christiaan Huygens, Leibniz spent most of his life as a librarian, diplomat, and counselor in the employ of the Electors of Hanover. He devoted much effort to researching and writing the genealogy of the Hanoverian dynasty.

Leibniz's career as a philosopher and scientist differed from those of most other early Enlightenment intellectuals. In his lifetime he published only one book under his own name, but made extensive contributions to periodicals. He was one of the first major figures to exploit the growing periodical press. Leibniz also corresponded widely. Most of his voluminous writings were in manuscript, written in Latin and French—the international languages of his time—rather than in German.

Leibniz was familiar with the writings of René Descartes (1596–1650) and other 17th-century "mechanical philosophers," and early in his career made important contributions to mechanics. He distinguished the concept of force from quantity of motion, and is considered a founder of the science of dynamics—a word he coined. Leibniz championed the idea of the conservation of force, and suggested than when an inelastic body came to rest after an impact, its motion was transferred to its individual parts. Leibniz met with Baruch Spinoza on multiple occasions and admired his work, but broke with him on the question of the freedom of God. Leibniz thought that God was not bound by Spinoza's strict determinism but only the moral necessity of creating the best possible world.

Leibniz asserted that his philosophy drew on what was good from ancient and medieval scholastic traditions rather than simply replacing them with a better philosophy. He was optimistic about scientific progress, which he hoped would make the world better, but he found contemporary physics too materialistic. Leibniz modified what he considered overly mechanical modern philosophy and science by turning it in a spiritual direction, reducing the world to "substances." According to Leibniz, material entities influenced by outside sources could not be substances. Leibniz, influenced by the Jewish mystical and magical philosophy of Kabbalah, theorized that the ultimate reality were monads, "simple substances" that combined to produce the world, essentially atoms that were not material but spiritual.

The monads—and therefore all nature—were alive and arranged in a harmony directed by God. This harmony of monads proved the existence of God.

Leibniz was a great supporter of academies and scientific societies. He urged the establishment of the Royal Academy of Berlin, the capital of Prussia. This Prussian scientific academy, which followed the model of the French Royal Academy of Sciences, was founded in 1700, and Leibniz presided over it in its early years. It would become a leading scientific body in the 18th century. Leibniz also encouraged the Russian Tsar Peter the Great (r. 1687–1725) to establish a scientific academy. Shortly after the Tsar's death, the Imperial Academy of Sciences of St. Petersburg was founded.

Leibniz's greatest rival was Isaac Newton. Both invented calculus around the same time, leading to a vicious priority dispute provoked and waged rather unscrupulously by Newton, who accused Leibniz of having stolen his ideas. The English mostly took Newton's side for nationalistic reasons and deference to Newton's position as head of the Royal Society. For decades, English mathematicians stubbornly refused to use Leibniz's superior system for calculus, but French, German, and other continental mathematicians used it with great success. English mathematics would lag behind until the early 19th century.

Leibniz also disagreed with other aspects of Newton's science and philosophy. He found the idea of universal gravity to be suspect, as it seemed to involve two objects affecting each other at a distance with no attempt to explain how this was possible. He also distrusted Newton's use of space as an absolute rather than as a relative quality. Leibnizian physics defined motion and therefore space as relational. Leibniz had a famous exchange of letters over these questions with a follower of Newton's, the English clergyman Samuel Clarke (1675–1729), in 1715 and 1716. Leibniz, again like Newton, saw his philosophy in religious terms. He placed great emphasis on the perfection of the world as created by God and criticized Newton and Clarke for their belief that God had to interfere on occasion to keep the universe running. This did not mean that any world God created would by definition be perfect, as Leibniz believed in standards of good and evil independent of God's will. Because God is both good and omnipotent, the world he chose to create from all possible worlds that he had the power to create had to be the best of all possible worlds.

Leibniz was savagely mocked for this by Voltaire in his novel *Candide* (1759). In the novel, Candide's advisor, the relentlessly optimistic Dr. Pangloss, is a caricature of Leibniz. This mockery and other attacks on Leibniz as an optimist rely on a distortion of his position. He was working with a different definition of goodness than the ordinary definition. Leibniz defined goodness as combining the maximum diversity of phenomena with the maximum simplicity of laws, rather than providing a pleasant life. Human happiness was only one among many considerations for God, and could be sacrificed for more important things.

Leibniz was a great believer in ecumenism, and spent much of his career promoting good relations between the various Protestant churches of Europe and the Roman Catholic Church. Much of his philosophy was designed to resolve the difficulties that existed between the churches. He also was interested in Chinese philosophy, and corresponded with Catholic Jesuit missionaries in China. Leibniz was one of the first Europeans to make a serious study of Chinese thought, although he had to rely on translations.

Leibniz died at Hanover in 1716. He never was very influential in England, where the Newtonians despised him; and in France his philosophy was considered insufficiently mechanical, although his mathematics were admired. (One exception to this French lack of interest in Leibniz's natural philosophy was the Marquise du Châtelet, who integrated Leibnizian and Newtonian ideas in physics.) Leibniz was always influential in Germany, particularly in the German universities. Some religious authorities found Leibniz suspect as a determinist who denied the possibility of humans having free will, but versions of Leibniz's philosophy were quite popular in 18th-century Germany.

See also: Enlightenment Views of Asian Civilizations; Châtelet, Émilie du; Germany, the Enlightenment in; Newton, Isaac; Science; Voltaire.

Further Reading

Antognazza, Maria Rosa, *Leibniz: An Intellectual Biography* (Cambridge and New York: Cambridge University Press, 2009).

Hall, A. Rupert, *Philosophers at War: The Quarrel Between Newton and Leibniz* (Cambridge and New York: Cambridge University Press, 1980).

Jolley, Nicholas, *The Cambridge Companion to Leibniz* (New York and Cambridge: Cambridge University Press, 1995).

LESSING, GOTTHOLD EPHRAIM (1729–1781)   Gotthold Ephraim Lessing was the foremost representative of the Enlightenment in mid-18th-century Germany. The eldest son of a Protestant pastor, he was born on January 22, 1729, in Kamenz, Germany. He was expected to follow his father's profession, but instead became a dramatist and writer. As a dramatist, Lessing conceived the mission of liberating German drama from slavish imitation of the highly rule-governed, formalized style of French neoclassical drama. His first successful play, *Miss Sara Sampson*, premiered in 1755. Its English characters and setting represented a conscious turning away from aristocratic French drama to "bourgeois" English models.

Lessing became a professional writer and translator, among the earliest Germans to make a living by using his pen. His hopes of patronage from the "enlightened despot," Frederick the Great of Prussia, were dashed partly by Frederick's lack of interest in German culture, and partly by the enmity of Frederick's friend and ally Voltaire. Lessing distrusted Voltaire's irreligion, and Voltaire suspected that Lessing was planning to publish a "pirate" translation, paying nothing to the original author, of Voltaire's *Century of Louis XIV.* Lessing also found Voltaire's tragedies too formal and emotionless, comparing them unfavorably to Shakespeare's plays. After years of seeking, in 1770 Lessing finally received a steady position as librarian to the Duke of Brunswick.

Lessing's *Laocoon* (1766) was the most important work of aesthetic criticism to emerge from the Enlightenment. The book's title comes from an ancient statue of the mythological character Laocoon and his two sons being strangled by snakes. Ironically, Lessing never saw the statue and instead worked from engravings of it. In *Laocoon,* Lessing argued against the notion—handed down from the ancient Greeks and Romans—that poetry and painting were sister arts, and instead argued that they were radically separate. Poetry, he claimed, was the stronger and more versatile art due to its ability to present the passage of time rather than only a single moment.

Lessing was interested in the Bible, which he did not believe to be a sacred text handed down from God. Like many of the Enlightened, he viewed the Bible as a historical document created by human beings. His research into the origin of the Gospels was too daring to be published in Germany, but he strongly advocated religious tolerance, not only among Christians but between Christians and Jews as well. His play *Nathan the Wise,* which premiered in 1778, was set at the time of the Crusades and had for its central character a wise and admirable Jew, modeled after Lessing's close friend Moses Mendelssohn. In it, Lessing showed that character was more important than particular religious beliefs and that religious prejudice was a destructive force in society.

Many of Lessing's later writings dealt with religion, and caused controversy with religious authorities in Brunswick. Lessing became a follower of Baruch Spinoza, accepting the Spinozist beliefs in pantheism and the illusory nature of human free will. Lessing's *The Education of the Human Race* (1780) presented a picture of human history as spiritually progressive in which religion plays an important role, not as a revelation of final truth but as an inspiration of human progress. He also was a Freemason. Lessing died on February 15, 1781, in Brunswick. A few years after his death, he became a subject of controversy as his Spinozist beliefs became known more generally.

See also: Germany, the Enlightenment in; Mendelssohn, Moses; Spinoza, Baruch; Theater.

Further Reading

Fischer, Barbara and Thomas C. Fox (eds.), *A Companion to the Works of Gotthold Ephraim Lessing* (Rochester, NY: Camden House, 2005).

Nisbet, H. B., *Gotthold Ephraim Lessing: His Life, Works and Thought* (Oxford: Oxford University Press, 2013).

Robertson, Ritchie (ed.), *Lessing and the German Enlightenment* (Oxford: Voltaire Foundation, 2013).

LISBON EARTHQUAKE One of the most destructive earthquakes in European history occurred at the Portuguese capital of Lisbon on November 1, 1755. Much of the city was destroyed by the quake and the subsequent fires and tsunamis, and tens of thousands of people were killed. The loss of life and the destruction caused by the earthquake was a challenge to the view of nature as being fundamentally benevolent and attracted attention throughout Europe. The disaster inspired a poem by Voltaire, *Poem on the Disaster at Lisbon* (1756), which scathingly criticizes philosophical optimism and the belief in a Divine Providence just or merciful in its relations with human beings. One scene in Voltaire's satirical novel, *Candide* (1759), another attack on optimism, has a scene set in Lisbon during the earthquake, and it also figures in Denis Diderot's posthumously published novel *Jacques the Fatalist* (1796). Jean-Jacques Rousseau used the earthquake as evidence against the wisdom of living in cities, and the young Immanuel Kant was fascinated with the subject, developing a theory of earthquakes as caused by the release of subterranean gases.

The center of Lisbon was rebuilt along the lines of Enlightened urbanism under the leadership of the Enlightened statesman the Marquis of Pombal. A grid pattern replaced the previous tangle of streets, and various measures to minimize damage in the case of a future earthquake were put in place. The neighborhood still is referred to as the "Baxia Pombal" or "Pombaline Lower Town."

See also: Nature; Pombal, Sebastião José de Carvalho e Melo, 1st Marquis of; Religion; Voltaire.

Further Reading

Johns, Alessa (ed.), *Dreadful Visitations: Confronting Natural Catastrophe in the Age of the Enlightenment* (New York: Routledge, 1999).

LITERATURE The dominant aesthetic philosophy at the beginning of the Enlightenment was the classicism that had been developed in late

17th-century France. Classicists exalted the following of rules. Voltaire, when he became the first French writer to discuss the works of William Shakespeare, admired Shakespeare's genius but deprecated his ignorance of the rules which governed tragedy. Seventeenth-century French tragedians such as Racine would never have mixed comedy with tragedy in the manner of the porter's scene in *Macbeth*. Although French classicism had comparatively little effect on England, it had a great deal of influence outside France on the European continent. Germany in the early part of the century literarily was dominated by France, a pattern which suited the tastes of the Enlightenment monarch Frederick the Great, a well-known despiser of German literature and even of the German language. Beginning in mid-century, German writers such as Gottfried Ephraim Lessing began the emancipation of German literature from French hegemony.

Genres of literature that are now considered motivated primarily by aesthetic goals had a didactic purpose in the 18th century. The Enlightened English physician Erasmus Darwin (1731–1802) was the author of *The Loves of the Plants* (1789), an epic poem on the latest scientific ideas about the sexual behavior of plants.

The most remarkable phenomenon in the literary history of the 18th century was the rise of the novel, a phenomenon that interacted in complex ways with the Enlightenment. Several Enlightenment writers, notably Voltaire, Rousseau, and Diderot were novelists, and Enlightenment philosophers read and were impressed by the leading novelists of the time, including Samuel Richardson, the author of *Pamela* (1740) and *Clarissa* (1747–1748), and Laurence Sterne, the author of *Tristram Shandy* (1759–1767). The novel appealed to a broader reading public that included members of the middle and working classes and women, the same public that many Enlightenment writings appealed to. The novel also was difficult to assimilate into the canon of neoclassical aesthetics.

Although some novels, such as Voltaire's *Candide* (1759) or Diderot's *Jacques the Fatalist* (1796), appealed primarily to the intellect, many of the most successful novels of the 18th century were "sentimental" novels, appealing to the emotions and, at their most successful, drawing tears from the reader. Many of the most successful novelists, such as Richardson, appealed to the emotions rather than to reason, but they were admired by Enlightened readers regardless. Diderot wrote a tribute to Richardson whom he admired for leading his readers to passionately admire the virtues of his protagonists while staying true to life. The most successful sentimental novelist among the leaders of the Enlightenment was Jean-Jacques Rousseau, whose *The New Heloise* (1761) was among the most popular novels of the 18th century.

The growth of the sentimental novel was connected with the growth of a literary market among women, many of whom were fans of Rousseau. Despite their appeal to the emotions, Rousseau saw the purpose of his novels as fundamentally didactic, teaching the right ideas about education, the subject of *Émile, or a Treatise on Education* (1762), and domestic life. Other novels, such as Cholderos de Laclos's *Dangerous Liaisons* (1782) made a backhanded appeal to virtue by focusing on corrupt and evil protagonists. The novel had a later start in Germany, but *The Sorrows of Young Werther* (1774) by Johann Wolfgang von Goethe (1749–1832) was a popular success and even was credited with setting off a fashion for suicide in emulation of its hero, although the evidence for this is weak.

The novel also was more open to the contributions of women than were many older genres. Many women became popular novelists in both English and French, and women often were considered a primary audience for novels.

See also: Diderot, Denis; Rousseau, Jean-Jacques; Theater; Voltaire.

Further Reading

Jones, Tom, and Rowan Boyson (eds.), *The Poetic Enlightenment: Poetry and Human Science, 1650–1820* (London: Pickering and Chatto, 2013).

London, April, *The Cambridge Introduction to the Eighteenth-Century Novel* (Cambridge and New York: Cambridge University Press, 2012).

Rex, Walter E., *The Attraction of the Contrary: Essays on the Literature of the French Enlightenment* (Cambridge and New York: Cambridge University Press, 1987).

LOCKE, JOHN (1632–1704) John Locke was an English physician and philosopher who pleaded for religious toleration and the basing of political authority on the idea of a contract between the government and people. He was born on August 29, 1682, in the English town of Wrington.

As a political philosopher, Locke often is considered a founder of the liberal tradition. Locke denied that the original source of political power was the power God had given Adam, and suggested that it derived instead from the voluntary agreement of the governed. He also argued that when people were severely misgoverned, the contract was being broken and the people had a right to rebel. His *Two Treatises on Government* (published in 1689, but written earlier) expressed this position, and the second treatise has become a recognized classic of political thought. Locke's work influenced the Enlightenment and the American revolutionaries, although scholars still disagree on the extent of his influence. Locke was a supporter of the Whig party in late

17th-century England. His close relation to the Whig leader Anthony Ashley Cooper (1621–1683), First Earl of Shaftesbury, whom he served as physician forced him into exile in the Dutch Republic following the Tory ascendancy in 1683. Locke was a supporter of the English Revolution of 1688, which led to his return to England. His political philosophy sometimes was read as a justification of that revolution, although much of it was developed before the revolution.

Locke's religious position came close to Deism, without ever renouncing Christianity entirely. He was a member of the Church of England. His posthumously published *Discourse on Miracles* (1706) treated the miracles of Jesus as the strongest evidence for Christianity, a popular position in early Enlightenment religious apologetics. Locke was a strong supporter of religious toleration, and his three *Letters on Toleration* (1689–1692) remained influential well into the 18th century. Locke's endorsement of toleration was limited, however. He made an exception for Roman Catholics (the Whigs of Locke's time were strongly anti-Catholic), arguing that they could not be trusted as their loyalty lay with the Pope, the ruler of a foreign state. He made another exception for atheists, believing that their lack of belief in a supernatural authority meant that their word could not be trusted.

Locke also made important contributions to psychology, and attempted to devise a new philosophical style compatible with the new science of the 17th century. Locke viewed the philosopher's mission not as the setting up of a comprehensive system answering all questions about the universe, but as clearing away mental errors and preconceptions, thus enabling people to think more clearly. This view became quite influential in the Enlightenment, which shared Locke's hostility to "system-building." Locke's *Essay Concerning Human Understanding* (1690) analyzed the human mind in terms of the reception and combination of sense-impressions—Locke strongly opposed the theory, which goes back to the ancient Greek philosopher Plato, that certain ideas were inborn or "innate" in the human mind. Locke's argument that impressions were taken in through the senses by human minds that combined them into complex ideas would be the basis of Enlightenment psychology. (It is sometimes referred to as the "blank slate" or *tabula rasa* theory.) Because the outside world, and not our own minds, is the ultimate source of truth, it was important that it be observed thoroughly and conscientiously. Locke analyzed the distinction between "primary" qualities existing in a thing in itself such as mass, and "secondary" qualities created by our perceptions (e.g., of color), a distinction fundamental to Enlightenment and modern science. He also wrote on education, the "reasonableness of Christianity," and economics. Although an acquaintance and correspondent of Isaac Newton, with whom he served on a committee on problems of the English coinage, Locke was skeptical of grand theories in the sciences, believing that they often exceeded the boundaries of what was knowable.

Locke died on October 28, 1704, at the English village of High Laver. Locke and Newton together would be exalted as the founders of the Enlightenment in the 18th century.

See also: England, the Enlightenment in; Political Philosophy; Religion.

Further Reading

Ashcraft, Richard, *Revolutionary Politics and Locke's "Two Treatises of Government"* (Princeton: Princeton University Press, 1986).

Hirschmann, Nancy J., and Kirstie M. McClure (eds.), *Feminist Interpretations of John Locke* (University Park, PA: Pennsylvania State University Press, 2007).

Woolhouse, Roger, *Locke: A Biography* (Cambridge and New York: Cambridge University Press, 2007).

MENDELSSOHN, MOSES (1729–1786)   Moses Mendelssohn was the most important leader of the Jewish Enlightenment or "Haskalah," and a friend and associate of leaders in the German Enlightenment, including Gottfried Ephraim Lessing and Immanuel Kant. (Lessing modeled the Jewish hero of his play, *Nathan the Wise*, after Mendelssohn.) Mendelssohn was born on September 6, 1729, in the German town of Dessau. Mendelssohn's father was a teacher at a Jewish school and his formal education as a boy and young man was traditionally Jewish. Like other Jewish boys, he learned Hebrew and the Torah—the sacred scripture of the Jews—along with the Talmud, the extensive body of interpretations of Jewish law. He also was self-taught in modern European languages and the literature of ancient pagan and Christian philosophers and thinkers.

Mendelssohn published extensively in both German and Hebrew. As a philosopher he was an heir of the German philosophers Gottfried Wilhelm Leibniz and Christian Wolff (1679–1754), although he was not afraid to depart from them in considering specific issues. Like them, Mendelssohn was a rationalist believing that fundamental universal truths—such as the existence of God, the immortality of the soul, and the basic precepts of morality—were reachable through human reason. His most successful book, *Phaedo* (1767), was an updating of the ancient Greek philosopher Plato's dialogue on the immortality of the soul. (Mendelssohn was a hunchback, and his combination of bodily deformity with philosophical wisdom led him to be nicknamed the Jewish Socrates or the Berlin Socrates after the famously ugly Greek philosopher who was Plato's teacher.) It was widely translated in Continental Europe.

Mendelssohn spent his adult life in Berlin, the capital of Prussia, during the reign of Frederick the Great. He worked as a bookkeeper and later was the partner of a Jewish silk merchant. In 18th-century Prussia, Jews had religious freedom but suffered from legal inequality. Mendelssohn faced opposition both within the Jewish community—suspicious of his applications of non-Jewish learning to Jewish questions and his translation of books from the Hebrew Bible into German—and from Christians, some of whom hoped that the widely admired Mendelssohn would convert to Christianity. In 1769, he had a controversy with the Swiss pastor Johann Caspar Lavater (1741–1801), who demanded that Mendelssohn explain his reasons for not converting. Mendelssohn's most important book, *Jerusalem* (1783)—written after his controversy with Lavater—combined an argument for religious toleration with an attempt to demonstrate the compatibility of Judaism with natural religion. He claimed that Judaism, unlike Christianity, lacked the concept of religious coercion—making it a religion ideally suited for Enlightened sensibilities. Mendelssohn's Enlightened Judaism required questioning the legitimacy of the power held by rabbis in Jewish communities.

Mendelssohn's later years were marred by a controversy over the beliefs and character of his deceased friend Lessing. Lessing had been charged with "Spinozism," being a follower of Baruch Spinoza, a position widely—though incorrectly—identified with atheism. Defending Lessing's character brought Mendelssohn into opposition with several prominent German intellectuals. Mendelssohn died on January 4, 1786, in Berlin. Despite Mendelssohn's passionate loyalty to Judaism, his descendants—including the composer Felix Mendelssohn (1809–1847), who wrote his biography—assimilated to German society by becoming Christians.

See also: Enlightenment Views of Jews and Judaism; Germany, the Enlightenment in; Jewish Enlightenment; Lessing, Gotthold Ephraim; Religion.

Further Reading

Feiner, Shmuel, *Moses Mendelssohn: Sage of Modernity,* translated by Anthony Berris (New Haven: Yale University Press, 2010).

Sorkin, David, *Moses Mendelssohn and the Religious Enlightenment* (Berkeley: University of California Press, 1996).

MONTESQUIEU, CHARLES-LOUIS DE SECONDAT, BARON DE (1689–1755)

The Baron de Montesquieu was born on January 18, 1689, as a member of the hereditary nobility of French judges and lawyers known as the "nobility of the robe." As was traditional in his family, he served actively in the criminal division of the *Parlement,* or judiciary, of the French province of Bordeaux. His first book—published anonymously—was *Persian Letters* (1721). *Persian Letters* employed the literary device of having European society described by a fictional foreigner; during the Enlightenment this device was very popular. *Persian Letters* consists of the letters between two imaginary Persians, mocking what they see as the irrationality of European society. The mockery is not only of Europeans, however, as the Persian Muslim Usbek—perceptive in his denunciations of tyranny in Europe—is shown acting like a tyrant over his harem in Persia. The book was extremely popular.

Montesquieu was a firm believer in many of the principles of the Enlightenment, such as the necessity of a government serving the people and religious toleration. The issue of toleration was particularly important to him, as he was a Catholic married to a Calvinist. He strongly supported toleration of Jews as well as of different Christian sects. Montesquieu wrote a historical study of Ancient Rome, *Consideration of the Causes of the Greatness and Decay of the Romans* (1734), which influenced Gibbon's *The Decline and Fall of the Roman Empire*. He also contributed to the *Encyclopédie*.

In 1725, Montesquieu retired from the bench. He spent some years traveling through Europe observing different social institutions and, in 1731, began to work on his masterpiece, *The Spirit of the Laws*, which was published in 1748. *The Spirit of the Laws* is the first great comparative study of social and legal institutions. Montesquieu believed that laws and institutions should be judged not against an abstract standard of perfection but in terms of how they were adapted to different peoples. Seemingly irrational laws might well have a rational function in their society.

Given that adaptation of laws to peoples, legal reform should be undertaken very carefully. Strengthening the power of the French monarch against the nobility, for example, as many reformers of the Enlightenment wished to do, would be harmful in that it would remove a check on the monarch's power. This possibly could lead France from being a monarchy (of which Montesquieu approved) to despotism, which Montesquieu despised and which he associated with non-western rulers, such as the Sultan of the Ottoman Empire.

Monarchy and despotism—which differs from monarchy in that the despot has no responsibility to follow the laws—are two of Montesquieu's three basic types of government. The third is the republic, which could take the form of the democracy where the people rule, or the aristocratic state ruled by a few. Except for despotism—which is innately corrupt—each of these governments can appear in both good and corrupt forms. Democratic republics were particularly vulnerable to corruption, as their maintenance required a great number of people to sustain an unnatural degree of civic virtue.

To protect individual freedom and to guard against corruption, it is necessary that all power in a polity not be concentrated in the same place.

Montesquieu distinguished between legislative, executive, and judicial power. He believed that is was best that these powers be separated, as bringing them all into the same hands could lead to despotism. Montesquieu was a great admirer of the English government which balanced the power of the king with the legislative power of parliament. Montesquieu had little interest in the quest for an ideal or "utopian" government; he believed that a limited government that left people to carry out their own affairs without excessive interference was the best that could be desired.

Montesquieu's analysis of how different types of governments are formed and maintained includes consideration of physical factors, such as climate, as well as cultural factors such as religion. The theory that human societies were shaped by climate was not original to him, and dates back to the 16th century. Harsh countries are less tempting to invaders, and the hard work required to cultivate them is linked to virtue and republican government. The indolence of dwellers in hot climates contributes to their alleged propensity for despotism. However, Montesquieu was not a climactic determinist—other factors such as the influence of a great legislator or a religion could overcome the influence of climate. Montesquieu analyzed religion in *The Spirit of the Laws* principally in relation to its social utility—different religions are adapted to different societies, as Protestantism is to republics, Catholicism is to monarchies, and Islam is to despotisms. Montesquieu's book was condemned by the Catholic Church and placed on the "Index of Forbidden Books," but it passed the French censorship and circulated freely in France. It would influence later political thought, including that of the American founding fathers. Montesquieu died of a fever on February 10, 1755, in Paris.

See also: Enlightenment Views of Asian Civilizations; Enlightenment Views of Muslims and Islam; France, the Enlightenment in; Political Philosophy.

Further Reading

Rahe, Paul A., *Montesquieu and the Logic of Liberty* (New Haven: Yale University Press, 2009).

Shackleton, Robert, *Essays on Montesquieu and the Enlightenment* (Oxford: Voltaire Foundation, 1988).

Shklar, Judith, *Montesquieu* (Oxford: Oxford University Press, 1987).

NATURE There were many disagreements and contradictions in Enlightenment views about nature, but a few themes can be picked out. The Enlightenment built on the Christian tradition of thinking about nature by concentrating on its usefulness for humans. The use of land for the maximum benefit of humanity was both a moral value and a criterion for ranking civilizations. Scottish thinkers such as Adam Ferguson (1723–1816) and Adam Smith divided human history into four stages defined by a relationship with the land—hunter-gathering, pastoral, agricultural, and commercial. Progress through the stages was seen as a process of improvement. "Rise" through the stages, however, was not simply a matter of peaceful development. It continued in the Enlightenment's own time through the often violent displacement of herding peoples, hunter-gatherers, and other people not making the full use of their land—such as Scottish Highlanders and Native Americans—by more "civilized" folk. The process by which unproductive wilderness was turned into productive agricultural land often involved the transformation of unowned or communally owned land into "private property" on the European model, and was considered justification for conquest. Those natural features which prevented agriculturalists from making full use of land, such as mountains or economically useless trees, were condemned as blemishes.

None of this means that the thinkers of the Enlightenment were universally hostile to or contemptuous of nature. The tradition of natural theology—of using nature to demonstrate the existence and attributes of God—remained powerful in the 18th and early 19th century, and increasingly drew from the evidence of natural history as well as physics. The beauty and glories of nature were widely praised, particularly by botanists and zoologists such as Georges-Louis Leclerc de Buffon (1707–1788), director of the Royal Botanical Garden in Paris, and the Swedish inventor of modern biological classification Carolus Linnaeus (1707–1778). The writings of 18th-century naturalists such as the Anglican minister Gilbert White (1720–1793) reflect a deep love of nature, as shown in the close observations recounted in his frequently reprinted *The Natural History and Antiquities of Selborne* (1789). The study of nature was regarded as a way of improving the mind, and natural history in particular became a popular avocation among many men and women of a variety of social backgrounds.

Gardens and parks were widely distributed, and public ones such as London's Hyde Park were popular recreation spots, although generally were not available to poor and working-class citizens. Many wealthy landowners devoted a large portion of their land and wealth to the creation of ornamental gardens, such as Thomas Jefferson's gardens at Monticello. The point of 18th-century gardens and parks, however, was to show nature as shaped by the hand of humanity. The lack of interest in preserving the land in its original state can be seen in the wide popularity of exotic plants as garden ornaments. The rigid geometry of the formal garden of the age of Louis XIV (r. 1643–1715) had been abandoned in favor of something more adapted to the contours of the land, but no one would mistake the 18th-century garden for a wilderness. The activity that did promote keeping large areas of land in something close to their natural state was the sport—and often the obsession—of European male (and a few female) aristocrats and kings: hunting. The Enlightenment monarch, Frederick the Great of Prussia, was one of the few European rulers who disliked hunting.

Many believed that the cultivation of the land improved not merely the land but the cultivator. Voltaire's novel *Candide* (1759) ends with the famous line "let us cultivate our garden" ("il faut cultiver notre jardin"), which shows that Candide has given up his world-spanning ambitions and has settled on a poor but contented life. The image of the virtuous farmer in contrast with the corrupt city-dweller occurs frequently in the propaganda of the American Revolutionary era, as in Hector St. John de Crevecouer's *Letters from an American Farmer* (1782) or John Dickinson's *Letters from a Farmer in Pennsylvania* (1767–1768). The farmer in real life, particularly the European peasant, however, often was not seen as a fountain of wisdom or even someone who had perfected a craft but as someone who would benefit from advice from better-educated people. Agricultural improvement was a popular cause in the 18th century, spawning numerous societies and publications even if its impact on actual farming practices was limited. Some groups working for agricultural improvement were gatherings of local landowners, and others, such as the Paris-based Royal Society of Agriculture founded in 1761, were backed with state power and resources.

One area in which much of the Enlightenment—particularly the radical and skeptical Enlightenment—differed from mainstream Christianity was that it saw humanity as part of nature, rather than separated from it by the possession of a spiritual soul. As such, humanity, like animals and plants, was shaped by its natural environment. Montesquieu's *The Spirit of the Laws* (1748) ascribed many aspects of human society to the different climates in which different societies had developed, although some people, such as Voltaire, criticized this approach, preferring to place more emphasis on social factors such as religion. The emphasis on the "natural" body rather than the spiritual soul opened the door for arguments about the relative worth of different human subgroups based on the differences of their bodies. This expressed itself in both racial and gendered terms, as the body of European white men was considered the norm and other bodies, even the bodies of American white men, were defined in opposition to it.

See also: Gender; Lisbon Earthquake; Rousseau, Jean-Jacques; Science.

Further Reading

Daston, Lorraine and Gianna Pomata (eds.), *The Faces of Nature in Enlightenment Europe* (Berlin: BWV, Berliner Wissenschafts-Verlag, 2003).

Gerbi, Antonello, *The Dispute of the New World: History of a Polemic, 1750–1900*, translated by Jeremy Moyle (Pittsburgh: University of Pittsburgh Press, 1973).

Wolloch, Isaac, *History and Nature in the Enlightenment: Praise of the Mastery of Nature in Eighteenth-Century Historical Literature* (Farnham: Surrey, 2011).

NEWTON, ISAAC (1642–1727)   Isaac Newton—the most admired man of the Enlightenment—set a frame of reference for physical science that remained in place until the early 20th century. Newton made fundamental contributions to mechanics, optics, and mathematics. Newton's most famous contributions are the invention of calculus, the theory of universal gravitation, and the three laws of motion. Newton also served successfully as head of the English Mint and as president of the Royal Society—England's leading scientific organization—from 1703 to his death.

Newton was born on December 25, 1642, into a family of yeoman farmers far removed from England's elite, although well above the very poorest. Newton's father died before Isaac was born, which increased the family's financial difficulties. Newton's intelligence was noticed early in his life, and he attended Cambridge University on a scholarship. The period from 1665 to 1666 often is identified as Newton's *annus mirabilis*—the most productive phase of his career. In that time, Newton experimentally established the diffraction of light, discovered the general form of the binomial theorem, laid the foundations of differential and integral calculus, and began his work on universal gravitation. In 1668, Newton applied his work on optics to invent the first successful reflecting telescope.

Newton's enormously influential approach to science is based on the belief that a divine lawgiver handed down the natural laws—expressible in mathematical form—which govern the universe. The most famous of all Newton's laws is the law of gravity, as set forth in his *Mathematical Principles of Natural Philosophy* (1687). Newton's theory of gravity states that two objects attract each other with a strength varying directly with their mass and inversely with the square of their distance from each other. Newton's establishment that this formula could explain both the falling of a dropped object on the earth and the movements of planets around the sun was vital in establishing that the entire universe was governed by the same set of laws.

Newton also established the three laws of motion. The first law is that an object in a uniform motion tends to stay in that motion unless it encounters an external force. This is also known as the law of inertia. The second law defines force as mass times acceleration ($f = ma$). The third law is that every action has an opposite and equal reaction.

Newton was devout but unorthodox in his religion. He did not believe in the Trinity—a heretical position in early modern England. He discretely concealed his real beliefs. The aged Newton spent most of his intellectual efforts on interpreting Biblical prophecies, which puzzled many of his secularly minded Enlightenment admirers who saw it as the folly of an otherwise brilliant man. Newton's scientific work contributed to his prophetic interpretation, as he believed that comets could play a key role in the prophesied devastation of the earth. He also spent an enormous amount of time working out the chronologies of the various ancient kingdoms mentioned in the Bible.

Newton's closing decades were marked by nasty feuds, particularly one with his great German rival, Gottfried Wilhelm Leibniz. Newton and Leibniz quarreled over who deserved the credit for the invention of calculus, but Newton also viewed Leibniz's philosophy and theology with grave suspicion. The feud—during which Newton rallied the support of the British scientific establishment—had disastrous consequences for British mathematics. It delayed the acceptance of the superior Leibnizian calculus for a century.

Newton died in London on March 31, 1727. His funeral a week later was a state occasion, and the farmer's son was buried in Westminster Abbey among England's greatest citizens. The fact that, in England, a person of humble origins such as Newton could rise to a peak of universal respect impressed many in the Enlightenment, especially Voltaire, who might have attended the funeral. Newton's amazing accomplishments in science made him a model for the Enlightenment and an example of what the human mind can achieve.

See also: Academies and Learned Societies; Bible, the; Châtelet, Émilie du; England, the Enlightenment in; Leibniz, Gottfried Wilhelm; Religion; Science; Voltaire.

Further Reading
Dobbs, B. J. T., and Margaret Jacob, *Newton and the Culture of Newtonianism* (Atlantic Highlands, NJ: Humanities Press, 1993).
Hall, A. Rupert, *Philosophers at War: The Quarrel between Newton and Leibniz* (Cambridge and New York: Cambridge University Press, 1980).
Westfall, Richard S., *The Life of Isaac Newton* (Cambridge: Cambridge University Press, 1994)

PAINE, THOMAS (1737–1809)   Thomas Paine was born on February 9, 1737, in the English village of Thetford in the county of Norfolk. He became one of the leading political and religious radicals of the late Enlightenment, and at some time or another was at odds with virtually every government he encountered. Ironically, considering his later career, in England Paine was a tax collector for the English Excise, an "exciseman." Paine became an activist for the excisemen—one of the most despised groups in English society—arguing in *The Case of the Officers of the Excise* (1772) that the best way to combat corruption in the excise was to increase excisemen's pay. Shortly afterwards, Paine was fired from his job. On the advice of Benjamin Franklin, Paine set off for the American colonies, arriving in Franklin's city of Philadelphia.

In Philadelphia, Paine found his way into the profession in which he would excel—journalism. His pamphlet, *Common Sense*, published in January 1776 before the adoption of the Declaration of Independence, argued for separation from Great Britain and denounced monarchy. *Common Sense* was an immediate best seller, selling more than 150,000 copies. The pamphlet helped influence the climate of American opinion towards independence. Paine served in the Continental Army during the American Revolution and continued to propagandize for the rebel cause in a series of pamphlets collectively titled *The American Crisis*.

Paine opposed slavery but he was never a serious campaigner against it and counted American slave owners such as Thomas Jefferson and the South Carolinian statesman Henry Laurens (1724–1792) among his friends and political allies. Despite Paine's contribution to the revolutionary cause, some of the more conservative revolutionaries, such as John Adams (1735–1826), despised him.

Temporarily fading into obscurity and poverty after the American Revolution, Paine went back to Britain to find financial support for a new method of building bridges that he had devised. Paine rose to even greater fame and faced more condemnation during the French Revolution. His two-part *The Rights of Man* (1791, 1792) was a response to the Irish politician Edmund Burke's denunciation of the Revolution and all its works, published in *Reflections on the Revolution in France* (1790). In the *Declaration of the Rights of Man* (1789), Paine supported the idea of natural rights as embodied. The book was extremely popular, but its impassioned call for revolution attracted condemnation from the British government, forcing Paine, who was living in Britain at the time, to flee to revolutionary France. In France he was made an honorary citizen and a delegate to the French National Convention, where he opposed the execution of Louis XVI and supported the abolition of the monarchy. Paine was imprisoned by the radical Jacobins, but was released at the end of the Reign of Terror. Paine thought that the American government had not done enough to get him out of prison in France, and thus became embittered and wrote a vitriolic attack on American President George Washington. Paine remained in France and even was readmitted to the National Convention. After his release, he published *The Age of Reason* (two parts; 1794, 1795), an argument for rational, Deistic religion that was directed at Christianity.

Paine did not return to the United States until 1802, after his friend Thomas Jefferson had become president and invited him to the White House. Paine, however, still faced much opposition from American clergy and other Christians. Paine died of a stroke on June 8, 1809, in New York City.

See also: American Revolution and Founding; Bible, the; French Revolution; Political Philosophy; Religion.

Further Reading

Foner, Eric, *Tom Paine and Revolutionary America,* 2nd ed. (Oxford: Oxford University Press, 2005).

Fruchtman, Jack, *Thomas Paine and the Religion of Nature* (Baltimore: Johns Hopkins University Press, 1993).

Speck, W. A., *A Political Biography of Thomas Paine* (London: Pickering and Chatto, 2013).

POLITICAL PHILOSOPHY   Ideas associated with the Enlightenment—secularism and anti-clericalism, turning a skeptical eye towards tradition and custom in favor of the application of reason and expertise to public affairs and, to a lesser extent, democracy—have played a prominent role in political thought in the 18th century and later.

The Enlightenment continued the secularization of European political philosophy that had begun in the Renaissance with the work of Florentine Niccolo Machiavelli (1469–1527). It also drew on the political thought of the English Revolution of the mid-17th century, which had seen the temporary overthrow of the monarchy. Enlightenment philosophers did not believe that rulers received their authority directly or indirectly from God, as Christian political thinkers—both Protestant and Catholic—had asserted. Authority had to be justified in other ways, such as the consent of the people, or the ruler's capacity to rule for the benefit of all—a benefit defined in terms of earthly prosperity rather than eternal salvation. Much of this theory derived from the English Revolution of the mid-17th century and the "contractual" political thought of the English political philosophers Thomas Hobbes (1588–1679) and John Locke, who probably had more influence on mainstream Enlightenment political thinking than did any other philosophers.

"Contractual" theories saw political authority as originating in a contract, either between a people and a sovereign (as asserted by Hobbes and Locke) or among the people themselves (as asserted by Jean-Jacques Rousseau). Contractualists also rejected the idea of sovereignty as being analogous to the authority of a father in a family, a concept known as the "patriarchal theory of authority." Locke's *Two Treatises on Government* were written to refute the patriarchal theorist Sir Robert Filmer (1588–1653).

The theory of the origin of political authority in a contract was most fully developed in the Enlightenment by Rousseau. Rousseau's *The Social Contract* (1762) put forth a democratic theory of authority in which the power of the sovereign was derived from the consent of the people. Rousseau's contract was between equal individuals, unlike those of Hobbes and Locke that were between the people and a sovereign. Rousseau's ideal society was based on equality of rights among its citizens (although Rousseau strongly distinguished between the rights and functions of men and women) and obedience to "the general will," which was not always the will of the majority.

The secularization of political philosophy went along with a suspicion of any involvement of church and state. No state in 18th-century Europe separated church and state prior to the French Revolution, and many of the areas now thought as falling within the purview of the state—such as the legitimation of marriage—where controlled by official churches. Although not all Enlightenment philosophers went so far as to advocate a fully secular state, all distrusted the political power of the clergy. China—idealized as a place governed by wise magistrates who had marginalized the priesthood—often was put forth as a model in this regard. Religious domination was wrong and unjustified not only in that it stifled human freedom, but it also held back economic development, an argument with a long history that had been made in Locke's influential *Letters on Toleration*. A favorite example of many French Enlightenment philosophers was King Louis XIV's expulsion of the French Protestants (Huguenots) from France in 1685. Some argued that the expulsion had been an economic catastrophe, depriving the country of many skilled workers. Voltaire's influential *Letters on England* (1734) traced England's economic prosperity to its religious toleration, an implicit contrast with Voltaire's own France, in which religions other than Catholicism were legally forbidden, if tolerated on a *de facto* basis. The culmination of this Enlightenment approach to politics is the First Amendment to the Constitution of the United States, with its guarantee of religious freedom and prohibition of the establishment of a church by the federal government (although the First Amendment initially was considered compatible with established churches and religious discrimination in the states). The idea that a state could be religiously neutral was one of the most radical (and controversial) innovations of the American founding—an innovation fully in harmony with the ideals of the Enlightenment. Religious toleration also was included in the 1789 *Declaration of the Rights of Man* from the early, liberal phase of the French Revolution.

The idea of political and social power as justified by tradition also found little favor among the Enlightened. Eighteenth-century European society was a complex structure of groups and classes claiming privileges on the basis of custom and tradition. The nobility possessed many social and legal privileges that varied greatly across European societies, as did the definition of nobility itself. Even the vaunted British parliament was elected on a crazy quilt of franchises based on historic traditions rather than on abstract political logic.

Enlightenment philosophers—many of whom came from the middle class—attacked local traditions and privileges in the name of the universal values of reason and justice. They pointed out the fundamental irrationality of a system that distributed essential responsibilities on the basis of birth rather than ability. Enlightenment philosophers even approved of some revolutions, including the English Revolution of 1688, the failed Genevan revolution of 1770, and the American and French Revolutions. The French Revolution was the most dramatic example in Europe of an attempt to put the ideas of the Enlightenment into practice with the abolition of religious intolerance and hereditary privilege, although the radicalism of the later stages alienated many of the Enlightened. (The Irish politician Edmund Burke (1729–1797), who had supported the American Revolution, was repulsed by the French Revolution's renunciation of traditional authority, which he connected to its violence.)

Enlightenment philosophers, however, did not value revolution for its own sake or think it innately preferable to other methods for social reform. They condemned revolutionary movements driven by traditionalism and religion, such as Pugachev's rebellion from 1773 to 1775 in Russia. Rulers affected by the Enlightenment, such as Frederick II of Prussia and Catherine II of Russia, had to deal with the power of the nobility and often were reluctant to attack this formidable group directly, and even increased some of its privileges.

Hereditary monarchy itself was the most obvious example of traditional privilege, and Enlightenment opinion was split on the subject. More radical philosophers opposed it, but moderates often found it pragmatically best to accept kingship as an institution and to work with monarchical reformers such as Frederick or Catherine. The ability of a strong monarch to defy the church and overcome vested interests and traditions was appealing to many philosophers including Voltaire, who hoped for a strong French king to put the Enlightenment program into practice. The Enlightenment conceived of monarchy as the calling of an individual to work for the good of the people, an important element in the presentation of such Enlightened rulers as Frederick. Monarchy must be subordinated to laws, and moderate enlightenment thinkers such as the Baron de Montesquieu sharply distinguished between lawful monarchy and despotism which acknowledged no law. To live under despotism such as that of the contemporary Ottoman Empire was to be no better off than a slave.

Philosophers supported radical reform of the judicial system which, in addition to upholding aristocratic privilege, still admitted—and in some cases, relied on—evidence obtained by torture. Enlightenment philosophers pressed—with some success—for the abolition of torture and moderation in the use of the death penalty. The work of Cesare Beccaria was particularly influential in legal reform. The protracted and expensive nature of legal proceedings was another favorite target. Voltaire (who had a passionate hatred of injustice) and other French Enlightenment philosophers attacked France's hereditary magistrate class, the "Nobles of the Robe," for being more concerned with its own privileges than with the administration of justice. Voltaire's defense of the judicially murdered Protestant Jean Calas was as much directed against judicial incompetence as religious intolerance. Despite skepticism towards the ability of the judiciary to actually produce justice, philosophes still preferred due process of law to arbitrary actions, such as the French king's power to imprison subjects merely by producing a *lettre de cachet*, a practice that smacked of despotism. Persons living under arbitrary rule could not be free.

Enlightenment philosophers also were suspicious of war, although they usually accepted it as an inevitable feature of human society. The idea of waging war for glory was vehemently condemned. Rulers who preferred waging war to advance their own prestige over providing their subjects with economic prosperity epitomized bad ruling. Another monarchical flaw was excessive addiction to building splendid palaces, and Louis XIV of France's expenditure on the vast palace of Versailles was condemned frequently.

Despite the sometimes grudging acceptance of monarchy there was a strong republican strain in the Enlightenment, particularly marked in the works of Rousseau and Thomas Paine (a champion of both the American and French Revolutions). Philosophers and historians admired the ancient republics of Greece and Rome, and viewed the overthrow of the Roman Republic in favor of the Roman Empire as a political tragedy. (The centrality of ancient Greece and Rome in the schooling of elite European men meant that this point of view affected many others besides the philosophers and historians themselves.) The republics of 18th-century Europe, however, did not inspire much passion; many of them, including such fabled states as the Dutch Republic and the Venetian Republic, were rapidly declining as powers. (It was the actual experience of republics during Montesquieu's visits to Italy and the Netherlands that cured him of his early republicanism.) The example of the United States, however, revived interest in republics in the late 18th century—a revival that would culminate in the establishment of the French

Republic after the French Revolution. Before the French Revolution, however, only a few radicals such as Paine went fully in the direction of supporting democracy—and even then, democracy was limited to the male population. Many others, including Voltaire, were suspicious of the uneducated and religious common people. The term "democracy" itself usually carried negative connotations associated with mob rule.

Much Enlightenment political philosophy was subordinated to the Enlightenment agenda of practical reform. Rulers that enacted Enlightened reforms always could count on support from some Enlightenment thinkers, no matter how despotic they were as sovereigns or how limited their Enlightened policies. Frederick of Prussia and Catherine of Russia, along with many other rulers, won Enlightenment support despite their authoritarian—and militaristic—policies.

See also: American Revolution and Founding; Beccaria, Cesare; Catherine II, "the Great," of Russia; Condorcet, Marie-Jean-Antoine-Nicolas Caritat, Marquis de; Frederick II, "the Great," of Prussia; French Revolution; Joseph II of Austria; Locke, John; Montesquieu, Charles-Louis de Secondat, Baron de; Paine, Thomas; Pombal, Sebastião José de Carvalho e Melo, 1st Marquis of; Rousseau, Jean-Jacques; Voltaire.

Further Reading
Bradley, James E., and Dale K. Van Kley (eds.), *Religion and Politics in Enlightenment Europe* (Notre Dame: University of Notre Dame Press, 2001).
Cranston, Maurice, *Philosophers and Pamphleteers: Political Theorists of the Enlightenment* (Oxford: Oxford University Press, 1986).
Israel, Jonathan, *A Revolution of the Mind: Radical Enlightenment and the Intellectual Origins of Modern Democracy* (Princeton: Princeton University Press, 2010).

POMBAL, SEBASTIÃO JOSÉ DE CARVALHO E MELO, 1ST MARQUIS OF (1699–1782)   Eighteenth-century Portugal was peripheral to the Enlightenment and produced no significant Enlightenment writers. It did, however, produce one of the most radical statesmen of the period, the Marquis of Pombal, often viewed as a prototypical "Enlightened despot."

Sebastião José de Carvalho e Melo was born on May 13, 1699, in the Portuguese capital of Lisbon. He was educated at the University of Coimbra—Portugal's leading university—and entered the diplomatic service, serving as Portuguese minister to Great Britain and Austria. His rise to power was the result of his relationship with King Joseph I (r. 1750–1777), who put Pombal in power almost immediately after his ascension to the throne in 1750. Pombal particularly distinguished himself by his cool-headed response to the massive destruction of Lisbon following the earthquake of 1755, and his leadership role in the great rebuilding of the city. As the most powerful man in Portugal, under the king, Pombal emphasized economic development and governmental financial efficiency. Pombal led in the creation of a Royal Treasury for Portugal in 1761 and appointed himself its first inspector general. Under Pombal, the Portuguese government was an early adopter of double-entry bookkeeping for government accounts.

Pombal wanted to weaken the grip that the Catholic Church had on Portuguese life and institutions. The establishment of a royal censorship board, for example, was less directed at the Portuguese press than it was at the existing, church-dominated censorship process. The Marquis was a staunch opponent of the Jesuits, who had a very strong position in Portugal. The "Tavora affair" of 1758—an attempt to assassinate King Joseph—furnished Pombal the pretext needed to move against the Jesuits, and he asserted that they were linked to the assassination conspiracy. The expulsion of the Jesuits from Portugal in 1758 was the beginning of the process which eventually led to their suppression by the Pope in 1773, and was followed by attempts to secularize the clerically dominated educational system. Pombal brought the Portuguese Inquisition—the centuries-long obsession with rooting out Portuguese subjects of Jewish ancestry, and a practice which Pombal regarded as a menace to economic development—under firmer state control.

The savagery with which Pombal repressed all opposition alienated some of the Enlightened outside of Portugal who had first supported him. More importantly, Pombal's reforms won the hatred of the devout Catholics and the conservative Portuguese aristocrats who maintained a great deal of influence at court. King Joseph, however, continued to back Pombal, granting the title of "Marquis of Pombal" by which he is known starting in 1770. The death of Joseph in 1777, and the succession of the pious, Jesuit-influenced Queen Maria I (r. 1777–1816), led to Pombal's downfall and his exile to his country estates. He was further banished from coming within several miles of the queen. He died on May 8, 1782, at his estate of Pombal.

See also: Jesuits; Lisbon Earthquake; Political Philosophy.

Further Reading
Maxwell, Kenneth, *Pombal: Paradox of the Enlightenment* (Cambridge and New York: Cambridge University Press, 1995).

PRIESTLEY, JOSEPH (1733–1804)   Born on March 24, 1733, in the village of Birstall, England, the English teacher and schoolmaster Joseph Priestley was a passionate political and religious radical as well as one of the most important chemists of the 18th century. Like many leaders of the English Enlightenment he was a Protestant Dissenter, opposed to the established Church of England. In science, he was particularly known for his work in pneumatic, or gaseous, chemistry, particularly the discovery of oxygen or "dephlogisticated air" in 1774. Priestley's most important political book, *An Essay on the First Principles of Government, and on the Nature of Political, Civil and Religious Liberty* (1768) built on the legacy of John Locke to distinguish between civil and political liberty. Civil liberty was the right of individuals to have government stay out of their lives, and was more important to Priestley than political liberty, the power to vote or serve in office.

In 1773, Priestley was hired as a librarian and tutor in the household of William Petty, Earl of Shelburne (1737–1805), a statesman and, like Priestley himself, a supporter of conciliation with the American colonists. (Priestley also was a friend of Benjamin Franklin, sharing his scientific interests.) While working for the Earl, Priestley wrote political pamphlets opposing the religious discrimination that he and his fellow Dissenters suffered, as well as opposing English oppression of the Americans. In 1780, Priestley moved to Birmingham, where he became a leading minister and the scientific star of the city's informal gathering of Enlightened minds, the Lunar Society. Priestley's dissenting background, radical political and religious beliefs, and orientation to Northern England meant that—despite his achievements—he was never a member of England's London-based scientific establishment, although he was admitted to the Royal Society.

Priestley always was a religious believer. On a visit to Paris, he was shocked to discover that not only were the leading French scientists not Christians, but that they found it hard to believe that he was Christian. Priestley was an unusual philosophical hybrid—a Christian materialist. A defender of the argument from design against David Hume, he was an open Unitarian Christian and publicly avowed the denial of Christ's divinity, behavior that technically was illegal in England. Priestley thought that many objections to Christianity were based on the idea of a non-material, "spiritual," reality. For example, a materialist Christianity would substitute a miraculous resurrection of the body for the superstitious belief in the immortality of the soul. Priestley also was a millenarian, interpreting the Bible as claiming that the French Revolution and the rise of Napoleon were signs of a forthcoming apocalypse. The reaction against the French Revolution in Britain made Priestley's religious and political radicalism increasingly dangerous. In 1791, a conservative "Church and King" mob, tacitly supported by local magistrates and Church of England clergy, attacked Priestley's dwelling in Birmingham. Facing continuing hostility, in 1794 Priestley with his family immigrated to the United States.

Priestley's move to America did not remove him from controversy. He was alarmed by the conservatism and hostility toward revolutionary France that the American government exhibited under Federalist President John Adams, and thus Priestley aligned himself politically with the anti-Federalists. He defended his political opinions in *Letters to the Inhabitants of Northumberland* (1799). Some in the American government argued for Priestley's expulsion as a seditious foreigner but this never occurred, possibly due to respect for his eminence as a scientist and religious thinker. His religious opinions also exposed him to hostility from many American clergymen. Priestley was disappointed in his attempts to found a college near his new home in Northumberland, Pennsylvania. Priestley was, by this time, as isolated in his scientific beliefs as in his political and religious ones, being among the last important chemists to support the phlogiston theory of combustion, recently overthrown by the French chemist Antoine-Laurent Lavoisier (1743–1794).

Although he never sought American citizenship, Priestley became more at home in the country during the presidential administration of Adam's successor, Thomas Jefferson, an admirer and correspondent of Priestley. Priestley's religious writings were particularly important to Jefferson in forming his own "enlightened" version of Christianity. Priestley died in poverty at his home in Northumberland on February 6, 1804.

See also: England, the Enlightenment in; French Revolution; Religion; Science.

Further Reading

Rivers, Isabel, and David L. Wykes (eds.), *Joseph Priestley, Scientist, Philosopher, and Theologian* (Oxford and New York: Oxford University Press, 2008).

Schofield, Robert W., *The Enlightened Joseph Priestley: A Study of His Life and Work from 1773 to 1804* (University Park, PA: Pennsylvania State University Press, 2004).

Uglow, Jenny, *The Lunar Men: Five Friends Whose Curiosity Changed the World* (New York: Farrar, Straus, and Giroux, 2002).

RELIGION   With the exception of the territories in its southeast ruled by the Muslim Ottoman Empire, Europe at the dawn of the 18th century remained what it had been for many centuries—a society dominated by Christianity. Whatever the government, it proclaimed that its power came from the God of Christianity, and it restricted political participation to professed Christians, usually of one particular church. In many European countries, including France, to follow a form of Christianity other than that which dominated the government was illegal (although these laws were falling into disuse in many places). Even in religiously tolerant countries, blasphemy laws existed and were intermittently enforced. The only substantial non-Christian minority in Christian countries west of Russia—the Jewish community—faced many restrictions in most parts of Europe and was debarred from institutional political power in all. Many areas of life now governed by secular law, such as marriage, fell into the jurisdiction of churches that had their own set of laws and courts rather than that of governments. Education systems, particularly universities, were dominated by churches and staffed largely by clerics, who were also well-represented in elite intellectual institutions such as the French Academy. Churches, particularly in Catholic countries, held extensive property in land, money, and movable goods—much of which was exempt from taxes. The Enlightenment overthrew very little of this, but it challenged nearly all of it.

Divisions within religious communities often were too deep for communities to unite against the Enlightenment. The ongoing conflict between Catholicism and Protestantism continued to occupy much attention, and some Protestants were willing to accept anticlerical philosophes such as Voltaire as fellow combatants in the struggle against the Pope. In addition to traditional orthodoxy, many parts of Europe and America were marked in the 18th century by the rise of a more emotional piety, centered on a passionate relationship with God rather than belief in correct dogma or adherence to conventional morality.

In America, there was a series of evangelical revivals known as the "Great Awakening." Britain also saw huge revivals, along with John Wesley's founding of the Methodist movement in the mid-18th century. Lutheran Germany was racked by conflict between traditional pastors and professors and the "Pietist" movement. The Church in Catholic France was challenged by the Jansenist movement with its roots in the 17th century. Jansenism emphasized devotion and charity and was viewed by the leaders of the French church and state as far more of a threat than the Enlightenment. In Eastern Europe, the rabbinic Jewish establishment faced Yisroel ben Eliezer (1698–1760), known as the "Baal Shem Tov" or "Master of the Good Name," and his followers in the Hasidic movement he founded. The Hasidic emphasis on ecstatic worship rather than meticulous observance of Jewish law drove some traditional rabbis towards a more rational, Enlightenment-influenced piety.

In addition to the growing religious diversity of Europe itself, Europeans were becoming more aware of the religious diversity of humanity. The expansion of the British, French, Dutch, Spanish, and other colonial empires and the growth of global trade were exposing the thinkers of the Enlightenment to the religions of the Middle East, India, China, and Native America. Knowledge of Hinduism, Islam, Buddhism, and Confucianism was growing.

Growing knowledge of the multiplicity and complexity of humanity's religious life led to a tendency to analyze religions not according to their claims to divine truth but to their historical and social impact. Leaders in this development were the legal and social analyst Montesquieu and the historian Edward Gibbon.

One of the most prominent features of the 18th-century Enlightenment was the hostility that many of its thinkers (but not all) displayed to organized religion. This opposition took a variety of forms, from fighting for religious tolerance to outright atheism. Hostility to religion also varied greatly between different countries in the Enlightenment. Generally, England with its relatively tolerant established church saw the least hostility between the Enlightenment and the Church, and France saw the most. Opposition to religion tended to be stronger in societies that combined an Enlightened intelligentsia with a powerful institutional church, such as in France and parts of Italy. Although many of the leaders of the Enlightenment were religiously educated or even were clergymen themselves and included high-ranking officials in the Church, they were skeptical of the power wielded by organized Christianity.

Belief in religious tolerance was a distinguishing mark of the Enlightenment, shared by nearly everyone connected to it. The killing, torture, or imprisonment of persons for following the wrong faith epitomized everything Enlightenment thinkers detested about organized religion. The era of religious wars in the 16th and 17th centuries demonstrated the destructiveness of religious conflict, and although religious wars had ended by the 18th century, religious intolerance still could kill, as in the Calas case of 1761, one of several cases of religious persecution that attracted the attention of Voltaire and other French Enlightenment leaders. After his involvement in the Calas case, Voltaire in his correspondence started using the slogan, "Ecrasez l'infame" ("crush the infamy"), referring either to Christianity or to religion.

The critique of religious intolerance extended into a broader anticlerical critique of the economic, cultural, and institutional power of Christian churches. Enlightened thinkers did not invent anticlericalism—which had a long history in Europe—and Enlightened anticlericalism was limited by the fact that many Enlightened philosophers themselves were Catholic priests or Protestant ministers. Many aspects of clerical power, however, such as censorship, the repression of sexuality, and the hostility toward the theater, were targets of Enlightened criticism.

Radical Enlightened thinkers did not just criticize the actions of churches but also the philosophical basis of religion itself—particularly those religions they were most familiar with: Christianity and Judaism. The Bible was attacked as the superstitious work of ancient savages, far inferior to modern writings as well as to the works of the pagan Greeks and Romans. As science developed the idea of a rationally ordered world, less and less credibility could be given to miracles. David Hume argued that not only was there usually insufficient testimony for miracles to be believed, but that it was more likely that a person would lie or be mistaken than that a miracle—a violation of the laws of nature—actually would occur. This argument, unlike previous Protestant attacks on Catholic miracle accounts, was directed against the miracles of Jesus and other Biblical accounts as well as more modern accounts. (Hume's argument was not pressed with such vehemence as to prevent him from being friends with leaders of the established Presbyterian Church of Scotland, many of whom—including the historian William Robertson (1721–1793)—were themselves supporters of the Enlightenment.)

The Enlightenment critique of religion was not restricted to negative attacks, but also included positive alternatives. One popular alternative to Christianity, endorsed by Voltaire and, less publicly, by several of America's founding fathers, was Deism. Deism, with its roots in the writings of Baruch Spinoza and late 17th-century England, was the belief in a single God (Deists denied the Christian Trinity), all powerful and all good. Deists believed that all the necessary truths about God could be discovered through reason, rather than from the scriptural revelations of the Jewish and Christian Bibles. Deists were not a unified movement, and their opinions varied on issues such as whether God took note of human affairs or was indifferent to them. Deistic religion reached its height in the "Cult of the Supreme Being," established in the French Revolution.

An even more radical opposition to Christianity was atheism, the position of a small minority among the philosophers of the Enlightenment, the most prominent being the Baron d'Holbach. The modern definition of atheism, a flat denial of God's existence, emerged in the 18th century. Before the Enlightenment, the most common definition of atheism was indifference to God rather than denial of God's existence. Atheism always was a minority position, despite the popularity of many atheistic tracts including those of d'Holbach. Many philosophers, including Voltaire, found the argument of design—the claim that the universe itself could not have come into existence by chance—to be convincing proof of the existence of a god, even if the philosopher's god bore little resemblance to the personal God of Christianity. Atheism also was forbidden from practice in European countries, and so it had to be expressed in anonymous or pseudonymous tracts. Atheism was closely allied with philosophical materialism—the belief that the physical world is all that there is. Materialists denied the existence of a soul as well as of God. There were a few exceptions, including materialists such as Joseph Priestley, for whom materialism was compatible with belief in God and even a highly unorthodox Christianity.

Much of the Enlightened critique of Christianity was elitist; it was not intended to influence behavior beyond the middle and upper classes. Some Enlightenment philosophers endorsed religion as a way to regulate the behavior of the lower classes and of women. They idealized those purportedly nonreligious civilizations, such as China or ancient Greece and Rome whose governing elites did not share in the superstition of the people.

Not all philosophes opposed Christianity; attitudes toward religion varied by country. The French Enlightenment was more hostile to Christianity than was the Enlightenment in Britain or Germany. Some who found the rationality of deism attractive but still considered themselves Christians became Unitarians—rejecting the "absurd" concepts of the Trinity and the man-god Jesus Christ in favor of a belief in only one god, identified with "God the Father" in Christianity. This belief had roots in the Protestant Reformation, but spread among English-speaking intellectuals during the Enlightenment. Prominent English thinkers who held Unitarian ideas included Isaac Newton and Joseph Priestley. These beliefs—illegal in Britain and scorned in America—could be held but required employing some discretion.

Immanuel Kant attempted to save Christianity in a form compatible with the scientific thinking of the Enlightenment. His *Religion within the Limits of Reason Alone* (1793) expounded an Enlightenment-friendly, non-miraculous Christianity largely by attempting to disentangle religion and science completely. Kant shifted the argument about God's existence from a relationship to nature to a relationship with morality. He rejected both revealed and natural theology to prove the existence of God and life after death through an argument based on moral obligation. God was the *Summum Bonum*—the good to which virtue was oriented. True worship was the attempt to lead a moral life pleasing to God. Kant found Christianity to be the only religion propounding a truly moral life, although Christians often mistook specifically ecclesiastical duties—such as church attendance and belief in correct dogma—for the true religious obligations, which were moral. Despite Kant's support for Christianity, in the conservative reaction to the French Revolution, his emphasis on reason led the Prussian government to warn him not to publish further on religious topics. The leader of the German-Jewish Enlightenment, Kant's friend Moses Mendelssohn, performed a similar function in making Judaism compatible with the Enlightenment.

Christianity was further challenged by the revolutions of the late 18th century. The American Revolution resulted in the creation of the first "western" state that was not officially Christian since the establishment of the Roman Empire. The vast majority of the population of the new nation, however, was Christian and Christianity was central to public life. The French Revolution in its more radical phases went much further, into a campaign of "de-Christianization" and attempts to establish a Deistic "religion of reason" dedicated to the Supreme Being in place of Christianity. Even the Cathedral of Notre Dame in Paris was rededicated as a temple of the Supreme Being. (Atheism, conversely, was strongly condemned by the Republic as being "aristocratic.") Condorcet, in his *Sketch for a History of the Progress of the Human Mind* (written when he was hiding from the revolutionaries) portrayed religion in general and Christianity in particular as completely negative forces in human development. The institutional reaction against Christianity was short-lived, however, and France returned to official Catholicism under the rule of Napoleon Bonaparte in the early 19th century. The more enduring growth of secularism in Europe in the 19th century built upon the work of the Enlightenment.

See also: Bible, the; Calas Case; Enlightenment Views of Jews and Judaism; Enlightenment Views of Muslims and Islam; Political Philosophy.

Further Reading

Burson, Jeffrey D., *The Rise and Fall of Theological Enlightenment: Jean-Martin de Prades and Ideological Polarization in Eighteenth-Century France* (Notre Dame: University of Notre Dame Press, 2010).

Curran, Mark, *Atheism, Religion, and Enlightenment in Pre-Revolutionary Europe* (Woodbridge, Suffolk and Rochester, NY: Boydell Press, 2010).

Hudson, Wayne, Diego Lucci, and Jeffrey R. Wigelsworth (eds.), *Atheism and Deism Revalued: Heterodox Religious Identities in Britain, 1650–1800* (Farnham, Surrey: Ashgate, 2014).

Sorkin, David, *The Religious Enlightenment: Protestants, Jews, and Catholics from London to Vienna* (Princeton: Princeton University Press, 2011).

ROUSSEAU, JEAN-JACQUES (1712–1778) Jean-Jacques Rousseau shared many of the principles of the Enlightenment while also looking forward to the era of Romanticism. Born June 8, 1712, in the independent French-speaking city-state of Geneva, Rousseau had a difficult youth. His mother died giving birth to him and his father, a watchmaker, deserted him. Like Edward Gibbon—with whom he did not share many other qualities— Rousseau converted to Catholicism as a young man. He was saved from poverty by Madame Francoise-Louise de Warens (1699–1762), another convert to Catholicism who saw to his education and served as a mother figure for the motherless Rousseau. She later became his lover.

Rousseau's earliest published writings were on music, a subject on which he contributed several articles to Diderot's *Encyclopédie*. (Rousseau also composed operas.) Rousseau made a spectacular entrance into mainstream Enlightenment intellectual life in 1750 with the publication of his essay, *Discourse on the Art and Sciences*, which originally had been submitted to a contest in the hope of winning a prize. In the essay, Rousseau argued that the development of the arts and sciences had helped corrupt human society by moving it from its original state of equality. Rousseau continued his critique of inequality in 1755, with the publication of *Discourse on Inequality* in which he argued that human beings originally had been equal but the development of property had led to the end of this state. He became identified with the idea of going back to nature—Voltaire famously stated that reading Rousseau made him want to go on all fours—but Rousseau did not believe that a return to this natural state of equality really was possible.

Rousseau's political writings culminated in 1762 with the publication of *The Social Contract,* which included the now-famous first line, "Man is born free, yet everywhere he is in chains." *The Social Contract* deals with how people are to live in society in an equal way. Rousseau argues that society is founded on a contract between equal individuals, not between the people and a sovereign as argued by earlier contractarian theorists. The ideal society Rousseau presents is based on equality of rights among its citizens (although Rousseau strongly distinguished between the rights and functions of men and women) and obedience to what he defined as "the general will," which is not always the will of the majority. Political philosophers still argue whether Rousseau was a precursor of democracy, with his emphasis on equality and the responsibility of government to the people, or of totalitarianism, emphasizing the subordination of the individual to the general will. *The Social Contract* helped revive Republican thinking in Europe and influenced some of the leaders of the French Revolution, including the leader of the Jacobin Terror, Maximilien Robespierre (1758–1794). Rousseau himself took pride in being a citizen of the independent Republican city-state of Geneva.

Religiously, Rousseau sympathized with Deism but, unlike many Deists, he had no interest in the idea of a "religion of reason." In a way that anticipated the later Romantic movement, Rousseau exalted the "heart" (passion and emotion) over the "head" (reason). He believed that the best religion for the state was a minimal Deistic civil religion, emphasizing morality that is compatible with a variety of religious practices and beliefs on the part of individuals and communities within the state.

Rousseau also was a successful novelist. His multi-volume work, *Julie, or the New Heloise* (1761), featured a love triangle between three people who would rather talk about their passions than indulge in them and also painted a picture of the "ideal domestic woman." The work was extraordinarily popular and caused many readers to think that they had forged a personal bond with the author. His second novel, *Émile, or On Education,* was published in the same year as *The Social Contract*. Education was one of Rousseau's major concerns. *Émile* shows in the education of its hero the creation of a citizen fit to live in the ideal state discussed in *The Social Contract,* and the male counterpart to the virtuous woman, Julie. It was a controversial book that was banned by the French Parlement, and forced Rousseau to flee persecution for several years. Rousseau's personal life did not match the morality presented in his books; the five children he had with his partner Thérèse Levasseur (1721–1801) were abandoned and sent to an orphanage; their fate is unknown.

Rousseau's posthumously published autobiography, *Confessions*, appeared in two parts in 1782 and 1789. It often is identified as the first modern autobiography. In *Confessions*, Rousseau spoke of his life with an unprecedented frankness. Rousseau hoped to justify himself by presenting an account of his life that included his faults and offenses. Unlike many autobiographies of the 18th century, it represents the author's interior emotional life as well as the events in which he participated. *Confessions* also was unusually open about Rousseau's personal life, including his fetish for being spanked by women and his abandonment of his children—which he tried to justify by claiming that the Foundling Hospital would do a better job of raising them. It was one of the first works to treat childhood experience as central to the formation of the adult personality. He began this work in the late 1750s and completed it by 1770, but wanted it to be published only after his death.

Rousseau had a difficult and highly suspicious personality. He also frequently quarreled with his friends, including leaders of the Enlightenment such as Jean Le Rond d'Alembert, David Hume, and the Baron Holbach. He became convinced that Holbach was the leader of a conspiracy against him that included many of the major figures of the Enlightenment and Thérèse Levasseur's mother. He was extremely fond of his dogs, which he claimed that he found to be superior in character to most humans. Rousseau died on July 2, 1778, at Eremenonville, France, two months after the death of his friend, enemy, and rival Voltaire.

See also: France, the Enlightenment in; French Revolution; Literature; Nature; Theater.

Further Reading

Cranston, Maurice, *Jean-Jacques: The Early Life and Work of Jean-Jacques Rousseau, 1712–1754* (New York: Norton, 1983).

Cranston, Maurice, *The Noble Savage: Jean-Jacques Rousseau 1754–1762* (Chicago: University of Chicago Press, 1991).

Cranston, Maurice, *The Solitary Self: Jean-Jacques Rousseau in Exile and Adversity* (Chicago: University of Chicago Press, 1997).

Riley, Patrick (ed.), *The Cambridge Companion to Rousseau* (Cambridge and New York: Cambridge University Press, 2001).

SALONS   The salon—a regularly scheduled gathering of intellectuals (and others) held at a private home—was a characteristic institution of the French Enlightenment. It had roots in the early 17th century, when the idea was imported from Italian Renaissance courts. Salons originally were a way of introducing the courtly refinement characteristic of the Italian elite to the comparatively crude French court. Salons were held on a weekly or biweekly basis in a space specifically set aside for the purpose. The 17th-century salon space was richly decorated, with mirrors, comfortable armchairs, porcelain, and an emphasis on refinement. Gatherings were held for the purpose of conversation, which had to follow certain forms in terms of vocabulary and forms of address. The purification of the French language was one of the missions of the early salons.

Salons usually were sponsored and regulated by hostesses, upper-class women, and provided a space for female intellectual activity. Although few 17th-century French salon hostesses were writers themselves, they sometimes fostered female talent—such as the novelist Madeline de Scudery (1607–1701), who was a member of the Rambouillet circle before becoming a salon hostess herself. The growth of female intellectual activity and the opposition it aroused in men can be seen in two plays written by popular French comic playwright Molière (1622–1673) and which ridiculed educated women—*Les Précieuses Ridicules* (1659) and *Les Femmes Savantes* (1672). Both were quite successful as plays and are considered classics of French literature, but they did not stop the growth of salons or women's intellectual culture.

The intellectual salon of the 18th century—basically a Parisian phenomenon—was less aristocratic and less concerned with the refinement of manners and language than its 17th-century predecessors. It was a place where male middle-class and noble intellectuals could meet on a basis of social equality. The hostess was a gatekeeper, determined who was admitted, facilitated introductions, and functioned as an authority keeping the conversation under control. (There were occasional male-run salons, the most notable being d'Holbach's, but they were very much the exception.) Running a salon required a substantial commitment of time, energy, and money. Would-be salon hostesses were drawn from the social and economic elite and often attended other salons, sometimes for decades before opening their own. Parisian salons made an important contribution to the culture of the Enlightenment, and admittance to a salon was an important step in the career of the young Parisian professional intellectual.

In addition to the prestige of salon membership, a salon was a good place to read one's works, circulate manuscripts, and facilitate contacts. Certain salon hostesses were influential in securing admittance to the Parisian academies, such as the French Academy and the Royal Academy of Sciences. At the other end of the scale, hostesses competed for the participation of major intellectual stars who would lend glamour to their salons. In 1764, when Jeanne Julie Éléonore de Lespinasse (1732–1776) left the salon of her aunt, the Marquise du Deffand (1697–1780), to establish her own, she took with her one of Deffand's stars, Jean Le Rond D'Alembert. This led to a violent split with Deffand that forced salon habitués to choose one or the other.

Many male visitors to Paris—such as David Hume and Benjamin Franklin—were particularly delighted by the conversation of the salons and the close female attention given to major intellectuals, a phenomenon not nearly as common in the Anglophone world. This delight was not universal; Jean-Jacques Rousseau came to despise the salon hostesses, whom he saw as having abandoned the female duty of domestic life to corrupt the virtue of the male public with artificiality.

The salon was one of the few institutional venues for freedom of speech in Old Regime France. Salon culture generally was identified with the Enlightenment against its conservative opponents. Within this broad consensus, salons often were identified with an intellectual or political party. The salon of Suzanne Necker (1737–1794) helped advance the career of her husband, the Genevan banker Jacques Necker (1732–1804), who—despite his Protestantism—became the director-general of French finances. The salon of Mademoiselle de Lespinasse was known for attracting many of the leading contributors to the *Encyclopédie*, including d'Alembert and Condorcet; d'Holbach's salon was notorious for its atheism. Not much evidence survives as to what people in salons actually discussed. There was somewhat less emphasis on the female intellectual contribution in the 18th century than in the 17th-century salons. The principal literary art followed by 18th-century salon hostesses was correspondence, and many of them became well-known for their letters, which were intended to be circulated after being read by their recipient. Madame du Deffand's correspondence with the English writer Horace Walpole (1717–1797) is one example, and a vastly different example is the passionate love letters of Mademoiselle de Lespinasse to the French general and military writer Jacques Antoine Hippolyte, the Comte du Guibert (1743–1790).

Although France was at the heart of salon culture, salons were found in other countries as well. The Countess Caterina Vignati di San Gillio (1714–1800) ran a popular salon in Turin—the capital of the Kingdom of Piedmont in northwestern Italy—which was particularly attractive to English people passing through Italy. By the late 18th century, Berlin was the home of an active salon community. Jewish women, such as Rahel Varnhagen (1771–1833), adopted the role of hostess for salons—which were one of the few places where Jewish and Christian Germans could mingle. By contrast, salon culture never occupied an important role in Britain, where much of the Enlightened socializing in both Scotland and England took place in all-male groups.

See also: France, the Enlightenment in; Gender.

Further Reading

Craveri, Benedetta, *Madame du Deffand and Her World,* translated by Theresa Waugh (Boston: Godine, 1994).

Goodman, Dena, *The Republic of Letters: A Cultural History of the French Enlightenment* (Ithaca: Cornell University Press, 1994).

Sutton, Geoffrey V., *Science for a Polite Society: Gender, Culture, and the Demonstration of Enlightenment* (Boulder, CO: Westview Press, 1995).

SCIENCE   The Enlightenment followed the remarkable period in the growth of European science known as "the Scientific Revolution," culminating in the new mathematical physics of Isaac Newton. Enlightenment thought was shaped by science and its success—one of the achievements of modern society which Enlightenment thinkers found most impressive and which they identified as an area in which modern society definitely had exceeded that of antiquity. Many thinkers and writers of the Enlightenment came from scientific backgrounds, and even those who did not often took an informed interest in scientific developments. Enlightenment thinkers who made considerable contributions to science include mathematician Jean Le Rond d'Alembert; electrical theorist Benjamin Franklin; and chemist, physicist, and discoverer of oxygen Joseph Priestley.

A common career pattern for an Enlightened thinker was to establish a reputation in the sciences before turning to social or political questions. This path was followed by d'Alembert, Immanuel Kant, and the German philosopher and aphorist Georg Christoph Lichtenberg (1742–1799), among others. Benjamin Franklin—although he established a reputation as a journalist in Philadelphia before he began his electrical experiments—first became known in Europe as a scientific experimenter. (Franklin had the advantage of working in electricity, a cutting-edge field that attracted a great deal of public interest, partly due to the dramatic effects electrical experimenters created.) More importantly, the progress of science furnished a model for the Enlightenment itself. As many Enlightened thinkers saw it, science had made enormous advances by throwing off traditional authorities—the ancient Greek philosopher Aristotle and the Catholic Church—and boldly assuming the right to think and speak freely. It was the thinkers of the Enlightenment—and not the Scientific Revolution itself—that freely applied the term "revolution" to the changes in early modern science. Even if some scientific ideas would become obsolete or disproven, Enlightenment thinkers believed that the empirical and mathematical methods of modern science could be applied to other problems and would result in similar intellectual progress.

The Enlightenment also saw the rise of the heroic image of the scientist. Among the moderns, Newton in particular was virtually deified as the greatest man who ever lived. Newtonian mathematical physics, which continued to develop during the Enlightenment after Newton's death, was seen as the highest achievement of the human mind. Many Enlightenment thinkers, however, attacked what Newton himself had seen as the central feature of his system—the alliance between the system of a law-governed nature and the fundamentally religious truth of the providence of God. Radical philosophers invoked science not as a support but as an alternative system of validation to religion and tradition. Many Enlightenment thinkers (including Voltaire) contrasted an idealized version of a scientific community interested only in truth with a demonized picture of theologians and systematic abstract philosophers as motivated by hate, anger, and jealousy. However violent the polemical struggle between the "Cartesian" supporters of Rene Descartes's physics and Newtonians became in early 18th-century France, not a drop of blood was shed—in remarkable contrast to the struggle between Catholics and Protestants in the previous two centuries. Whatever the actual reality of scientific practice, the idealized version of science, like the idealized version of trade, offered a model of internationalism and people with different religious beliefs working together. Although the poor and, with a few scattered exceptions, women were excluded, science also was more socially egalitarian than many other aspects of 18th-century society. Some leading scientists, such as the great French chemist Antoine-Laurent Lavoisier (1743–1794), were noblemen, but the privilege of nobility meant little in evaluating a scientist's ideas.

The spread of true science was necessary for social and intellectual reform, and thus was not a matter for scientists alone. True scientific knowledge had to spread, not to the entire population, but to the men and women of the literate classes. One of the greatest of the early modern popularizers was Bernard de Fontenelle, whose *Discourse on the Plurality of Worlds* (1686) was reprinted and translated throughout the 18th century and furnished the model for subsequent popularizing works. Such was the importance of the spread of scientific knowledge, that Voltaire, although not particularly gifted mathematically, took it upon himself (with the help of the Marquise du Châtelet, a mathematical physicist) to spread the true Newtonian system of the world in France, against the dominant Cartesian school. Voltaire and other Enlightenment thinkers at times also were capable of regretting that the passion for science was driving out that for the equally valuable pursuits of literature and art. At worst, however, this was seen as a regrettable necessity, and certainly not a reason to reject science.

Science was a much more radicalizing ideology in France than it was in Britain or Germany. Early Enlightenment French propagandists (such as Voltaire) often linked the discoveries of Newton and other eminent English scientists to the greater degree of personal freedom enjoyed by English people. French philosophes struggled long and hard to displace the churchmen and the more conservative scholars from their dominating position in French intellectual life. In the process, their criticism of the domination of the Roman Catholic Church and the aristocracy grew more extreme. Such was the radicalization of French Enlightenment science, that some of it developed in the direction of materialism. (The influence of Cartesianism also encouraged the growth of materialism.) Enlightenment scientific interest in treating human beings as material rather than spiritual creatures was clearly incompatible with traditional religion. Additionally, by the late 18th century some French philosophes, such as Claude-Adrien Helvetius (1715–1771), were openly calling themselves atheists. This tendency was rejected by other philosophes, and Denis Diderot complained that an overemphasis on the vastness of space should not challenge the centrality of humanity and morality.

Jean Jacques Rousseau made a more radical critique of the cultural role of science. Prefiguring the later Romantic reaction against the Enlightenment, Rousseau stated in his *Discourse on the Arts and Sciences* (1750) that the progress of the sciences had not made people happier, but had made them more corrupt and farther from nature. Even Rousseau, however, did not see a return to the primitive state and the abandonment of scientific knowledge and the scientific endeavor as practical possibilities.

The philosophers of the Enlightenment hoped to make philosophy scientific, thus avoiding what they saw as the sterility of the Aristotelian Scholastic metaphysics that still influenced European thinking, particularly in the Catholic world. David Hume's (1711–1776) *Treatise of Human Nature* (1739–1740) was advertised as "[a]n attempt to introduce the experimental method of reasoning into moral subjects" and he described Scholastic "school divinity" as worthy only to be burnt. Immanuel Kant's philosophy began as an attempt to provide a solid metaphysical grounding for the natural sciences.

The hope of building a science of man—both man as an individual and man living in society—was characteristic of the Enlightenment. Enlightenment social science, one of the major 18th-century achievements, began in the claim to apply scientific criteria to thought about society. The "human sciences" could be founded on a scientific and empirical basis, with the study of a variety of human societies in both space and time. Even the established humanistic discipline of history could be improved by what were believed to be the methods of the natural sciences. This Enlightenment social science was not morally neutral. The philosophes hoped to found moral philosophy—and thus morality—on a scientific rather than a religious basis.

See also: Academies and Learned Societies; Châtelet, Émilie du; Franklin, Benjamin; Leibniz, Gottfried Wilhelm; Newton, Isaac; Priestley, Joseph.

Further Reading

Hankins, Thomas L., *Science and the Enlightenment* (Cambridge: Cambridge University Press, 1985).

Jacob, Margaret, *Scientific Culture and the Making of the Industrial West* (New York and Oxford: Oxford University Press, 1997).

McClellan, James E., III, *Science Reorganized: Scientific Societies in the Eighteenth Century* (New York: Columbia University Press, 1985).

Paul, Charles B., *Science and Immortality: The Éloges of the Paris Academy of Sciences (1699–1791)* (Berkeley and Los Angeles: University of California Press, 1980).

SCOTLAND, THE ENLIGHTENMENT IN The Enlightenment in Scotland rivaled that of France for its brilliance, but its culture and institutions were very different. Universities—marginal in French and English Enlightenment culture—were central in Scotland. Salons played no role and their place as centers of intellectual conversation was taken by male clubs and drinking circles. Filling the role that Paris played in France as the center of Enlightenment was Edinburgh, the capital of Scotland and the home of its leading university.

Unlike the French, who knew themselves at the center of European civilization, the Scots were self-consciously marginal, not only in Europe but in the British Isles. Scotland and England, joined at first when James VI of Scotland became James I of England in 1603, were further joined into a single country, the Kingdom of Great Britain, by the Act of Union passed through the English and Scottish Parliaments in 1707. Although the Act of Union abolished the Scottish Parliament in favor of the Parliament of Great Britain sitting in London and dominated by England, separate legal systems and established churches remained. Not all Scots were happy with the Union, which was one reason why many of them supported Prince Charles Stuart (Bonnie Prince Charlie) when he invaded Scotland as the first stage of his attempt to recover the British crown for his family in 1745. The Prince's army was drawn principally from the Highlands, but successfully occupied the Scottish lowlands including the capital of Scotland and the center of the Scottish Enlightenment, Edinburgh.

After a predominantly English army defeated the Stuart forces at the battle of Culloden on April 16, 1746, it became clear to most Scots that there was no alternative to the Union. The leaders of the Scottish Enlightenment also were supporters of the Union, despite the hostility which many English continued to display to Scots throughout the century. The capitulation of Edinburgh—although dominated by the Whig opponents of the Stuarts—to the Stuart army without a struggle was a source of shame, however, and much effort subsequently was put into identifying the sources of civic virtue and valor and instilling them among the lowland Scots. Many of the Enlightened would support the formation of a Scottish militia aimed at instilling patriotism and martial virtue among Scottish youth, a project always blocked by the suspicion of the British government in London.

Like other Britons, the Scots had the advantage of not facing a censorship. However, the Church of Scotland remained a very powerful force in Scottish life. In 1697, church influence actually had procured the execution of a young Scottish man, Thomas Aikenhead, for blasphemy. Fortunately, the mid-18th-century Enlightened were allied with a powerful faction in the church itself, the "moderates," whose leader for much of the period was the Enlightenment historian the Reverend William Robertson (1721–1793). The opponents of the moderates, the "evangelicals," were more popular among the Scottish people and made great polemical use out of the association of the moderates with such religiously suspect persons as David Hume. On the great issue that divided the Scottish Church in the 18th century, "patronage"—whether a parish clergyman should be appointed by a patron who had the legal right to appoint or selected by a congregation—the moderates and the Enlightened were firmly on the side of the patrons, hoping that patronage would introduce an educated and civil clergy into Scottish communities.

The Scottish Enlightened thinkers believed that the future of their country lay in the development of a more modern civilization—more like that of England and France and less bound by the strictures of tradition and religion. Sometimes this got them into trouble, as in 1756 when in an attempt to promote an indigenous Scottish theater, leading moderates and Hume supported the play, *Douglas*, a tragedy written by John Home (1722–1808), a clergyman of the Church of Scotland. It was produced at Edinburgh's Canongate Theater. The play was violently condemned, both for being authored by a clergyman and also because of the values it promoted. *Douglas* was based on a Scottish ballad because one characteristic of 18th-century Scottish elite culture was an increased interest in Scottish folk culture. The heroine, Lady Randolph, commits suicide after her husband kills her son. The play's opponents argued that she should have displayed Christian patience rather than pagan despair. The controversy provoked church condemnation of the play, the theater generally, and the play's sponsors. The moderates controlled the General Assembly (the Church's highest council), and were able to contain the damage, although Home himself was forced to quit the ministry. (The play itself was extremely successful in England.)

Scottish concern with modernization contributed to interest in the historical development of society, a subject that emerges frequently in Scottish Enlightenment writing, from the histories of Hume and Robertson to Adam Ferguson's *An Essay on the History of Civil Society* (1767), and Adam Smith's *The Wealth of Nations* (1776). Hume's history of England and Robertson's numerous works, including *The History of Scotland* (1759), *The History of the Reign of the Emperor Charles V* (1769), *The History of America* (1777), and *Historical Disquisition Concerning the Knowledge the Ancients Had of India* (1791) gave Scotland the reputation of "the historical nation." The close proximity of the Highlands—a highly rural society still built on herding and, for much of the century, war—and the commercial cities of Edinburgh and Glasgow made the contrast between different types of society particularly apparent. Scottish social theory was particularly known for its "four-stage" theory of social development—hunter-gatherer, pastoral, agricultural, and commercial.

Scotland began the 18th century without a culture of academies or scientific societies. More informal groups such as the "Poker Club," a group formed to agitate for the formation of a Scottish militia, took their place. (The name was based on the analogy of a poker stirring up a fire in a fireplace, as the club hoped to "stir up" the militia question.) Several leaders of the Scottish Enlightenment also were members of the Poker Club, including Hume, Smith, Ferguson, and Robertson.

The first formal society to leave much of a mark was the Society for Improving Arts and Sciences, founded in 1737 and commonly known as the Edinburgh Philosophical Society. The Society's existence was interrupted by the 1745 rising, but it continued to exist until it was absorbed in the founding of the Royal Society of Edinburgh in 1783. Hume was a member of the Edinburgh Philosophical Society. The Royal Society of Edinburgh was a chartered body based on the model of London's Royal Society, although it initially was divided into a scientific section and a literary section, rather than specializing in science as did the London group. It brought together many of

Scotland's foremost Enlightened intellectuals including Robertson, Ferguson, the chemist Joseph Black (1728–1799), and the rhetorician Hugh Blair (1718–1800). The organization exists today.

The conservative cultural and political reaction in Scotland after the French Revolution was a severe blow to the openness on which the Scottish Enlightenment had thrived. In addition to the growth of repression and controls over intellectual life, this period also saw the skeptical philosophy of Hume challenged successfully by the "Common Sense" philosophy of Thomas Reid (1710–1796)—Adam Smith's successor as Professor of Moral Philosophy at the University of Glasgow. Reid insisted that there were certain intellectual structures of the mind manifested in the structure of languages and shared by all humanity, and thus were "common." The universality of common sense indicated that things could be known with certainty.

See also: England, the Enlightenment in; Hume, David; Smith, Adam.

Further Reading

Buchan, James, *Crowded with Genius: The Scottish Enlightenment: Edinburgh's Moment of the Mind* (New York: Harper Collins, 2003).

Porter, Roy, *The Creation of the Modern World: The Untold Story of the British Enlightenment* (New York and London: W. W. Norton, 2000).

Sakamoto, Tatsuya, and Hideo Tanaka (eds.), *The Rise of Political Economy in the Scottish Enlightenment* (London and New York: Routledge, 2003).

Sher, Richard, *Church and University in the Scottish Enlightenment: The Moderate Literati of Edinburgh* (Princeton: Princeton University Press, 1985).

SEX Enlightenment thought challenged the prevailing sexual order in Christian Europe in its secularity and generally positive view of sex and sexual pleasure. It did not, however, challenge the established customs of male domination or the dominant emphasis on the procreative purpose of sex.

For many Enlightenment thinkers, sexual desire was not sinful lust, but natural and praiseworthy. Enlightenment thinkers rejected the traditional Christian suspicion of sex, particularly the Catholic idea that celibacy was spiritually superior to being sexually active. (Protestants, with their married clergy, were somewhat less anti-sexual than Catholics.) Most, however, did not believe in unfettered license. Sex should be regulated, but not by the Bible or the church. Instead, nature's laws should be the supreme authority. Although many took a tolerant attitude toward different sexual behaviors, belief in natural law often entailed rejecting not only celibacy but also other sexual practices considered "unnatural," because they are not procreative. Many Enlightened thinkers, including Voltaire, Jean-Jacques Rousseau, and Immanuel Kant, for example, endorsed the violent, medically based hostility toward masturbation which emerged in 18th-century Europe. Champions of the Enlightenment also employed homophobic attacks against their enemies, particularly the Jesuits, whose frequent role as schoolmasters had left them with a bad reputation for abusing the boys under their charge. (Voltaire charged his Jesuit masters with having raped him as a child, and in his novel *Candide* he depicted the Jesuits as pedophiles.) Another reason that celibacy was blameworthy was that it fostered same-sex relations among both men and women, as described in Denis Diderot's novel of convent life, *The Nun*. The work was so scandalous that it was not published until 1796, long after Diderot's death.

Adopting a more positive attitude regarding sexuality was part of the Enlightenment program of social reform. Many Enlightenment thinkers—particularly in France—believed that an expanding population was a mark of social health and that their society was underpopulated. (David Hume wrote an essay refuting the commonly held idea that Europe had been more densely populated in ancient times.) Sexual repression contributed to this problem, particularly the institutionalized celibacy practiced by tens of thousands of priests and members of male and female religious orders in the Catholic world. Celibates were parasites on society in their refusal to participate in the creation of the next generation. Abolition of celibacy and the acceptance of sex as a natural phenomenon would lead to an increase in population, thus strengthening the state. Some, including Benjamin Franklin, advocated abolition of the stigma against unmarried mothers for the same reason. Pregnancy and childbirth, however, were very risky for women's health. The classic work of Enlightenment pornography, *Thérèse Philosophe* (1748), endorsed mutual masturbation and coitus interruptus as being less dangerous for women, although the probable author of the anonymous work was a man, Jean-Baptiste de Boyer, Marquis d'Argens (1704–1771).

Enlightenment philosophers emphasized the positive role of sex and relations between men and women in creating and sustaining human society. Sociability was an important enlightenment value. (Enlightenment belief in sociability also was another reason for rejecting masturbation—the act was not merely unnatural, but antisocial.) Social interactions between men and women were "civilizing," and societies which secluded women from men were viewed as less civilized or not civilized at all.

In the 18th century, Diderot was among the most radical opponents of the sexual order. His series of dialogues entitled *Supplement to the Voyage of Bougainville* (1772) paints an imaginary picture of Tahiti. The island only recently had been encountered by Europeans. Louis-Antoine de Bougainville (1729–1811) was the captain of a French expedition in the South Pacific and the author of a popular account of the journey. Tahiti was depicted as a utopia of sexual freedom, and the book contrasted the Tahitians' frank acceptance of sex with the repression and hypocrisy of European visitors who brought both sexual shame and sexually transmitted disease.

Diderot even endorsed intergenerational incest, particularly if a father begets children with a daughter too ugly to attract men. Diderot's ethic was not one of unlimited license, however, and like the European establishment, Diderot put forth a different standard for men and for women. For Diderot and his fictional Tahitians, sex largely was valuable because it leads to the conception and birth of children. The "Tahitians" in the book frown on men having sex with women who cannot conceive. Sterile or menstruating women wear particular clothing to indicate their sexual unavailability, and sterile women who have sex are punished severely.

Enlightenment thinkers such as Diderot usually did not challenge the tradition of male dominance in society, marriage, and the law. Unlike traditional Christians they did not root male dominance in divine commandment but in the "naturally" different functions of the sexes. Woman's natural function was domestic—as a wife and mother—and man's was public, a position that was particularly influential during the French Revolution. For some Enlightenment thinkers, sexual desire was as natural and praiseworthy for women as it was for men, particularly because a common form of heterosexual sex led to motherhood.

Although many male Enlightenment thinkers had affairs with married women and showed some sympathy for women trapped in unhappy marriages, few men questioned the double standard—the idea that oaths of marital fidelity are more binding on wives than on husbands. The idea of virtuous women as lacking sexual desire also persisted in some Enlightenment circles. In describing his sexual relationship with the idealized mother figure, Madame de Warens, in his *Confessions*, Rousseau emphasized that de Warens was not motivated by—and did not feel—sexual pleasure.

See also: Gender; Nature.

Further Reading
Darnton, Robert, *The Forbidden Best-Sellers of Pre-Revolutionary France* (New York and London: Norton, 1996).
Goodden, Angelica, *Diderot and the Body* (Oxford: Legenda, 2001).
Stengers, Jean, and Anne van Neck, *Masturbation: The History of a Great Terror,* translated by Kathryn A. Hoffman (New York: Palgrave, 2001).

SLAVERY   During the Enlightenment, the term "slavery" had a broader meaning than it does today. Frequently the subjects of despotic regimes or even mildly repressive regimes were referred to as "slaves." Enlightenment thinkers, however, also were aware of slavery as an institution—the use of forced, unfree labor of people treated as property. The 18th century was marked by the flourishing of a slavery-based "plantation" economy throughout many European colonies in the Americas—from Brazil to Virginia. Midway through the century, an "abolitionist" movement to abolish the practice and free the slaves arose. Slavery also existed outside plantation economies. Leading countries in the Enlightenment—including Britain and France—were also leaders in the slave trade and the exploitation of slaves in their colonies. Britain imported more slaves than any other country, and France's St. Domingue sugar colony was among the Caribbean's most profitable by the late 18th century.

Along with the growth of slavery came criticism of the institution and its practices. A broad spectrum of Europeans, Africans, and Americans participated in the debate, many of them—such as the founder of Methodism, John Wesley (1703–1791)—were opponents of both slavery and the Enlightenment. The Enlightenment's principal impact on the controversy over slavery and its abolition was to promote humanitarian anti-slavery arguments and secular, non-Biblical arguments both for and against the institution.

Many Enlightenment thinkers expressed at least a verbal opposition to chattel slavery. Attacks on the misery of slaves and the hypocrisy and cruelty of those who exploited them or defended slavery were common Enlightenment rhetoric. Enlightenment philosophers combined denunciation of slavery's cruelty with the assertion that it violated the natural and inalienable rights which slaves, like all people, possessed—the same rights that would be asserted in classic Enlightenment-influenced political documents, such as the American Declaration of Independence and the French Declaration of the Rights of Man (neither of which led to the abolition of slavery, however). Montesquieu pointed out that the legendary cruelty of Atlantic slavery was an inevitable result of the slave system's corruption of the morals of slave owners.

The Enlightened of Europe, however, never campaigned against slavery as vigorously as they did against evils that were closer to home, such as religious intolerance and judicial torture. The American Enlightened community also was not strongly committed on the issue of slavery until the time of the American Revolution. For much of the 18th century, the fight against slavery was led by Quakers, such as the Philadelphian Anthony Benezet (1713–1784), and religiously conservative thinkers, such as Wesley and the English Evangelical Christian, William Wilberforce (1759–1833), or by ex-slaves such as Olaudah Equiano (1745?–1797), rather than by Enlightenment intellectuals such as Benjamin Franklin.

Although Enlightenment writers frequently attacked the enslavement of Africans in the Atlantic trade, denunciation of slavery was not always correlated with egalitarian ideas about race. David Hume strongly opposed slavery but held extreme views on black intellectual inferiority, comparing blacks who had acquired proficiency in European intellectual disciplines to trained parrots. Hume and other late-18th century thinkers (particularly in Scotland) also emphasized the pragmatic argument against slavery, claiming that it was economically harmful and that slave societies were not as wealthy or productive as those with free labor. Adam Smith, in *The Wealth of Nations* (1776), argued that free laborers ultimately were more efficient than slaves because they required less supervision.

One Enlightened group that organized against slavery rather than merely denouncing it was the Society of the Friends of the Blacks, a French group that was organized in early 1788, but which was most active during the French Revolution. Influenced by English and American anti-slavery movements, the Society was led by Jacques-Pierre Brissot (1754–1793), a pamphleteer and revolutionary politician who supported many Enlightenment programs. It included the Marquis de Condorcet among its other Enlightened members. It was a small, elitist group, however—at its peak it had less than 150 members—and it did not attempt the popular organizing characteristic of abolitionist groups in the English-speaking world. The Society, which agitated for equal political rights for free men of African descent as well as for slave emancipation, dissolved in 1793 (Brissot was executed by his political enemies the same year). When the National Convention did finally abolish slavery in the French Caribbean colonies in 1794, it was not due to the activities of the Society of the Friends of the Blacks, but rather to the success of the slave uprising in St. Domingue that became the Haitian Revolution. By the end of the century, the focus of the abolitionist movement was on abolishing the slave trade from Africa to the Americas rather than slavery itself.

Although some Enlightened leaders such as Condorcet and Franklin attacked slavery, defenders of slavery also phrased their arguments in Enlightened terms, arguing that Africans were simply inferior and best suited for slavery—in essence using the vocabulary of 18th-century science rather than the Biblical and religious justifications that would become more common in the 19th century. Although he was sometimes ambiguous about slavery, this was the position of American slave owner and Enlightened philosopher, Thomas Jefferson (1743–1826), in *Notes on the State of Virginia* (1785), a work published in Paris for a European audience. The organization of slave plantations concerned with the maximization of the labor value of each slave without regard for tradition or religious concerns also can be conceived of as "Enlightened" in the broad sense.

See also: American Revolution and Founding; Colonialism; Enlightenment Views of Africa and Africans; French Revolution.

Further Reading

Davis, David Brion, *The Problem of Slavery in the Age of Revolution, 1770–1823* (New York: Oxford University Press, 1999).
Manning, Susan, and Peter France (eds.), *Enlightenment and Emancipation* (Lewisburg, PA: Bucknell University Press, 2006).
Roberts, Justin, *Slavery and the Enlightenment in the British Atlantic* (Cambridge and New York: Cambridge University Press, 2013).

SMITH, ADAM (1723–1790) Although the Scottish philosopher and professor Adam Smith is best-known as the intellectual founder of free-market economics, he had a broad range of interests that included rhetoric, jurisprudence, and moral philosophy. Smith was born in Kircaldy in Scotland, and was educated at the Universities of Glasgow and Oxford. He was successively professor of logic and of moral philosophy at Glasgow, following a series of public lectures on moral philosophy that he had given in Edinburgh. Smith was one of the most popular professors at Glasgow. In 1750, while at Glasgow he began a close friendship with David Hume that lasted until Hume's death.

In his first book, *The Theory of Moral Sentiments* (1759), Smith principally was concerned with the origin of moral feelings rather than trying to set up a standard of morality. His position was similar to Hume's; he argued that much of moral feeling was founded on sympathy—the ability to put oneself in another's place—rather than on an innate moral sense. The book was quite successful. It was translated into French, and this subsequently enabled Smith to resign his academic position and travel to France as the tutor of a young Scottish nobleman, the Duke of Buccleuch.

In France, Smith met many leaders of the Enlightenment including Voltaire, Jean-Jacques Rousseau, and Jean Le Rond d'Alembert. He also met some of the leading French economists, members of the "physiocrat" movement. Economics was the subject of his next book, *An Inquiry into the Nature and Causes of the Wealth of Nations* (1776). Smith argued that individual prudent self-interest worked for the overall benefit of society. He traced the increasing wealth of European countries to the division of labor which enabled people to produce more than if everyone tried to do everything. Smith also argued against the "mercantilist" idea that governments should regulate international trade so as to promote domestic industries and to keep foreign goods out. Instead he claimed that overall prosperity would be promoted by buying goods at the best price, wherever that could be found. For that reason he argued that it was not worth the effort for Britain to keep its North American colonies—that both Britain and the colonies would prosper more if Britain did not try to control American markets. The publication of *The Wealth of Nations* often is considered to be the founding date of "classical economics." Smith, however, showed little awareness of the great economic transformation about to hit Britain and the world via the Industrial Revolution.

After the success of *The Wealth of Nations,* Smith received a post as commissioner of customs of Scotland—a job that required little effort and to which he was appointed to provide him with an income. His life was uneventful, save for a controversy following the death of Hume in 1776. (Hume lived long enough to see the publication of *The Wealth of Nations,* which he praised to Smith.) Smith wrote a letter—that became public—praising his late friend's character and suggesting that Hume had neared moral perfection more than any other person Smith had known. Given Hume's well-known rejection of Christianity, many were shocked by Smith's approval of his character.

Smith placed high demands on his own work, publishing only his two books in his lifetime and ordering most of his manuscripts to be burned shortly before his death. He died on July 17, 1790, in Edinburgh.

See also: American Revolution and Founding; Economics; Hume, David; Scotland, the Enlightenment in.

Further Reading

Griswold, Charles L., *Adam Smith and the Virtues of Enlightenment* (Cambridge and New York: Cambridge University Press, 1999).

Minowitz, Peter, *Profits, Priests, and Princes: Adam Smith's Emancipation of Economics from Politics and Religion* (Stanford: Stanford University Press, 1993).

Phillipson, N. T., *Adam Smith: An Enlightened Life* (New Haven: Yale University Press, 2010).

Rothschild, Emma, *Economic Sentiments: Adam Smith, Condorcet, and the Enlightenment* (Cambridge, MA: Harvard University Press, 2001).

SPINOZA, BARUCH (1632–1677)   Baruch Spinoza was a Jew born in Amsterdam, the center of world trade, on November 24, 1632. He spent his life in the relatively tolerant community of the Dutch Republic, part of a family of Jews that had been exiled from Portugal. The family subsequently imported dried fruit. Spinoza was educated in the excellent Portuguese-Jewish school in Amsterdam, but in 1656 was expelled from the local Portuguese-Jewish community for reasons which remain unclear, but which were prompted by his (then unpublished) religious opinions. Spinoza's philosophy was deterministic, allowing no room for free will, and monistic, allowing for no distinction between material and spiritual reality. Mind and body are not different substances. God was immanent in the universe rather than transcendent outside of it, a position sometimes known as "pantheism."

The doctrine espoused the idea that God did not have any personality traits—including those such as justice and mercy which traditionally are ascribed to God in both Christianity and Judaism. Spinoza rejected the tendency shared by Christians and Jews alike to "anthropomorphize" God—to endow God with the body or the personality traits of a human being. Spinoza believed that God had not "chosen" the Jews, nor did Jewish religious law enjoy any divine sanction. The Hebrew Bible was not of divine origin, and in fact probably was a corrupted text. Spinoza also denied the immortality of the soul—an open question within Judaism, but one supported by leaders of the Portuguese-Jewish community as well as being a fundamental tenet of Christianity. He also denied freedom of will, and Spinoza's philosophy became heavily identified with determinism—the belief that the course of events, including human being's "choices," is predetermined.

In his natural philosophy, Spinoza was a follower of the French philosopher René Descartes (1596–1650), about whom he had published *Principles of the Philosophy of René Descartes* (1663). Although he disagreed with Descartes on many other issues—most notably Descartes's division of reality into spiritual and material—his presentation of his philosophy as a series of logical arguments and deductions was influenced heavily by Cartesianism.

Spinoza's most influential work published during his lifetime was *Tractatus Theologico-Politicus*, published anonymously in 1670. It argued for religious toleration and against the idea that political authority was derived from God. Politically, Spinoza supported democracy.

After his expulsion from the Jewish community, Spinoza made his living as a lens-grinder. His intellectual reputation grew but he was not able to support himself as a writer. Baruch Spinoza died at the Hague on February 21, 1677, of a lung disease common among lens-grinders who breathed in tiny fragments of glass for many years. His *Ethics,* setting forth his complete philosophical system, was published later that year along with his other posthumous works. Spinoza's ethics were based on the idea of reason overcoming, although not extinguishing, the passions.

After his death, Spinoza became identified with the most radical Enlightenment positions: materialist, atheist, and Republican. "Spinozist" became an abusive term. Although many leaders of the Enlightenment thought Spinoza was a "system-builder" overly obsessed with logic, his ideas of toleration and democracy influenced some of the greatest thinkers of the Enlightenment, such as Denis Diderot, who moved from a position of hostility to an admiring attitude. Spinoza remained controversial into the late Enlightenment, when

Gotthold Ephraim Lessing was posthumously accused of being a "Spinozist," setting off a major controversy in Germany.

See also: Bible, the; Lessing, Gotthold Ephraim; Religion.

Further Reading

Garrett, Don (ed.), *The Cambridge Companion to Spinoza* (Cambridge and New York: Cambridge University Press, 1996).

Israel, Jonathan I., *Radical Enlightenment: Philosophy and the Making of Modernity, 1650–1750* (Oxford and New York: Oxford University Press, 2001).

Schwartz, Daniel B., *The First Modern Jew: Spinoza and the History of an Image* (Princeton: Princeton University Press, 2012).

THEATER　　The drama, not as written but as performed, was among the most controversial—and popular—arts in the 18th century. Many of the leading writers of the Enlightenment—such as Voltaire and Gotthold Ephraim Lessing—were successful playwrights. At the beginning of the period, the artistic canons of French neoclassicism remained dominant throughout much of Continental Europe. The 17th-century French tragedians Jean Racine (1639–1699) and Pierre Corneille (1606–1684), and their fellow countryman the comic playwright Molière (1622–1673), were regarded as the exemplars of their art and their work continued to be staged. The rules of tragedy were particularly strict. The five rules created by Aristotle to classify a tragedy are that all plays must have catharsis, a tragic hero, and have a change in fortune within a character (the "unities"); must be poetic; must occur in one location; must occur in a single day; and it is all closely related. Additionally, tragedies only could deal with persons of the upper classes—preferably characters from classical antiquity.

The neoclassical unities were weakest in England. In England, the 18th century saw the canonization of William Shakespeare—who had ignored the neoclassical rules—as the supreme dramatist and greatest writer not only in drama but across all genres. Voltaire, a lover of 17th-century French drama but one of the first writers to introduce Shakespeare to a French audience, admired his talents but deplored the Englishman's neglect of the neoclassical laws. Shakespeare's mixing of comedy and tragedy, with characters such as the porter in *Macbeth* and the gravedigger in *Hamlet*, was particularly worthy of scorn.

In addition to his hegemony over England, Shakespeare had an influence on the continent, where writers such as Lessing saw him as an alternative to the sterility of the French classical tradition. A neoclassical reaction in England produced Joseph Addison's *Cato* (1713), an account of an ancient

Roman hero. The story followed the classical rules, but its popularity did not remake the English dramatic tradition.

Anti-theatrical prejudice—based on the fact that actors were people who for a living pretended to be something they were not—had a long history and was strong throughout many areas in Europe, both Protestant and Catholic. It was strengthened by the association between the theater and sexual promiscuity. In Catholic countries, including France, theatrical performers could not be buried in consecrated ground, a fact that horrified many of the Enlightened. Voltaire contrasted France—where the body of the great tragic actress (and Voltaire's friend) Adrienne Lecouvreur (1692–1730), was buried in unhallowed ground on the banks of the Seine river—unfavorably with England, where the actress Anne Oldfield (1683–1730) was buried in Westminster Abbey. The removal of the legal disabilities of actors in France, however, had to wait until the French Revolution. Voltaire was the author of several successful plays, and got into trouble with the civic authorities in Geneva for the theatricals performed in his own home outside of the city. In a controversy over whether a theater should be built in the city of Geneva, Voltaire supported the theater and Jean-Jacques Rousseau, a Genevan himself, took the opposite side, arguing in *A Letter to d'Alembert on Spectacles* that the contemporary theater corrupted the morals of a community, even adducing the alleged ridicule of good morality in *The Misanthrope*, by Voltaire's beloved Molière.

In England, the cult of Shakespeare helped ensure the respectability of the drama. The late 17th-century Restoration comedy, with its vicious characters and attacks on popular standards of morality, was replaced in the 18th century by the more moral sentimental drama. In Scotland, the Enlightened supported the development of a Scottish drama while the anti-Enlightened Evangelical faction in the Church of Scotland strongly opposed it.

Germany was the scene of a protracted struggle to establish a native drama. In the eyes of many Germans, the principal obstacle to the creation of a German drama was not anti-theatrical prejudice but the dominance of French neoclassicism and the lack of interest in the theater shown by many Germans. The first noteworthy champion of a new German drama was Lessing, an admirer of Shakespeare. Lessing's "bourgeois tragedy" with an English setting, *Miss Sara Sampson*, was a hit at its premier in 1755 and was popularly seen as inaugurating a new day in the German theater. The work was even translated into French.

Theater could be a vehicle for the dissemination of Enlightenment values, as in the condemnation of religious intolerance in Voltaire's plays or the attack on social inequalities in the works of Pierre-Augustin Caron de Beaumarchais (1732–1799). Beaumarchais' plays, *The Barber of Seville* and its sequel, *The Marriage of Figaro,* attacked the prevailing social order by painting aristocrats as being full of undeserved privilege and their servants as being forced to use their superior intelligence against their masters. So controversial was *The Marriage of Figaro* that the French government banned its performance, although it did not ban its publication. Catherine the Great wrote plays herself and promoted the Russian theater so as to promote a more conservative version of the Enlightenment.

In addition to traditional theater, opera also was a popular genre in the 18th century, which saw some of the greatest operas ever composed in the work of Wolfgang Amadeus Mozart (1756–1791) and others. (Mozart adapted *The Marriage of Figaro* into a popular opera.) Beginning in 1752, the *War of the Buffoons* in Paris pitted the traditional, formal, and highly stylized French opera against the more informal and melodious opera coming out of Italy. Most of the French Enlightenment writers who took an interest, led by Jean-Jacques Rousseau, an opera composer himself, supported the Italian opera, a support reflected in the musical entries in the *Encyclopédie,* many of which were written by Rousseau. Rousseau even went so far as to declare the French language "unsingable."

See also: Lessing, Gotthold Ephraim; Literature; Rousseau, Jean-Jacques; Scotland, the Enlightenment in; Voltaire.

Further Reading

Caines, Michael, *Shakespeare and the Eighteenth Century* (Oxford: Oxford University Press, 2013).

Carlson, Marvin, *Voltaire and the Theater of the Eighteenth Century* (Westport, CN: Greenwood, 1998).

Howarth, William D., *Beaumarchais and the Theatre* (London and New York: Routledge, 1995).

VOLTAIRE (1694–1778)   If any single individual can be described as the leader of the Enlightenment, it surely is the French philosopher and polymath Francois-Marie Arouet, better known by his adopted pseudonym, "Voltaire." Voltaire was born in Paris on November 21, 1694, into a wealthy family of Parisian commoners. He retained a strong consciousness as a "bourgeois" and opponent of the aristocracy throughout his life. His father hoped that his son would follow in his footsteps by becoming a notary, a prestigious profession at the time. Voltaire was educated by Jesuits at the College of Louis the Great (Louis XIV) in Paris. He later would charge his Jesuit teachers with having sexually abused him as a child, and he carried a grudge against the Jesuits for the rest of his life.

After making a start as a poet and dramatist, Voltaire was forced to leave France after a quarrel with a noble—the Chevalier de Rohan (1683–1760)—who had his servants beat the poet, as he was not the social equal that Rohan could have engaged in a duel. In England, from 1726 to 1729, Voltaire became fascinated by the thoughts of Isaac Newton and John Locke, as well as the relative political and religious freedom and social equality of England. Upon his return to France, Voltaire became a missionary for English thought—notably in the advancement of Newtonian science against the dominant Cartesian tradition of France. (His girlfriend, the Marquise du Châtelet, was his partner in this project, supplying the mathematical expertise Voltaire himself lacked.) His *Letters on England* (1732) were addressed to a French audience and praised English thought, political institutions, and culture. It helped set off a wave of "Anglomania" that marked the early Enlightenment in France. Although the book was banned in France, it circulated widely. Voltaire, who continued to publish stories, poems, and dramas, began to climb the French social ladder under the patronage of the king's mistress, Madame du Pompadour (1721–1764). Voltaire also began corresponding with Frederick the Great of Prussia—a relationship which worked better than when Voltaire actually tried to live in Frederick's capital of Berlin, and the two men quarreled bitterly.

Voltaire was fired by a hatred of repression, particularly religious repression. His powerful pen transformed the Calas Case (a Protestant father wrongly charged with killing his son) from a local scandal into a national issue. Voltaire sometimes signed his letters with the words "ecrasez l'infame" meaning "crush the infamy." "The infamy" referred to organized religion. His personal beliefs were Deist, believing in an all-powerful deity who had created and oversaw the world, but not believing in any religion. He was troubled by the rise of materialism and atheism in the later French Enlightenment. Voltaire believed that the universe was too clearly designed for the existence of God to be denied, and that belief in God furnished a necessary ground for morality—not just among the common people but among princes and statesmen, as well. It is in the context of morality that Voltaire made his famous statement that "if God did not exist it would be necessary to invent him."

Politically, Voltaire supported a strong French monarchy that could modernize the country and sweep away the accumulated irrationalities of the centuries. He distrusted the parlements, the hereditary law courts which served as one of the few checks on royal power, and the power and privileges of the French aristocracy generally. He received several honors from the French government, including an appointment as Royal Historiographer in 1745 and Gentlemen-in-ordinary to the King, which came with rooms at the royal palace at Versailles and nomination to the French Academy. Although he never got the reforming government he and other French philosophes hoped for, he continued to distrust the masses of the people as well, viewing them as corrupted by Christianity and potentially criminal.

Voltaire's dislike of Christians extended to Jews. He found little to admire in the Jews of the Old Testament, and believed that the Jews of his own time were overly influenced by this "barbaric document," which he thought inferior to the works of the Greeks and Romans. He criticized the traditional European historiography of the ancient world for its excessive interest in this one small and barbarous people. Voltaire described the Jews of his own time as materialistic, dishonest, and corrupt but believed that some of these qualities could be moderated if Jews assimilated to Christian community, not religiously but in terms of abandoning specifically Jewish practices such as dietary restrictions. He was friendly to some individual Jews, however, and believed that Jews—like everyone else—were entitled to religious freedom. Voltaire even on rare occasions praised Jews and Judaism on some points where they diverged from Christians, such as the Jewish religion's disinterest in making converts.

Voltaire was a great master of French prose. His most important writings include the short novel, *Candide* (1759), a story of a young man who has all sorts of hair-raising adventures, designed to combat the philosophical optimism Voltaire blamed on Gottfried Wilhelm Leibniz. It concludes "Let us cultivate our garden" expressing Voltaire's preference for concrete action, even on a modest scale, over useless speculation. Another popular book was the *Philosophical Dictionary* (1764), setting forth much of the philosophy of the Enlightenment in a reference book that could be carried around in one's pocket, as opposed to the massive multi-volume *Encyclopédie* (to which Voltaire also was a contributor). His many works—published both legally and clandestinely—sold massively all over France for decades.

As a historian, Voltaire was a "philosophical historian" who investigated the past to make broad claims about human nature and civilization, rather than an "antiquarian" who viewed the recovery of facts and their accurate arrangement as the historian's primary task. His *The Century of Louis XIV* (1751) was one of the first books to integrate cultural and social with political history, examining how France changed during the time of Louis XIV (r. 1643–1715), which Voltaire regarded as one of the peaks of human culture, rather than simply recounting the king's battles and achievements. Voltaire's *Essay on Customs and the Spirit of the Nations* (1756) was an early attempt to write a history not focused on politics. It broke from the European and Christian-centric tradition of European historiography by beginning not with the Biblical narrative or the ancient Greeks but with China, which Voltaire regarded as the most ancient of civilizations.

To his contemporaries, however, Voltaire perhaps was best known as a dramatist. Many of his plays were performed by the Comédie Francaise, France's leading dramatic company. His first play was *Oedipe* and is based on the Greek myth of Oedipus. It first appeared in 1718 and was the first work to appear with the pen name, "Voltaire." It premiered at the Comédie Française and received praise from the Prince Regent of France, the Duke of Orléans (1674–1723), even though some considered the play—with its theme of incest—a hint at the rumors that Orléans was having an affair with his daughter the Duchess of Berry (1695–1719). The play was frequently revived.

Among the most successful of Voltaire's dramas was *Zaire*, set during the crusades and showing how religious intolerance, in this case between Christians and Muslims, leads to tragedy. It premiered at the Comédie Française on August 13, 1732. It received numerous performances and was also popular in England, where a translated version, *Zara*, appeared in 1736. *Zaire* was among the first French tragedies to include French characters, as French tragedy usually drew its subject matter from classical Greece and Rome or the Bible. Other noted plays by Voltaire include *Mahomet* (1736) which portrayed the founder of Islam as an unscrupulous tyrant, although Voltaire would claim that the real target of the drama was intolerant Christians. He also turned to a historical subject early in his career in his epic poem the *Henriade* (1723), with its hero King Henry IV of France (1553–1610) viewed as a champion of religious toleration. Although the poem was quite popular in Voltaire's lifetime and frequently was reprinted, it is not often read today nor is his subsequent satirical poem about Joan of Arc, *The Maid*, which took too many liberties with a French national icon to be published in full during Voltaire's life. Like many of the Enlightened thinkers, Voltaire also was a voluminous correspondent who left behind approximately 20,000 letters.

Voltaire died in Paris on May 30, 1778. His death seems to have been peaceful but it became surrounded by controversy, as false deathbed legends of his reconciliation with the church or dying in great torment as he awaited eternal damnation were spread by the faithful and continue to be spread more than two centuries later. For many Christian believers, Voltaire became the archetypal "infidel," but he became a hero to skeptics, anticlericals, and atheists. Even his remains became an object of cultural contention. The church did not wish for him to be buried in consecrated ground, so he was smuggled out of Paris by a clerical relative who buried him at a remote abbey in Champagne. After the French Revolution, he was reburied among the great of France in the Pantheon at Paris, established by the revolutionaries to honor the illustrious dead. In the tumult, pieces of his body such as teeth were removed to be venerated as relics. Although rumors later spread that his body had been dug up and desecrated by conservative Royalists, an exhumation performed in 1897 showed his remains mostly intact.

See also: Calas Case; Châtelet, Émilie du; Enlightenment Views of Asian Civilizations; Enlightenment Views of Jews and Judaism; Enlightenment Views of Muslims and Islam; Enlightenment Views of Native Americans; France, the Enlightenment in; Literature; Political Philosophy; Religion; Science; Theater.

Further Reading

Carlson, Marvin, *Voltaire and the Theater of the Eighteenth Century* (Westport, CN: Greenwood, 1998).

Cronk, Nicholas (ed.), *The Cambridge Companion to Voltaire* (Cambridge and New York: Cambridge University Press, 2009).

Davidson, Ian, *Voltaire: A Life* (London: Profile, 2010).

Gay, Peter, *Voltaire's Politics: The Poet as Realist* (Princeton: Princeton University Press, 1959).

Primary Documents

BARUCH SPINOZA

"On the Nature and Origin of the Emotions," from *Ethics* (1677)

Much of the Dutch-Jewish philosopher Baruch Spinoza's work can be seen as the extension of the scientific and mathematical methods that had been so successful in the investigation of nature to questions dealing with God and man. In this passage of the posthumously published *Ethics*, Spinoza calls for a science of the emotions less oriented to praising or blaming than to understanding.

Most writers on the emotions and on human conduct seem to be treating rather of matters outside nature than of natural phenomena following nature's general laws. They appear to conceive man to be situated in nature as a kingdom within a kingdom: for they believe that he disturbs rather than follows nature's order, that he has absolute control over his actions, and that he is determined solely by himself. They attribute human infirmities and fickleness, not to the power of nature in general, but to some mysterious flaw in the nature of man, which accordingly they bemoan, deride, despise, or, as usually happens, abuse: he, who succeeds in hitting off the weakness of the human mind more eloquently or more acutely than his fellows, is looked upon as a seer. Still there has been no lack of very excellent men (to whose toil and industry I confess myself much indebted), who have written many noteworthy things concerning the right way of life, and have given much sage advice to mankind. But no one, so far as I know, has defined the nature and strength of the emotions, and the power of the mind against them for their restraint.

I do not forget that the illustrious Descartes, though he believed that the mind has absolute power over its actions, strove to explain human emotions by their primary causes, and, at the same time, to point out a way by which the mind might attain to absolute dominion over them. However, in my opinion, he accomplishes nothing beyond a display of the acuteness of his own great intellect, as I will show in the proper place. For the present I wish to revert to those, who would rather abuse or deride human emotions than understand them. Such persons will, doubtless think it strange that I should attempt to treat of human vice and folly geometrically, and should wish to set forth with rigid reasoning those matters which they cry out against as repugnant to reason, frivolous, absurd, and dreadful. However, such is my plan. Nothing comes to pass in nature, which can be set down to a flaw therein; for nature is always the same, and everywhere one and the same in her efficacy and power of action; that is, nature's laws and ordinances, whereby all things come to pass and change from one form to another, are everywhere and always the same; so that there should be one and the same method of understanding the nature of all things whatsoever, namely, through nature's universal laws and rules. Thus the passions of hatred, anger, envy, and so on, considered in themselves, follow from this same necessity and efficacy of nature; they answer to certain definite causes, through which they are understood, and possess certain properties as worthy of being known as the properties of anything else, whereof the contemplation in itself affords us delight. I shall, therefore, treat of the nature and strength of the emotions according to the same method, as I employed heretofore in my investigations concerning God and the mind. I shall consider human actions and desires in exactly the same manner, as though I were concerned with lines, planes, and solids.

Source: Benedictus de Spinoza, *Improvement of the Understanding, Ethics and Correspondence.* Translated from the Latin by R.H.M. Elwes. New York: Willey Book Co., 1901, 127–128.

JOHN LOCKE

"Of the Beginnings of Political Societies," from *Second Treatise on Civil Government* (1689)

The 17th century in England was a time of intense political unrest and the questioning of established authority that produced much political theory. John Locke's *Second Treatise* emphasized the importance of rule by consent, in part by claiming that the origin of civil societies lay in the establishment of a contract between the ruler and the ruled. Locke was not the only contractarian theorist, but his version of the contract proved among the most influential in the Enlightenment, and Locke himself one of its intellectual heroes.

Sec. 95. MEN being, as has been said, by nature, all free, equal, and independent, no one can be put out of this estate, and subjected to the political power of another, without his own consent. The only way whereby any one divests himself of his natural liberty, and puts on the bonds of civil society, is by agreeing with other men to join and unite into a community for their comfortable, safe, and peaceable living one amongst another, in a secure enjoyment of their properties, and a greater security against any, that are not of it. This any number of men may do, because it injures not the freedom of the rest; they are left as they were in the liberty of the state of nature. When any number of men have so consented to make one community or government, they are thereby presently incorporated, and make one body politic, wherein the majority have a right to act and conclude the rest.

Sec. 96. For when any number of men have, by the consent of every individual, made a community, they have thereby made that community one body, with a power to act as one body, which is only by the will and determination of the majority: for that which acts any community, being only the consent of the individuals of it, and it being necessary to that which is one body to move one way; it is necessary the body should move that way whither the greater force carries it, which is the consent of the majority: or else it is impossible it should act or continue one body, one community, which the consent of every individual that united into it, agreed that it should; and so everyone is bound by that consent to be concluded by the majority. And therefore we see, that in assemblies, impowered to act by positive laws, where no number is set by that positive law which impowers them, the act of the majority passes for the act of the whole, and of course determines, as having, by the law of nature and reason, the power of the whole.

Sec. 97. And thus every man, by consenting with others to make one body politic under one government, puts himself under an obligation, to every one of that society, to submit to the determination of the majority, and to be concluded by it; or else this original compact, whereby he with others incorporates into one society, would signify nothing, and be no compact, if he be left free, and under no other ties than he was in before in the state of nature. For what appearance would there be of any compact? [W]hat new engagement if he were no farther tied by any decrees of the society, than he himself thought fit, and did actually consent to? This would be still as great a liberty, as he himself had before his compact, or any one else in the state of nature hath, who may submit himself, and consent to any acts of it if he thinks fit.

Sec. 98. For if the consent of the majority shall not, in reason, be received as the act of the whole, and conclude every individual; nothing but the consent of every individual can make any thing to be the act of the whole: but such a consent is next to impossible ever to be had, if we consider the infirmities of health, and avocations of business, which in a number, though much less than that of a commonwealth, will necessarily keep many away from the public assembly. To which if we add the variety of opinions, and contrariety of interests, which unavoidably happen in all collections of men, the coming into society upon such terms would be only like Cato's coming into the theatre, only to go out again. Such a constitution as this would make the mighty Leviathan of a shorter duration, than the feeblest creatures, and not let it outlast the day it was born in: which cannot be supposed, till we can think, that rational creatures should desire and constitute societies only to be dissolved: for where the majority cannot conclude the rest, there they cannot act as one body, and consequently will be immediately dissolved again.

Sec. 99. Whosoever therefore out of a state of nature unite into a community, must be understood to give up all the power, necessary to the ends for which they unite into society, to the majority of the community, unless they expressly agreed in any number greater than the majority. And this is done by barely agreeing to unite into one political society, which is all the compact that is, or needs be, between the individuals, that enter into, or make up a commonwealth. And thus that, which begins and actually constitutes any political society, is nothing but the consent of any number of freemen capable of a majority to unite and incorporate into such a society. And this is that, and that only, which did, or could give beginning to any lawful government in the world.

Source: John Locke, *Two Treatises of Government*. Edited by A. Millar et al. London. 1764.

GOTTFRIED WILHELM LEIBNIZ

The Leibniz-Clarke Correspondence (1717)

The Leibniz-Clarke Correspondence is an exchange of letters between Gottfried Wilhelm Leibniz and the English theologian Samuel Clarke. Clarke was widely believed to be a mouthpiece for his friend—and Leibniz's bitter enemy—Isaac Newton. Each tried to maneuver the other into a position that denied the perfection of God, linking his opponent with the materialists and Spinoza. In this passage, Leibniz attacks the Newtonian idea that God must actively intervene in the universe to keep it in operation.

1. IT is rightly observed in the Paper delivered to the Princess of Wales, which Her Royal Highness has been pleased to communicate to me, that, next to Corruption of Manners, the Principles of the Materialists do very much contribute to keep up Impiety. But I believe the Author had no reason to add, that the Mathematical Principles of Philosophy are opposite to those of the Materialists. On the contrary, they are the same; only with this difference, that the Materialists, in Imitation of Democritus, Epicurus, and Hobbes, confine themselves altogether to Mathematical Principles, and admit only Bodies; whereas the Christian Mathematicians admit also Immaterial Substances. Wherefore, not Mathematical Principles (according to the usual sense of that Word) but Metaphysical Principles ought to be opposed to those of the Materialists. Pythagoras, Plato, and Aristotle in some measure, had a

Knowledge of these Principles; but I pretend to have established them demonstratively in my Theodicæa, though I have done it in a popular manner. The great Foundation of Mathematicks, is the principle of Contradiction, or Identity, that is, that a Proposition cannot be true and false at the same time; and that therefore A is A, and cannot be not A. This single Principle is sufficient to demonstrate every part of Arithmetick and Geometry, that is, all Mathematical Principles. But in order to proceed from Mathematicks to Natural Philosophy, another Principle is requisite, as I have observed in my Theodicæa: I mean, the Principle of a sufficient Reason, viz. that nothing happens without a Reason why it should be so, rather than otherwise. And therefore Archimedes being to proceed from Mathematicks to Natural Philosophy, in his Book *De Æquilibrio*, was obliged to make use of a particular Case of the great Principle of a sufficient Reason. He takes it for granted, that if there be a [1] Balance, in which every thing is alike on both Sides, and if equal Weights are hung on the two ends of that Balance, the whole will be at rest. 'Tis because no Reason can be given, why one side should weigh down, rather than the other. Now, by that single Principle, viz. that there ought to be a sufficient Reason why Things should be so, and not otherwise, one may demonstrate the Being of a God, and all the other Parts of Metaphysicks or Natural Theology; and even, in some Measure, those Principles of Natural Philosophy, that are independent upon Mathematicks: I mean, the [2] Dynamick Principles, or the Principles of Force.

2. The Author proceeds, and says, that according to the Mathematical Principles, that is, according to Sir Isaac Newton's Philosophy, (for Mathematical Principles determine nothing in the present Case,) Matter is the most inconsiderable part of the Universe. The reason is, because he admits empty Space, besides Matter; and because, according to his Notions, Matter fills up only a very small part of Space. But Democritus and Epicurus maintained the same Thing: They differ'd from Sir Isaac Newton, only as to the Quantity of Matter; and perhaps they believed there was more Matter in the World, than Sir Isaac Newton will allow: Wherein I think their Opinion ought to be preferred; For, the more Matter there is, the more God has occasion to exercise his Wisdom and Power. Which is one Reason, among others, why I maintain that there is no Vacuum at all.

3. I find, in express Words, in the Appendix to Sir Isaac Newton's Opticks, that Space is the Sensorium of God. But the Word Sensorium hath always signified the Organ of Sensation. He, and his Friends, may now, if they think fit, explain themselves quite otherwise: I shall not be against it.

4. The Author supposes that the presence of the Soul is sufficient to make it perceive what passes in the Brain. But this is the very Thing which Father Mallebranche, and all the Cartesians deny; and they rightly deny it. More is requisite besides bare presence, to enable One thing to perceive what passes in another. Some Communication, that may be explained; some sort of influence, is requisite for this purpose. Space, according to Sir Isaac Newton, is intimately

present to the Body contained in it, and commensurate with it. Does it follow from thence, that Space perceives what passes in a Body; and remembers it, when That Body is gone away? Besides, the Soul being indivisible, its immediate presence, which may be imagined in the Body, would only be in one Point. How then could it perceive what happens out of that Point? I pretend to be the first, who has shown how the Soul perceives what passes in the Body.

5. The Reason why God perceives every thing, is not His bare Presence, but also his Operation. 'Tis because he preserves Things by an Action, which continually produces whatever is good and perfect in them. But the Soul having [5] no immediate Influence over the Body, nor the Body over the Soul; their mutual Correspondence cannot be explained by their being present to each other.

6. The true and principal Reason why we commend a Machine, is rather grounded upon the Effects of the Machine, than upon its Cause. We don't enquire so much about the Power of the Artist, as we do about his Skill in his Workmanship. And therefore the Reason alleged by the Author for extolling the Machine of God's making, grounded upon his having made it entirely, without wanting any Materials to make it of; That Reason, I say, is not sufficient. 'Tis a mere Shift the Author has been forced to have recourse to: And the Reason why God exceeds any other Artist, is not only because he makes the Whole, whereas all other Artists must have Matter to work upon. This Excellency in God, would be only on the account of Power. But God's Excellency arises also from another Cause, viz. Wisdom: whereby his Machine lasts longer, and moves more regularly, than those of any other Artist whatsoever. He who buys a Watch, does not mind whether the Workman made every Part of it himself, or whether he got the several Parts made by Others, and did only put them together; provided the Watch goes right. And if the Workman had received from God even the Gift of creating the Matter of the Wheels; yet the Buyer of the Watch would not be satisfied, unless the Workman had also received the Gift of putting them well together. In like manner, he who will be pleased with God's Workmanship, cannot be so, without some other Reason than that which the Author has here alleged.

7. Thus the Skill of God must not be inferior to that of a Workman; nay, it must go infinitely beyond it. The bare Production of every thing, would indeed show the Power of God; but it would not sufficiently show his Wisdom. They who maintain the contrary, will fall exactly into the Error of the Materialists, and of Spinoza, from whom they profess to differ. They would, in such case, acknowledge Power, but not sufficient Wisdom, in the Principle or Cause of all Things.

8. I do not say, the Material World is a Machine, or Watch, that goes without God's Interposition; and I have sufficiently insisted, that the Creation wants to be continually influenc'd by its Creator. But I maintain it to be a Watch, that goes without wanting to be Mended by him: Otherwise we must say, that God bethinks himself again. No; God has foreseen every thing; He has provided a Remedy for every thing before-hand; There is in his Works a Harmony, a Beauty, already pre-established.

Source: "Mr. Leibnitz's Second Paper." From Samuel Clarke, *A Collection of Papers, Which Passed Between the Late Learned Mr. Leibnitz, and Dr. Clarke, in the Years 1715 and 1716.* London: James Knapton, 1717.

MONTESQUIEU

"On Monarchies," from *The Spirit of the Laws* (1748)

Although Montesquieu as a young man had been attracted to republics, in the *Spirit of the Laws* he presents Monarchies as a better form of government. He was keen to distinguish monarchy from the worst form of government, despotism, however. Montesquieu thus emphasizes that in a proper monarchy the will of the monarch can be checked by other institutions. Not his monarchism but his emphasis on checks and balances would influence the framers of the American constitution.

CHAP. X.: Of the Expedition peculiar to the executive Power in Monarchies.
GREAT is the advantage which a monarchical government has over a republic. As the state is conducted by a single person, the executive power is thereby enabled to act with greater expedition: but, as this expedition may degenerate into rapidity, the laws should use some contrivance to slacken it: they ought not only to favour the nature of each constitution, but likewise to remedy the abuses that might result from this very nature.

Cardinal Richelieu advises monarchs to permit no such things as societies or communities that raise difficulties upon every trifle. If this man's heart had not been bewitched with the love of despotic power, still these arbitrary notions would have filled his head.

The bodies, intrusted with the depositum of the laws, are never more obedient than when they proceed slowly, and use that reflection in the prince's affairs which can scarcely be expected from the ignorance of a court, or from the precipitation of its councils.

What would have become of the finest monarchy in the world, if the magistrates, by their delays, their complaints, and entreaties, had not checked the rapidity even of their princes virtues, when these monarchs, consulting only the generous impulse of their minds, would fain have given a boundless reward to services performed with an unlimited courage and fidelity?

CHAP. XI.: Of the Excellence of a monarchical government.
MONARCHY has a great advantage over a despotic government. As it naturally requires there should be several orders or ranks of subjects, the state is more permanent, the constitution more steady, and the person of him who governs more secure.

Cicero is of opinion, that the establishing of the tribunes preserved the republic. "And, indeed, (says he,) the violence of a headless people is more terrible. A chief, or head, is sensible that the affair depends upon himself, and therefore he thinks; but the people, in their impetuosity, are ignorant of the danger into which they hurry (72) themselves." This reflection may be applied to a despotic government, which is a people without tribunes, and to a monarchy, where the people have some sort of tribunes.

Accordingly, it is observable, that, in the commotions of a despotic government, the people, hurried away by their passions, are apt to push things as far as they can go. The disorders they commit are all extreme; whereas, in monarchies, matters are seldom carried to excess. The chiefs are apprehensive on their own account; they are afraid of being abandoned; and the intermediate dependent powers do not choose that the populace should have too much the upper hand. It rarely happens that the states of the kingdom are entirely corrupted: the prince adheres to these; and the seditious, who have neither will nor hopes to subvert the government, have neither power nor will to dethrone the prince.

In these circumstances, men of prudence and authority interfere; moderate measures are first proposed, then complied with, and things at length are redressed; the laws resume their vigor, and command submission.

Thus all our histories are full of civil wars without revolutions, while the histories of despotic governments abound with revolutions without civil wars.

The writers of the history of the civil wars of some countries, even those who fomented them, sufficiently demonstrate the little foundation princes have to suspect the authority with which they invest particular bodies of men; since, even under the unhappy circumstance of their errors, they sighed only after the laws and their duty, and restrained, more than they were capable of inflaming, the impetuosity of the revolted.

Cardinal Richelieu, reflecting perhaps that he had too much reduced the states of the kingdom, has recourse to the virtues of the prince and of his ministers for the support of government: but he requires so many things, that indeed there is none but an angel capable of such attention, such resolution, and knowledge; and scarce can we flatter ourselves ever to see such a prince and ministers, no not while monarchy subsists.

As people, who live under a good government, are happier than those who, without rule or leaders, wander about the forests; so monarchs, who live under the fundamental laws of their country, are far happier than despotic princes, who have nothing to regulate either their own passions or those of their subjects.

CHAP. XII.: The same Subject continued.
LET us not look for magnanimity in despotic governments. The prince cannot impart a greatness which he has not himself: with him there is no such thing as glory.

It is in monarchies we behold the subjects encircling the throne, and cheered by the irradiancy of the sovereign: there it is that each person, filling, as it were, a larger space, is capable of exercising those virtues which adorn the soul, not with independence, but with true dignity and greatness.

Source: Secondat, Charles de, Baron de Montesquieu. *The Spirit of Laws*, Book V. Translated by Thomas Nugent. London: J. Nourse and P. Vaillant, 1750.

DAVID HUME

An Enquiry into the Principles of Morals (1751)

It was common in the Enlightenment for philosophers to reach out to the ancient thinkers of pagan Greece and Rome, across the gap of centuries of Christianity. Here, the Scottish skeptical philosopher David Hume hints that "modern philosophers," influenced by Christianity, had degenerated from the ancients, or "heathens." By confusing moral philosophy with theology, Christians—"divines" rather than philosophers—have hopelessly muddled the subject.

In general, we may observe, that the distinction of voluntary or involuntary was little regarded by the ancients in their moral reasonings; where they frequently treated the question as very doubtful, *whether virtue could be taught or not* [Vid. Plato in Menone, Seneca de otio sap. cap. 31. So also Horace, Virtutem doctrina paret, naturane donet, Epist. lib. I. ep. 18. Aeschines Socraticus, Dial. I.]? They justly considered that cowardice, meanness, levity, anxiety, impatience, folly, and many other qualities of the mind, might appear ridiculous and deformed, contemptible and odious, though independent of the will. Nor could it be supposed, at all times, in every man's power to attain every kind of mental more than of exterior beauty.

And here there occurs the fourth reflection which I purposed to make, in suggesting the reason why modern philosophers have often followed a course in their moral enquiries so different from that of the ancients. In later times, philosophy of all kinds, especially ethics, have been more closely united with theology than ever they were observed to be among the heathens; and as this latter science admits of no terms of composition, but bends every branch of knowledge to its own purpose, without much regard to the phenomena of nature, or to the unbiased sentiments of the mind, hence reasoning, and even language, have been warped from their natural course, and distinctions have been endeavoured to be established where the difference of the objects was, in a manner, imperceptible. Philosophers, or rather divines under that disguise, treating all morals as on a like footing with civil laws, guarded by the sanctions of reward and punishment, were necessarily led to render this circumstance, of voluntary or involuntary, the foundation of their whole theory. Every one may employ terms in what sense he pleases: but this, in the meantime, must be allowed, that sentiments are every day experienced of blame and praise, which have objects beyond the dominion of the will or choice, and of which it beho[o]ves us, if not as moralists, as speculative philosophers at least, to give some satisfactory theory and explication.

A blemish, a fault, a vice, a crime; these expressions seem to denote different degrees of censure and disapprobation; which are, however, all of them, at the bottom, pretty nearly all the same kind of species. The explication of one will easily lead us into a just conception of the others; and it is of greater consequence to attend to things than to verbal appellations. That we owe a duty to ourselves is confessed even in the most vulgar system of morals; and it must be of consequence to examine that duty, in order to see whether it bears any affinity to that which we owe to society. It is probable that the approbation attending the observance of both is of a similar nature, and arises from similar principles, whatever appellation we may give to either of these excellencies.

Source: David Hume, *Essays and Treatises on Several Subjects*. London: T. Cadell, 1772, 382–383.

DENIS DIDEROT

"Enjoyment" (Jouissance), from the *Encyclopédie* (1751–1765)

In addition to being the principal editor of the *Encyclopédie*, Denis Diderot was also one of the most productive of its many contributors. Although many of his articles were dry and factual, some were not, and used the reference book format to advance Enlightenment ideas. The attack on asceticism and emphasis on the goodness of pleasure was particularly important to Diderot. The term "jouissance" in French combines the meanings of pleasure in general and sexual climax in particular, a double meaning that Diderot plays with throughout the article.

Enjoyment. To enjoy is to know, to experience, to feel the advantages of possessing. We often possess without enjoyment. Whose magnificent palaces are these? Who planted these immense gardens? It is the sovereign. Who enjoys them? I do.

But let us leave the magnificent palaces that the sovereign has built, not for himself but for others; let us leave the enchanting gardens where he never strolls; let us stop at the voluptuousness that perpetuates the chain of living beings, that voluptuousness that we have come to call enjoyment.

Among the objects that nature offers to our desires from all sides—you who have a soul, tell me: Is there an object more worthy of our pursuit, whose possession and enjoyment can render us as happy, than the one who thinks and feels as you do, who has the same ideas, who experiences the same heat, the same delights, who carries his tender and delicate arms toward yours, who embraces you? Is there an object more worthy than one whose caresses are followed by the existence of a new being who will resemble you, who in his first movements will seek you to cuddle you, whom you will raise at your sides, whom you will love together, who will protect you in your old age, who will respect you at all times, and whose happy birth has already strengthened the bond that united you?

Crude, senseless, immobile beings deprived of life, who surround us, can serve our happiness; yet they do so without knowing it, and without sharing in it. Our sterile and destructive enjoyment alters them all but does not reproduce any happiness.

If any perverse Man may have taken offence at my praise of the most august and the most prevalent of passions, I would invoke Nature before him. I would have her speak and she would say to him: Why do you blush upon hearing the name of an exquisite pleasure ["volupté"] when you do not blush for having felt attracted by it in the shadow of the night? Do you not know its aim and what you owe it? Do you think that your mother would have risked her life in order to give you yours, if she had not attached an inexpressible charm to the embraces of her spouse? Be quiet, miserable one, and bear in mind that it is pleasure that pulled you out of oblivion.

The propagation of beings is the greatest goal of Nature. She solicits the two sexes imperiously in this aim, as soon as they have received what she designed for them in strength and in beauty. A vague and melancholic anxiety informs them of the moment; their mood becomes a mixture of pain and pleasure. That is when they listen to their senses, and they turn their awareness inward.

When an individual presents himself to another of the same species and a different sex, the feeling for all other needs is suspended; the heart palpitates; the limbs quiver; voluptuous images roam the brain; the torrents of the spirit flow into the nerves, irritate them and then move to the core of a new sense, which manifests itself and torments in turn. Vision is blurred, delirium is born; reason, a slave to instinct, contents itself with serving it, and Nature is satisfied.

This is how things occurred at the birth of the world, and how they occur again in the depths of the adult savage's lair.

But once woman began to discern, once she appeared to grow attentive to her choice, and once, among several men over whom passion cast its sights, one man stopped it, he could flatter himself for being preferred and believe to hold in a heart he esteemed, the esteem in which he held himself, and see in pleasure the reward for some merit. Once the veils, thrown on charms by modesty, gave blazing imagination the power to dispose of them at leisure, the most delicate of illusions competed with the most exquisite of senses to exaggerate happiness; the soul was seized by an almost divine enthusiasm; two young hearts overcome with love dedicated themselves, one to the other, forever, and the sky heard the first indiscreet vows.

How many happy instants in the day were lost before the instant when an entire soul sought to leap and lose itself in the soul of the loved one! We had enjoyments [pleasures] from the moment when we began to hope.

Yet confidence, time, nature and the liberty of caresses brought about self-lessness; having experienced the last exhilaration, we swore that there would be none other to compare; and this was found to be true every time sensitive and young organs, a tender heart, and an innocent soul who did not know suspicion nor remorse, were involved.

Source: Diderot, Denis (ascribed by Jacques Proust). "Enjoyment." *The Encyclopedia of Diderot & d'Alembert Collaborative Translation Project*. Translated by Anoush Terjanian. Ann Arbor: Michigan Publishing, University of Michigan Library, 2005. http://hdl.handle.net/2027/spo .did2222.0000.225. Originally published as "Jouissance," *Encyclopédie ou Dictionnaire raisonné des sciences, des arts et des métiers*, 8:889. Paris, 1765. Used by permission of Anoush Terjanian.

ROUSSEAU

From *Discourse on the Origin of Inequality* (1755)

Jean-Jacques Rousseau was fascinated by the idea of a "state of nature" that existed before the establishment of civil and political society. In this passage from *Discourse on the Origin of Inequality*, he defends man in the natural state from what he regards as the calumnies of the 17th-century theorist of the political contract, Thomas Hobbes. Hobbes's famous description of life in the state of nature as "poor, nasty, brutish and short" and his Christian-influenced picture of natural man as fundamentally vicious must be refuted to establish the natural state as an ideal from which subsequent society has (irreversibly) degenerated.

It appears, at first view, that men in a state of nature, having no moral relations or determinate obligations one with another, could not be either good or bad, virtuous or vicious; unless we take these terms in a physical sense, and call, in an individual, those qualities vices which may be injurious to his preservation, and those virtues which contribute to it; in which case, he would have to be accounted most virtuous, who put least check on the pure impulses of nature. But without deviating from the ordinary sense of the words, it will be proper to suspend the judgment we might be led to form on such a state, and be on our guard against our prejudices, till we have weighed the matter in the scales of impartiality, and seen whether virtues or vices preponderate among civilised men; and whether their virtues do them more good than their vices do harm; till we have discovered, whether the progress of the sciences sufficiently indem-nifies them for the mischiefs they do one another, in proportion as they are better informed of the good they ought to do; or whether they would not be, on the whole, in a much happier condition if they had nothing to fear or to hope from any one, than as they are, subjected to universal dependence, and obliged to take everything from those who engage to give them nothing in return.

Above all, let us not conclude, with Hobbes, that because man has no idea of goodness, he must be naturally wicked; that he is vicious because he does not know virtue; that he always refuses to do his fellow-creatures services which he does not think they have a right to demand; or that by virtue of the right he truly claims to everything he needs, he foolishly imagines himself the sole proprietor of the whole universe. Hobbes had seen clearly the defects of all the modern definitions of natural right: but the consequences which he deduces from his own show that he understands it in an equally false sense. In reasoning on the principles he lays down, he ought to have said that the state of nature, being that in which the care for our own preservation is the least prejudicial to that of others, was consequently the best calculated to promote peace, and the most suitable for mankind. He does say the exact opposite, in consequence of having improperly admitted, as a part of savage man's care for self-preservation, the gratification of a multitude of passions which are the work of society, and have made laws necessary. A bad man, he says, is a robust child. But it remains to be proved whether man in a state of nature is this robust child: and, should we grant that he is, what would he infer? Why truly, that if this man, when robust and strong, were dependent on others as he is when feeble, there is no extravagance he would not be guilty of; that he would beat his mother when she was too slow in giving him her breast; that he would strangle one of his younger brothers, if he should be troublesome to him, or bite the arm of another, if he put him to any inconvenience. But that man in the state of nature is both strong and dependent involves two contrary suppositions. Man is weak when he is dependent, and is his own master before he comes to be strong. Hobbes did not reflect that the same cause, which prevents a savage from making use of his reason, as our jurists hold, prevents him also from abusing his faculties, as Hobbes himself allows: so that it may be justly said that savages are not bad merely because they do not know what it is to be good: for it is neither the development of the understanding nor the restraint of law that hinders them from doing ill; but the peacefulness of their passions, and their ignorance of vice: *tanto plus in illis proficit vitiorum ignoratio, quam in his cognitio virtutis.*

There is another principle which has escaped Hobbes; which, having been bestowed on mankind, to moderate, on certain occasions, the impetuosity of egoism, or, before its birth, the desire of self-preservation, tempers the ardour with which he pursues his own welfare, by an innate repugnance at seeing a fellow-creature suffer. I think I need not fear contradiction in holding man to be possessed of the only natural virtue, which could not be denied him by the most violent detractor of human virtue. I am speaking of compassion, which is a disposition suitable to creatures so weak and subject to so many evils as we certainly are: by so much the more universal and useful to mankind, as it comes before any kind of reflection; and at the same time so natural, that the very brutes themselves sometimes give evident proofs of it. Not to mention the tenderness of mothers for their offspring and the perils they encounter to save them from danger, it is well known that horses show a reluctance to trample on living bodies. One animal never passes by the dead body of another of its species: there are even some which give their fellows a sort of burial; while the mournful lowing of the cattle when they enter the slaughter-house show the impressions made on them by the horrible spectacle which meets them. We find, with pleasure, the author of the Fable of the Bees obliged to own that man is a compassionate and sensible being, and laying aside his cold subtlety of style, in the example he gives, to present us with the pathetic description of a man who, from a place of confinement, is compelled to behold a wild beast tear a child from the arms of its mother, grinding its tender limbs with its murderous teeth, and tearing its palpitating entrails with its claws. What horrid agitation must not the eyewitness of such a scene experience, although he would not be personally concerned! What anxiety would he not suffer at not being able to give any assistance to the fainting mother and the dying infant!

Such is the pure emotion of nature, prior to all kinds of reflection! Such is the force of natural compassion, which the greatest depravity of morals has as yet hardly been able to destroy! [F]or we daily find at our theatres men affected, nay, shedding tears at the sufferings of a wretch who, were he in the tyrant's place, would probably even add to the torments of his enemies; like the blood-thirsty Sulla, who was so sensitive to ills he had not caused, or that Alexander of Pheros who did not dare to go and see any tragedy acted, for fear of being seen weeping with Andromache and Priam, though he could listen without emotion to the cries of all the citizens who were daily strangled at his command.

Source: Jean-Jacques Rousseau. *The Social Contract & Discourses*. Translated by G. D. H. Cole. New York: E. P. Dutton & Co., 1920, 195–198.

ADAM SMITH

From *The Theory of Moral Sentiments* (1759)

Few Enlightenment thinkers viewed human beings as passionless reasoning machines. Imagination and emotion were central to Enlightenment thought. Although the Scottish philosopher Adam Smith today principally is remembered as a founder of economics, in his own time he was highly regarded as a moral philosopher. Rather than viewing morality principally as a matter of following a "moral law," Smith rooted moral feeling in empathy, the ability of a person to vicariously feel the emotions—particularly the miseries—of another.

As we have no immediate experience of what other men feel, we can form no idea of the manner in which they are affected, but by conceiving what we ourselves should feel in the like situation. Though our brother is upon the rack, as long as we ourselves are at our ease, our senses will never inform us of what he suffers. They never did, and never can, carry us beyond our own person, and it is by the imagination only that we can form any conception of what are his sensations. Neither can that faculty help us to this any other way, than by representing to us what would be our own, if we were in his case. It is the impressions of our own senses only, not those of his, which our imaginations copy. By the imagination we place ourselves in his situation, we conceive ourselves enduring all the same torments, we enter as it were into his body, and become in some measure the same person with him, and thence form some idea of his sensations, and even feel something which, though weaker in degree, is not altogether unlike them. His agonies, when they are thus brought home to ourselves, when we have thus adopted and made them our own, begin at last to affect us, and we then tremble and shudder at the thought of what he feels. For as to be in pain or distress of any kind excites the most excessive sorrow, so to conceive or to imagine that we are in it, excites some degree of the same emotion, in proportion to the vivacity or dul[l]ness of the conception.

I.I.3

That this is the source of our fellow-feeling for the misery of others, that it is by changing places in fancy with the sufferer, that we come either to conceive or to be affected by what he feels, may be demonstrated by many obvious observations, if it should not be thought sufficiently evident of itself. When we see a stroke aimed and just ready to fall upon the leg or arm of another person, we naturally shrink and draw back our own leg or our own arm; and when it does fall, we feel it in some measure, and are hurt by it as well as the sufferer. The mob, when they are gazing at a dancer on the slack rope, naturally writhe and twist and balance their own bodies, as they see him do, and as they feel that they themselves must do if in his situation. Persons of delicate fibres and a weak constitution of body complain, that in looking on the sores and ulcers which are exposed by beggars in the streets, they are apt to feel an itching or uneasy sensation in the correspondent part of their own bodies. The horror which they conceive at the misery of those wretches affects that particular part in themselves more than any other; because that horror arises from conceiving what they themselves would suffer, if they really were the wretches whom they are looking upon, and if that particular part in themselves was actually affected in the same miserable manner. The very force of this conception is sufficient, in their feeble frames, to produce that itching or uneasy sensation complained of. Men of the most robust make, observe that in looking upon sore eyes they often feel a very sensible soreness in their own, which proceeds from the same reason; that organ being in the strongest man more delicate, than any other part of the body is in the weakest.

Source: Adam Smith, *The Theory of Moral Sentiments*. Part I, Section I. London: A. Millar. 1790.

VOLTAIRE

"Ancients and Moderns," from *Philosophical Dictionary* (1764)

The "Quarrel of the Ancients and Moderns," the debate about the relative achievements of the ancient civilizations of the Greeks and Romans and the modern civilization of 16th- and 17th-century Europe, began in the late 17th century, and continued into the 18th-century Enlightenment. Generally, the growing cultural confidence of the Enlightened put them firmly on the side of the moderns. In this article "Ancients and Moderns" from his *Philosophical Dictionary*, Voltaire champions the moderns against the English writer Sir William Temple (1628–1699), a leading "ancient." The modern achievements Voltaire praises include the French drama of the age of Louis XIV that he loved, as well as the new discoveries of the Scientific Revolution. He also shows his knowledge of the ancients. Voltaire suggests that the eloquence of the Athenian politician Demosthenes can be partially explained, not by his "ancientness," but by the democratic government of his city, contrasting it with the less free France of Cardinal Richelieu.

The great dispute between the ancients and the moderns is not yet settled; it has been on the table since the silver age succeeded the golden age. Mankind has always maintained that the good old times were much better than the present day. Nestor, in the "Iliad," wishing to insinuate himself as a wise conciliator into the minds of Achilles and Agamemnon, starts by saying to them—"I lived formerly with better men than you; no, I have never seen and I shall never see such great personages as Dryas, Cenaeus, Exadius, Polyphemus equal to the gods, etc."

Posterity has well avenged Achilles for Nestor's poor compliment. Nobody knows Dryas any longer; one has hardly heard speak of Exadius, or of Cenaeus; and as for Polyphemus equal to the gods, he has not too good a reputation, unless the possession of a big eye in one's forehead, and the eating of men raw, are to have something of the divine.

Lucretius does not hesitate to say that nature has degenerated (lib. II. v. 1159). Antiquity is full of eulogies of another more remote antiquity. Horace combats this prejudice with as much finesse as force in his beautiful Epistle to Augustus (Epist. I. liv. ii.). "Must our poems, then," he says, "be like our wines, of which the oldest are always preferred?"

The learned and ingenious Fontenelle expresses himself on this subject as follows: "The whole question of the pre-eminence between the ancients and the moderns, once it is well understood, is reduced to knowing whether the trees which formerly were in our countryside were bigger than those of to-day. In the event that they were, Homer, Plato, Demosthenes cannot be equalled in these latter centuries."

"Let us throw light on this paradox. If the ancients had more intellect than us, it is that the brains of those times were better ordered, formed of firmer or more delicate fibres, filled with more animal spirits; but in virtue of what were the brains of those times better ordered? The trees also would have been bigger and more beautiful; for if nature was then younger and more vigorous, the trees, as well as men's brains, would have been conscious of this vigour and this youth." ("Digression on the Ancients and the Moderns," vol. 4, 1742 edition.)

With the illustrious academician's permission, that is not at all the state of the question. It is not a matter of knowing whether nature has been able to produce in our day as great geniuses and as good works as those of Greek and Latin antiquity; but to know whether we have them in fact. Without a doubt it is not impossible for there to be as big oaks in the forest of Chantilli as in the forest of Dodona; but supposing that the oaks of Dodona had spoken, it would be quite clear that they had a great advantage over ours, which in all probability will never speak.

Nature is not bizarre; but it is possible that she gave the Athenians a country and a sky more suitable than Westphalia and the Limousin for forming certain geniuses. Further, it is possible that the government of Athens, by seconding the climate, put into Demosthenes' head something that the air of Clamart and La Grenouillere and the government of Cardinal de Richelieu did not put into the heads of Omer Talon and Jerome Bignon.

This dispute is therefore a question of fact. Was antiquity more fecund in great monuments of all kinds, up to the time of Plutarch, than modern centuries have been from the century of the Medicis up to Louis XIV, inclusive?

The Chinese, more than two hundred years before our era, constructed that great wall which was not able to save them from the invasion of the Tartars. The Egyptians, three thousand years before, had overloaded the earth with their astonishing pyramids, which had a base of about ninety thousand square feet. Nobody doubts that, if one wished to undertake to-day these useless works, one could easily succeed by a lavish expenditure of money. The great wall of China is a monument to fear; the pyramids are monuments to vanity and superstition. Both bear witness to a great patience in the peoples, but to no superior genius. Neither the Chinese nor the Egyptians would have been able to make even a statue such as those which our sculptors form to-day.

The chevalier Temple, who has made it his business to disparage all the moderns, claims that in architecture they have nothing comparable to the temples of Greece and Rome: but, for all that he is English, he must agree that the Church of St. Peter is incomparably more beautiful than the Capitol was.

It is curious with what assurance he maintains that there is nothing new in our astronomy, nothing in the knowledge of the human body, unless perhaps, he says, the circulation of the blood. Love of his own opinion, founded on his vast self-esteem, makes him forget the discovery of the satellites of Jupiter, of the five moons and the ring of Saturn, of the rotation of the sun on its axis, of the calculated position of three thousand stars, of the laws given by Kepler and

Newton for the heavenly orbs, of the causes of the precession of the equinoxes, and of a hundred other pieces of knowledge of which the ancients did not suspect even the possibility.

The discoveries in anatomy are as great in number. A new universe in little, discovered by the microscope, was counted for nothing by the chevalier Temple; he closed his eyes to the marvels of his contemporaries, and opened them only to admire ancient ignorance.

He goes so far as to pity us for having nothing left of the magic of the Indians, the Chaldeans, the Egyptians; and by this magic he understands a profound knowledge of nature, whereby they produced miracles: but he does not cite one miracle, because in fact there never were any. "What has become," he asks, "of the charms of that music which so often enchanted man and beast, the fishes, the birds, the snakes, and changed their nature?"

This enemy of his century really believes the fable of Orpheus, and has not apparently heard either the beautiful music of Italy, or even that of France, which in truth does not charm snakes, but does charm the ears of connoisseurs.

What is still more strange is that, having all his life cultivated belles-lettres, he does not reason better about our good authors than about our philosophers. He looks on Rabelais as a great man. He cites the "Amours des Gaules" as one of our best works. He was, however, a scholar, a courtier, a man of much wit, an ambassador, a man who had reflected profoundly on all he had seen. He possessed great knowledge: a prejudice sufficed to spoil all this merit.

There are beauties in Euripides, and in Sophocles still more; but they have many more defects. One dares say that the beautiful scenes of Corneille and the touching tragedies of Racine surpass the tragedies of Sophocles and Euripides as much as these two Greeks surpass Thespis. Racine was quite conscious of his great superiority over Euripides; but he praised the Greek poet in order to humiliate Perrault.

Molière, in his good pieces, is as superior to the pure but cold Terence, and to the droll Aristophanes, as to Dancourt the buffoon.

There are therefore spheres in which the moderns are far superior to the ancients, and others, very few in number, in which we are their inferiors. It is to this that the whole dispute is reduced.

Source: *Voltaire's Philosophical Dictionary*. New York: Carlton House, n.d., 17–20.

CESARE BECCARIA

From *On Crimes and Punishments* (1764)

Many Enlightenment thinkers, although by no means all, believed that society was improving and becoming more humane in their own time. This was connected to an idea that went back to the English philosopher Francis Bacon, that "modern times" essentially was defined by the introduction of new technologies, of which one of the most important was printing. Printing obviously made possible the creation of a market for books and periodicals on which many Enlightenment writers were financially dependent, but it had many other benefits as well. Here Cesare Beccaria, the Italian jurist and legal reformer, uses the fact that the law in his own time existed in an unchangeable, printed record to argue that the invention of printing has been essential in making the public better informed and more virtuous, along with having many positive effects on society as a whole.

Hence we see the use of printing, which alone makes the public, and not a few individuals, the guardians and defenders of the laws. It is this art which by diffusing literature, has gradually dissipated the gloomy spirit of cabal and intrigue. To this art it is owing that the atrocious crimes of our ancestors, who were alternately slaves and tyrants, are become less frequent. Those who are acquainted with the history of the two or three last centuries may observe, how from the lap of luxury and effeminacy have sprung the most tender virtues, humanity, benevolence, and toleration of human errors. They may contemplate the effects of what was so improperly called ancient simplicity and good faith; humanity groaning under implacable superstition, the avarice and ambition of a few staining with human blood the drones and palaces of kings, secret treasons and public massacres, every noble a tyrant over the people, and the ministers of the gospel of Christ bathing their hands in blood in the name of the God of all mercy. We may talk as we please of the corruption and degeneracy of the present age, but happily we see no such horrid examples of cruelty and oppression.

Source: Cesare Beccaria, *An Essay on Crimes and Punishments*. London: F. Newbery, 1769, 19–21. (Anonymous translation, published in Philadelphia in 1809. Via Google books.)

CATHERINE THE GREAT

From *Instructions to the Legislative Commission* (1767)

The Russian code of law current at the beginning of Tsarina Catherine's reign dated from 1649, well before the reforms of Tsar Peter I "the Great," and was increasingly archaic in a developing and westernizing Russia. Catherine planned a great reform of Russian law to bring it into closer harmony with modern European codes. The *Instructions to the Commission* that would carry out the reforms were aimed at a European audience as well as a Russian one. They were translated into numerous European languages including English, French, German, and Latin. They helped raise Catherine's presence and legitimacy in Europe as a reforming monarch. Catherine drew on her wide reading and familiarity with Enlightenment writers, particularly Montesquieu and Beccaria.

The Instructions of Catherine II to the Legislative Commission of 1767

The Instructions to the Commissioners for Composing a New Code of Laws

1. The Christian Law teaches us to do mutual Good to one another, as much as possibly we can.

2. Laying this down as a fundamental Rule prescribed by that Religion, which has taken, or ought to take Root in the Hearts of the whole People; we cannot but suppose that every honest Man in the Community is, or will be, desirous of seeing his native Country at the very Summit of Happiness, Glory, Safety, and Tranquillity.

3. And that every Individual Citizen in particular must wish to see himself protected by Laws, which should not distress him in his Circumstances, but, on the Contrary, should defend him from all Attempts of others that are repugnant to this fundamental Rule.

4. In order therefore to proceed to a speedy Execution of what We expect from such a general Wish, We, fixing the Foundation upon the above first-mentioned Rule, ought to begin with an Inquiry into the natural Situation of this Empire.

5. For those Laws have the greatest Conformity with Nature, whose particular Regulations are best adapted to the Situation and Circumstances of the People for whom they are instituted. This natural Situation is described in the three following Chapters.

Chapter I

6. Russia is a European State.

7. This is clearly demonstrated by the following Observations: The Alterations which Peter the Great undertook in Russia succeeded with the greater Ease, because the Manners, which prevailed at that Time, and had been introduced amongst us by a Mixture of different Nations, and the Conquest of foreign Territories, were quite unsuitable to the Climate. Peter the First, by introducing the Manners and Customs of Europe among the European People in his Dominions, found at that Time such Means as even he himself was not sanguine enough to expect.

Chapter II

8. The Possessions of the Russian Empire extend upon the terrestrial Globe to 32 Degrees of Latitude, and to 165 of Longitude.

9. The Sovereign is absolute; for there is no other authority but that which centers in his single Person that can act with a Vigour proportionate to the Extent of such a vast Dominion.

10. The Extent of the Dominion requires an absolute Power to be vested in that Person who rules over it. It is expedient so to be that the quick Dispatch of Affairs, sent from distant Parts, might make ample Amends for the Delay occasioned by the great Distance of the Places.

11. Every other Form of Government whatsoever would not only have been prejudicial to Russia, but would even have proved its entire Ruin.

13. What is the true End of Monarchy? Not to deprive People of their natural Liberty; but to correct their Actions, in order to attain the supreme Good.

14. The Form of Government, therefore, which best attains this End, and at the same Time sets less Bounds than others to natural Liberty, is that which coincides with the Views and Purposes of rational Creatures, and answers the End, upon which we ought to fix a steadfast Eye in the Regulations of civil Polity.

15. The Intention and the End of Monarchy is the Glory of the Citizens, of the State, and of the Sovereign.

16. But, from this Glory, a Sense of Liberty arises in a People governed by a Monarch; which may produce in these States as much Energy in transacting the most important Affairs, and may contribute as much to the Happiness of the Subjects, as even Liberty itself.

Chapter III

17. Of the Safety of the Institutions of Monarchy.

18. The intermediate Powers, subordinate to, and depending upon the supreme Power, form the essential Part of monarchical Government.

19. I have said, that the intermediate Powers, subordinate and depending, proceed from the supreme Power, as in the very Nature of the Thing the Sovereign is the Source of all imperial and civil Power.

20. The Laws, which form the Foundation of the State, send out certain Courts of judicature, through which, as through smaller Streams, the Power of the Government is poured out, and diffused.

21. The Laws allow these Courts of judicature to remonstrate, that such or such an Injunction is unconstitutional, and prejudicial, obscure, and impossible to be carried into Execution; and direct, beforehand, to which Injunction one ought to pay Obedience, and in what Manner one ought to conform to it. These Laws undoubtedly constitute the firm and immoveable Basis of every State.

Source: Documents of Catherine the Great: The Correspondence with Voltaire and the Instruction of 1767 in the English Text of 1768. Translated by W. F. Reddaway. Cambridge: Cambridge University Press, 1931, 215–217. Reprinted with the permission of Cambridge University Press.

EDWARD GIBBON

From *The Decline and Fall of the Roman Empire* (1776)

As a champion of Enlightenment, Edward Gibbon despised religious persecution; he also had little respect for Christianity. This meant that when Christians were persecuted by non-Christians, his feelings often were divided.

When his *The Decline and Fall of the Roman Empire* reached the discussion of the Roman persecution of the early Christians, he condemned the pagan persecutors, but asserted their superiority to subsequent Christian persecutors, such as the Holy Roman Emperor Charles V, or the King of France Louis XIV. Gibbon argues that the persecutions of the Christians were mild as compared to subsequent persecutions by Christians.

History, which undertakes to record the transactions of the past, for the instruction of future ages, would ill deserve that honorable office, if she condescended to plead the cause of tyrants, or to justify the maxims of persecution. It must, however, be acknowledged, that the conduct of the emperors who appeared the least favorable to the primitive church, is by no means so criminal as that of modern sovereigns, who have employed the arm of violence and terror against the religious opinions of any part of their subjects. From their reflections, or even from their own feelings, a Charles V or a Lewis XIV might have acquired a just knowledge of the rights of conscience, of the obligation of faith, and of the innocence of error. But the princes and magistrates of ancient Rome were strangers to those principles which inspired and authorized the inflexible obstinacy of the Christians in the cause of truth, nor could they themselves discover in their own breasts any motive which would have prompted them to refuse a legal, and as it were a natural, submission to the sacred institutions of their country. The same reason which contributes to alleviate the guilt, must have tended to abate the vigor, of their persecutions. As they were actuated, not by the furious zeal of bigots, but by the temperate policy of legislators, contempt must often have relaxed, and humanity must frequently have suspended, the execution of those laws which they enacted against the humble and obscure followers of Christ. From the general view of their character and motives we might naturally conclude: I. That a considerable time elapsed before they considered the new sectaries as an object deserving of the attention of government. II. That in the conviction of any of their subjects who were accused of so very singular a crime, they proceeded with caution and reluctance. III. That they were moderate in the use of punishments; and, IV. That the afflicted church enjoyed many intervals of peace and tranquility.

Source: Edward Gibbon. *The History of the Decline and Fall of the Roman Empire*, Vol II. London: Oxford University Press, 1907, 93–94.

THE DECLARATION OF INDEPENDENCE (1776)

The American Declaration of Independence draws from a number of traditions and discourses, including the Enlightenment. The "Committee of Five" which drafted the Declaration for submission to the Continental Congress included some of America's most Enlightened minds, such as Thomas Jefferson, the principal author, Benjamin Franklin, and John Adams. Enlightenment themes of the document include the appeal to "Nature's God" and the respect for the "opinions of mankind." The assertion of a right to change the government when it grew tyrannical rather than passively submitting to it was also consistent with the Enlightenment.

IN CONGRESS, July 4, 1776.

The unanimous Declaration of the thirteen united States of America,

When in the Course of human events, it becomes necessary for one people to dissolve the political bands which have connected them with another, and to assume among the powers of the earth, the separate and equal station to which the Laws of Nature and of Nature's God entitle them, a decent respect to the opinions of mankind requires that they should declare the causes which impel them to the separation.

We hold these truths to be self-evident, that all men are created equal, that they are endowed by their Creator with certain unalienable Rights, that among these are Life, Liberty and the pursuit of Happiness.—That to secure these rights, Governments are instituted among Men, deriving their just powers from the consent of the governed,—That whenever any Form of Government becomes destructive of these ends, it is the Right of the People to alter or to abolish it, and to institute new Government, laying its foundation on such principles and organizing its powers in such form, as to them shall seem most likely to effect their Safety and Happiness. Prudence, indeed, will dictate that Governments long established should not be changed for light and transient causes; and accordingly all experience hath shewn, that mankind are more disposed to suffer, while evils are sufferable, than to right themselves by abolishing the forms to which they are accustomed. But when a long train of abuses and usurpations, pursuing invariably the same Object evinces a design to reduce them under absolute Despotism, it is their right, it is their duty, to throw off such Government, and to provide new Guards for their future security.—Such has been the patient sufferance of these Colonies; and such is now the necessity which constrains them to alter their former Systems of Government. The history of the present King of Great Britain is a history of repeated injuries and usurpations, all having in direct object the establishment of an absolute Tyranny over these States. To prove this, let Facts be submitted to a candid world.

He has refused his Assent to Laws, the most wholesome and necessary for the public good.

He has forbidden his Governors to pass Laws of immediate and pressing importance, unless suspended in their operation till his Assent should be obtained; and when so suspended, he has utterly neglected to attend to them.

He has refused to pass other Laws for the accommodation of large districts of people, unless those people would relinquish the right of Representation in the Legislature, a right inestimable to them and formidable to tyrants only.

He has called together legislative bodies at places unusual, uncomfortable, and distant from the depository of their public Records, for the sole purpose of fatiguing them into compliance with his measures.

He has dissolved Representative Houses repeatedly, for opposing with manly firmness his invasions on the rights of the people.

He has refused for a long time, after such dissolutions, to cause others to be elected; whereby the Legislative powers, incapable of Annihilation, have returned to the People at large for their exercise; the State remaining in the mean time exposed to all the dangers of invasion from without, and convulsions within.

He has endeavoured to prevent the population of these States; for that purpose obstructing the Laws for Naturalization of Foreigners; refusing to pass others to encourage their migrations hither, and raising the conditions of new Appropriations of Lands.

He has obstructed the Administration of Justice, by refusing his Assent to Laws for establishing Judiciary powers.

He has made Judges dependent on his Will alone, for the tenure of their offices, and the amount and payment of their salaries.

He has erected a multitude of New Offices, and sent hither swarms of Officers to harass our people, and eat out their substance.

He has kept among us, in times of peace, Standing Armies without the Consent of our legislatures.

He has affected to render the Military independent of and superior to the Civil power.

He has combined with others to subject us to a jurisdiction foreign to our constitution, and unacknowledged by our laws; giving his Assent to their Acts of pretended Legislation:

For Quartering large bodies of armed troops among us:

For protecting them, by a mock Trial, from punishment for any Murders which they should commit on the Inhabitants of these States:

For cutting off our Trade with all parts of the world:

For imposing Taxes on us without our Consent:

For depriving us in many cases, of the benefits of Trial by Jury:

For transporting us beyond Seas to be tried for pretended offences

For abolishing the free System of English Laws in a neighbouring Province, establishing therein an Arbitrary government, and enlarging its Boundaries so as to render it at once an example and fit instrument for introducing the same absolute rule into these Colonies:

For taking away our Charters, abolishing our most valuable Laws, and altering fundamentally the Forms of our Governments:

For suspending our own Legislatures, and declaring themselves invested with power to legislate for us in all cases whatsoever.

He has abdicated Government here, by declaring us out of his Protection and waging War against us.

He has plundered our seas, ravaged our Coasts, burnt our towns, and destroyed the lives of our people.

He is at this time transporting large Armies of foreign Mercenaries to compleat the works of death, desolation and tyranny, already begun with circumstances of Cruelty & perfidy scarcely paralleled in the most barbarous ages, and totally unworthy the Head of a civilized nation.

He has constrained our fellow Citizens taken Captive on the high Seas to bear Arms against their Country, to become the executioners of their friends and Brethren, or to fall themselves by their Hands.

He has excited domestic insurrections amongst us, and has endeavoured to bring on the inhabitants of our frontiers, the merciless Indian Savages, whose known rule of warfare, is an undistinguished destruction of all ages, sexes and conditions.

In every stage of these Oppressions We have Petitioned for Redress in the most humble terms: Our repeated Petitions have been answered only by repeated injury. A Prince whose character is thus marked by every act which may define a Tyrant, is unfit to be the ruler of a free people.

Nor have We been wanting in attentions to our British brethren. We have warned them from time to time of attempts by their legislature to extend an unwarrantable jurisdiction over us. We have reminded them of the circumstances of our emigration and settlement here. We have appealed to their native justice and magnanimity, and we have conjured them by the ties of our common kindred to disavow these usurpations, which, would inevitably interrupt our connections and correspondence. They too have been deaf to the voice of justice and of consanguinity. We must, therefore, acquiesce in the necessity, which denounces our Separation, and hold them, as we hold the rest of mankind, Enemies in War, in Peace Friends.

We, therefore, the Representatives of the United States of America, in General Congress, Assembled, appealing to the Supreme Judge of the world for the rectitude of our intentions, do, in the Name, and by Authority of the good People of these Colonies, solemnly publish and declare, That these United Colonies are, and of Right ought to be Free and Independent States; that they are Absolved from all Allegiance to the British Crown, and that all political connection between them and the State of Great Britain, is and ought to be totally dissolved; and that as Free and Independent States, they have full Power to levy War, conclude Peace, contract Alliances, establish Commerce, and to do all other Acts and Things which Independent States may of right do. And for the support of this Declaration, with a firm reliance on the protection of divine Providence, we mutually pledge to each other our Lives, our Fortunes and our sacred Honor.

Source: U.S. National Archives.

IMMANUEL KANT

From *What Is Enlightenment?* (1784)

This famous essay by German philosopher Immanuel Kant originally was published in the *Berlin Monthly*, a periodical of the Wednesday Society, a leading Enlightened group in Prussia. It was part of a group of essays by German thinkers on the topic of Enlightenment. In it, Kant defines Enlightenment as the courage to think freely for oneself. He deals with the question of how widespread we can expect Enlightenment to be and how it would particularly affect clergymen, who were a major portion of the intelligentsia in Berlin as elsewhere in Europe.

Enlightenment is man's release from his self-incurred tutelage. Tutelage is man's inability to make use of his understanding without direction from another. Self-incurred is this tutelage when its cause lies not in lack of reason but in lack of resolution and courage to use it without direction from another. *Sapere aude!* "Have courage to use your own reason!"—that is the motto of enlightenment.

Laziness and cowardice are the reasons why so great a portion of mankind, after nature has long since discharged them from external direction (*naturaliter maiorennes*), nevertheless remains under lifelong tutelage, and why it is so easy for others to set themselves up as their guardians. It is so easy not to be of age. If I have a book which understands for me, a pastor who has a conscience for me, a physician who decides my diet, and so forth, I need not trouble myself. I need not think, if I can only pay—others will easily undertake the irksome work for me.

That the step to competence is held to be very dangerous by the far greater portion of mankind (and by the entire fair sex)—quite apart from its being arduous is seen to by those guardians who have so kindly assumed superintendence over them. After the guardians have first made their domestic cattle dumb and have made sure that these placid creatures will not dare take a single step without the harness of the cart to which they are tethered, the guardians then show them the danger which threatens if they try to go alone. Actually, however, this danger is not so great, for by falling a few times they would finally learn to walk alone. But an example of this failure makes them timid and ordinarily frightens them away from all further trials.

For any single individual to work himself out of the life under tutelage which has become almost his nature is very difficult. He has come to be fond of his state, and he is for the present really incapable of making use of his reason, for no one has ever let him try it out. Statutes and formulas, those mechanical tools of the rational employment or rather misemployment of his natural gifts, are the fetters of an everlasting tutelage. Whoever throws them off makes only an uncertain leap over the narrowest ditch because he is not accustomed to that kind of free motion. Therefore, there are few who have succeeded by their own exercise of mind both in freeing themselves from incompetence and in achieving a steady pace.

But that the public should enlighten itself is more possible; indeed, if only freedom is granted enlightenment is almost sure to follow. For there will always be some independent thinkers, even among the established guardians of the great masses, who, after throwing off the yoke of tutelage from their own shoulders, will disseminate the spirit of the rational appreciation of both their own worth and every man's vocation for thinking for himself. But be it noted that the public, which has first been brought under this yoke by their guardians, forces the guardians themselves to remain bound when it is incited to do so by some of the guardians who are themselves capable of some enlightenment—so harmful is it to implant prejudices, for they later take vengeance on their cultivators or on their descendants. Thus the public can only slowly attain enlightenment. Perhaps a fall of personal despotism or of avaricious or tyrannical oppression may be accomplished by revolution, but never a true reform in ways of thinking. Farther, new prejudices will serve as well as old ones to harness the great unthinking masses.

For this enlightenment, however, nothing is required but freedom, and indeed the most harmless among all the things to which this term can properly be applied. It is the freedom to make public use of one's reason at every point. But I hear on all sides, "Do not argue!" The Officer says: "Do not argue but drill!" The tax collector: "Do not argue but pay!" The cleric: "Do not argue but believe!" Only one prince in the world says, "Argue as much as you will, and about what you will, but obey!" Everywhere there is restriction on freedom.

Which restriction is an obstacle to enlightenment, and which is not an obstacle but a promoter of it? I answer: The public use of one's reason must always be free, and it alone can bring about enlightenment among men. The private use of reason, on the other hand, may often be very narrowly restricted without particularly hindering the progress of enlightenment. By the public use of one's reason I understand the use which a person makes of it as a scholar before the reading public. Private use I call that which one may make of it in a particular civil post or office which is entrusted to him. Many affairs which are conducted in the interest of the community require a certain mechanism through which some members of the community must passively conduct themselves with an artificial unanimity, so that the government may direct them to public ends, or at least prevent them from destroying those ends. Here argument is certainly not allowed—one must obey. But so far as a part of the mechanism regards himself at the same time as a member of the whole community or of a society of world citizens, and thus in the role of a scholar who addresses the public (in the proper sense of the word) through his writings, he certainly can argue without hurting the affairs for which he is in part responsible as a passive member. Thus it would be ruinous for an officer in service to debate about the suitability or utility of a command given to him by his superior; he must obey. But the right to make remarks on errors in the military service and to lay them before the public for judgment cannot equitably be refused him as a scholar. The citizen cannot refuse to pay the taxes imposed on him; indeed, an impudent complaint at those levied on him can be punished as a scandal (as it could occasion general refractoriness). But the same person nevertheless does not act contrary to his duty as a citizen, when, as a scholar, he publicly expresses his thoughts on the inappropriateness or even the injustices of these levies, Similarly a clergyman is obligated to make his sermon to his pupils in catechism and his congregation conform to the symbol of the church which he serves, for he has been accepted on this condition. But as a scholar he has complete freedom, even the calling, to communicate to the public all his carefully tested and well-meaning thoughts on that which is erroneous in the symbol and to make suggestions for the better organization of the religious body and church. In doing this there is nothing that could be laid as a burden on his conscience. For what he teaches as a consequence of his office as a representative of the church, this he considers something about which he has not freedom to teach according to his own lights; it is something which he is appointed to propound at the dictation of and in the name of another. He will say, "Our church teaches this or that; those are the proofs which it adduces." He thus extracts all practical uses for his congregation from statutes to which he himself would not subscribe with full conviction but to the enunciation of which he can very well pledge himself because it is not impossible that truth lies hidden in them, and, in any case, there is at least nothing in them contradictory to inner religion. For if he believed he had found such in them, he could not conscientiously discharge the duties of his office; he would have to give it up. The use, therefore, which an appointed teacher makes of his reason before his congregation is merely private, because this congregation is only a domestic one (even if it be a large gathering); with respect to it, as a priest, he is not free, nor can he be free, because he carries out the orders of another. But as a scholar, whose writings speak to his public, the world, the clergyman in the public use of his reason enjoys an unlimited freedom to use his own reason to speak in his own person. That the guardian of the people (in spiritual things) should themselves be incompetent is an absurdity which amounts to the eternalization of absurdities.

Source: Beck, Lewis White, *Immanuel Kant: Foundations of the Metaphysics of Morals*, 2nd ed. New York: Pearson Education, Inc., 1990.

THOMAS PAINE

From *The Age of Reason,* Part II (1795)

Thomas Paine's *The Age of Reason Part I*, published in 1794, had been received with scorn by many defenders of Christianity, although he viewed it as also directed against the "atheism" of the French Revolutionaries who had imprisoned him. In *Part II*, Paine responds to his Christian critics with a thoroughgoing attack on the morality, veracity, and authority of the Bible, focusing on the Old Testament. *Part III*, directed at the Biblical account of Jesus Christ, would not be published until 1807. Although few of Paine's arguments were original, the effectiveness of his mockery would be particularly noted by both his enemies and allies.

It has often been said that any thing may be proved from the Bible; but before any thing can be admitted as proved by Bible, the Bible itself must be proved to be true; for if the Bible be not true, or the truth of it be doubtful, it ceases to have authority, and cannot be admitted as proof of any thing.

It has been the practice of all Christian commentators on the Bible, and of all Christian priests and preachers, to impose the Bible on the world as a mass of truth, and as the word of God; they have disputed and wrangled, and have anathematized each other about the supposeable meaning of particular parts and passages therein; one has said and insisted that such a passage meant such a thing, another that it meant directly the contrary, and a third, that it meant neither one nor the other, but something different from both; and this they have called understanding the Bible.

It has happened, that all the answers that I have seen to the former part of "The Age of Reason" have been written by priests: and these pious men, like their predecessors, contend and wrangle, and understand the Bible; each understands it differently, but each understands it best; and they have agreed in nothing but in telling their readers that Thomas Paine understands it not.

Now instead of wasting their time, and heating themselves in fractious disputations about doctrinal points drawn from the Bible, these men ought to know, and if they do not it is civility to inform them, that the first thing to be understood is, whether there is sufficient authority for believing the Bible to be the word of God, or whether there is not?

There are matters in that book, said to be done by the express command of God, that are as shocking to humanity, and to every idea we have of moral justice, as any thing done by Robespierre, by Carrier, by Joseph le Bon, in France, by the English government in the East Indies, or by any other assassin in modern times. When we read in the books ascribed to Moses, Joshua, etc., that they (the Israelites) came by stealth upon whole nations of people, who, as the history itself shews, had given them no offence; that they put all those nations to the sword; that they spared neither age nor infancy; that they utterly destroyed men, women and children; that they left not a soul to breathe; expressions that are repeated over and over again in those books, and that too with exulting ferocity; are we sure these things are facts? Are we sure that the Creator of man commissioned those things to be done? Are we sure that the books that tell us so were written by his authority?

It is not the antiquity of a tale that is an evidence of its truth; on the contrary, it is a symptom of its being fabulous; for the more ancient any history pretends to be, the more it has the resemblance of a fable. The origin of every nation is buried in fabulous tradition, and that of the Jews is as much to be suspected as any other.

To charge the commission of things upon the Almighty, which in their own nature, and by every rule of moral justice, are crimes, as all assassination is, and more especially the assassination of infants, is a matter of serious concern. The Bible tells us, that those assassinations were done by the express command of God. To believe therefore the Bible to be true, we must unbelieve all our belief in the moral justice of God; for wherein could crying or smiling infants offend? And to read the Bible without horror, we must undo every thing that is tender, sympathising, and benevolent in the heart of man. Speaking for myself, if I had no other evidence that the Bible is fabulous, than the sacrifice I must make to believe it to be true, that alone would be sufficient to determine my choice.

But in addition to all the moral evidence against the Bible, I will, in the progress of this work, produce such other evidence as even a priest cannot deny; and show, from that evidence, that the Bible is not entitled to credit, as being the word of God.

But, before I proceed to this examination, I will show wherein the Bible differs from all other ancient writings with respect to the nature of the evidence necessary to establish its authenticity; and this is the more proper to be done, because the advocates of the Bible, in their answers to the former part of "The Age of Reason," undertake to say, and they put some stress thereon, that the authenticity of the Bible is as well established as that of any other ancient book: as if our belief of the one could become any rule for our belief of the other.

I know, however, but of one ancient book that authoritatively challenges universal consent and belief, and that is Euclid's *Elements of Geometry* [Euclid, according to chronological history, lived three hundred years before Christ, and about one hundred before Archimedes; he was of the city of Alexandria, in Egypt.—Author.]; and the reason is, because it is a book of self-evident demonstration, entirely independent of its author, and of every thing relating to time, place, and circumstance. The matters contained in that book would have the same authority they now have, had they been written by any other person, or had the work been anonymous, or had the author never been known; for the identical certainty of who was the author makes no part of our belief of the matters contained in the book. But it is quite otherwise with respect to the books ascribed to Moses, to Joshua, to Samuel, etc.: those are books of testimony, and they testify of things naturally incredible; and therefore the whole of our belief, as to the authenticity of those books, rests, in the first place, upon the certainty that they were written by Moses, Joshua, and Samuel; secondly, upon the credit we give to their testimony. We may believe the first, that is, may believe the certainty of the authorship, and yet not the testimony; in the same manner that we may believe that a certain person gave evidence upon a case, and yet not believe the evidence that he gave. But if it should be found that the books ascribed to Moses, Joshua, and Samuel, were not written by

Moses, Joshua, and Samuel, every part of the authority and authenticity of those books is gone at once; for there can be no such thing as forged or invented testimony; neither can there be anonymous testimony, more especially as to things naturally incredible; such as that of talking with God face to face, or that of the sun and moon standing still at the command of a man.

Source: Thomas Paine, *The Age of Reason*. London: Holyoake & Co., 1861, 33–34.

Key Questions

QUESTION 1: WAS THERE AN ENLIGHTENMENT FOR WOMEN?

The experiences of men and women in 18th-century Europe were vastly different. Men virtually monopolized political and religious power, and also controlled most of the wealth of society. They received vastly superior educations—at least among the European elite—wrote and published most of the books, and monopolized most intellectual institutions.

Given the overwhelming power of men, did the Enlightenment change things for women? Women played a central role in some Enlightenments, particularly the French, as salon hostesses; but much of what they did in salons was facilitate the careers and ideas of men rather than function as philosophers in their own right. A few Enlightenment champions, including women such as Mary Wollstonecraft and men such as the Marquis de Condorcet, did advocate a broadening of women's choices and public roles, but others—such as Jean-Jacques Rousseau—took exactly the opposite tack, holding that women already were too powerful in the public sphere and should devote their energies to their homes and families. The French Revolution initially incorporated elements of both approaches, but moved steadily in the direction of differentiating the male "public sphere" from which women were excluded, and the "female sphere" of home and family. The longtime Enlightenment project of the reform of French law culminated in the Napoleonic Code, which in many ways was a step backwards for women, and one that affected many countries in addition to France.

The movements for the legal emancipation and political and social equality for women that emerged in the 19th century had a complex relationship with the Enlightenment. Although some supporters of women put themselves in the tradition of the Enlightenment, others were at best suspicious of it. Today, the equality of men and women is sometimes identified as an "Enlightenment value" but this does not usually refer to the historical Enlightenment.

During the Enlightenment, women's experiences were diverse. Martin Manning concentrates on the anticlerical and anti-authoritarian values of the Enlightenment and the women who moved in the elite Enlightenment circles. Manning finds that the Enlightenment contributed to women's emancipation. Matthew Quest takes a broader look, including women not usually viewed as part of the Enlightenment narrative. Quest finds that the Enlightenment marginalized women's voices and sometimes appropriated their knowledge.

ANSWER: MARTIN J. MANNING, "YES, WOMEN PLAYED A CENTRAL ROLE IN THE ENLIGHTENMENT"

The importance of women to the Enlightenment highlights their roles in 18th century culture, particularly in post-French Revolution France which radicalized the role of women more than any other European country. Several developments helped create public debate about women and their intellectual potential, including a marked increase in literacy for both men and women; the establishment of the salon; the increasing growth of the print industry and the professionalization of women writers; more educational opportunities for girls; and the beginning of female activism in charitable works, in political action, and philosophical and scientific debates.

One of the Enlightenment's most important achievements was to radicalize thinking from contemporary religious ideology that worked against women's intellectual or political empowerment—the traditional female roles were wife, mother, daughter, and sister, all under male domination. For women who repudiated marriage or failed to make a suitable match in Roman Catholic countries, convent life was an option, but this life actually could be intellectually stimulating and publicly useful. Protestantism in England and in the United Provinces of the Netherlands promoted equality and mutual affection in marriage along with women's involvement in preaching and in good works. What little power women exerted—such as controlling family estates or working in certain commercial enterprises—and the economic independence it gave them often was severely limited to high-ranking women. On the whole, though, little thought was given to the idea of equality among the sexes. Major figures of the Enlightenment, such as Jean-Jacques Rousseau, the Baron de Montesquieu, and Immanuel Kant conceived of women as morally weak beings who lacked inventive imagination or genius, and were submissive. Others, like the Marquis de Condorcet, went further in championing women. He insisted that women were equal to men and just as capable as men in benefiting from education and political involvement. He endorsed women's education and their right to full citizenship.

According to Sarah Knott and Barbara Taylor, in *Women, Gender, and Enlightenment* (2005), historians long excluded women from any serious study of the Enlightenment. Modern research, however, now shows that woman and gender were key categories of Enlightenment thought, and that women themselves—as scientists and as salonnieres, bluestockings and governesses, feminists and novelists—contributed much to enlightened intellectual culture. Carla Hesse, in *The Other Enlightenment: How French Women Became Modern* (2001), notes that the French Revolution created a new cultural world that freed women from patriarchal censorship, even though it failed to grant them legal equality. Women burst into print in unprecedented numbers and became active participants in the great political, ethical, and aesthetic debates that gave birth to the individual as a self-creating, self-determining agent. Beginning with the Enlightenment, French women began to use writing to create themselves as modern individuals, from the marketplace fishwives (and their *poissarde*, or fishwives' speech) to the salon hostesses whose eloquence shaped many aspects of French culture.

Modern feminist theory originated in the Enlightenment and generally is associated with Mary Wollstonecraft (1759–1797) and her writings on feminism. Her biting attack on Edmund Burke's *Reflections on the Revolution in France* (1790), and her book, *A Vindication of the Rights of Woman* (1792), made her a central figure in the articulation of feminism. Wollstonecraft's first book, *Thoughts on the Education of Daughters* (1787), was a collection of essays on education targeting parents detailing the role of education in enabling women to overcome their humiliating domestic situation.

Wollstonecraft was the only woman to contribute regularly to the periodical, *Analytical Review*, and the only woman invited every week to attend the dinners that publisher Joseph Johnson gave for "his authors" and his circle of friends. Wollstonecraft's, *A Vindication of the Rights of Men: In a Letter to the Right Honourable Edmund Burke: Occasioned By His Reflections on the Revolution in France* (1790) responded to the changing education of—and literature for—women in the later decades of the 18th century.

The setting in which Enlightenment women most often were comfortable was the literary salon, defined as a regular intellectual gathering that is led by a woman. Salons primarily were located in France, Germany, and Italy. They were hosted by wealthy, literary women who influenced matters of taste and pleasure, but primarily served to facilitate discussions of philosophical, literary, and scientific issues. Salon hostesses invited the guests and proposed the subjects to be discussed, such as, for example, a reading of Voltaire's *L'orpelin de Chine* at the salon of Madame Geoffrin. Dena Goodman, in *The Republic of Letters: A Cultural History of the French Enlightenment* (1994), argues that women were essential to the Enlightenment in their role as salonnières. Salons "became the civil working spaces of the project of Enlightenment" (Goodman at 53) and salonnières, were "the legitimate governors of [the] potentially unruly discourse" (Goodman at 53) that took place within. In Germany, many salons took place in courts and were hosted by royal women, such as Queen Sophia Dorothea of Prussia, the mother of Frederick the Great. Queen Sophia hosted salons at her small private castle, Monbijou. Another court salon was led by Caroline von Hessen-Darmstadt at her palace in Darmstadt. The German-Jewish salon hostess, Rahel Levin (1771–1833), was married to the writer Kark August Varnhagen von Ense. Levin's writings were collected by her husband and published as, *Rahel: Ein Buch des Andenkens fur ihre Freunde* [*Rahel: A Book of Memories for Her Friends*] (Berlin, 1834).

In these settings, women were as vital to the Enlightenment as were men, but their roles generally were different. Often writers themselves, hostesses encouraged homage from prominent men. In France, women of letters such as Mademoiselle de Scudery and Madame de Sevigne aired their views on female education. In England, Elizabeth Montagu hosted what became known as the "Bluestocking Circle." This sober group of intellectuals included Hannah More, a prolific activist who wrote extensively on numerous topics and who campaigned on behalf of the miners, the uneducated poor, prostitutes, and slaves.

Probably the best known French Enlightenment woman was Émilie Le Tonnelier de Breteuil, marquise du Châtelet. Châtelet was a French mathematician, physicist, and author, whose achievement is considered to be her translation and commentary on Isaac Newton's work, *Principia Mathematica*. In her first independent work—the preface to her translation of Bernard Mandeville's *Fable of the Bees* (2d ed., 1725), du Châtelet argued strongly for women's education, particularly arguing in favor of providing women with the same challenging secondary education as was available for young men in the French collèges. In 1733, she met Voltaire—one of the most important figures of the Enlightenment. Throughout Châtelet and Voltaire's tumultuous 15-year relationship, they conducted scientific experiments; entertained leading thinkers; and developed radical ideas about topics including the nature of free will, the subordination of women, and the separation of church and state.

Women writers came into their own during the Enlightenment as publishing became central to the public sphere. For the first time, women were able to earn a respectable living entirely by writing. Between 1750 and 1799, there were approximately 580 English women-penned documents in print. In France, documents by 834 women were in print between 1750 and 1820, and French women produced a total of 657 publications between 1789 and 1800. The literary skills of several outstanding women still would have brought them fame even in other periods, but the Enlightenment made their accomplishments particularly bright.

Progressive 18th-century attitudes toward women's intellectual competence and moral worth tended to validate women's political and social involvement. In 1717, inoculation against smallpox was introduced into England from Turkey by Lady Mary Wortley Montagu. The prolific French writer, Louise Felicite Guynement de Keralio-Robert, published histories about female power and, in line with post-revolutionary rhetoric, represented women as masculinized, capable of leading armies, engaging in politics, and participating fully in civic life. In August 1789, Keralio-Robert launched her newspaper, *Le Journal du Citoyen ou le Mercure National,* and in 1793 she anonymously published her classic work, *The Crimes of the Queens of France* [*Les crimes des reines de France. . .*]. Playwright Olympe de Gouges published her pamphlet, "Declaration of the Rights of Women" (1791) which deployed the language of natural rights to call for political and civil rights for women in the new regime. Yet, in 1795, when France created a National Institute and Normal Schools, it excluded women from the professional study of philosophy. This exclusion remained in place until 1905.

The culture of sensibility also was important in shaping women's lives, as it promoted new ideals of female virtue, and discarded the outdated teaching that cast wives as the moral and religious guardians of wayward men. This culture of sensibility—especially as it developed in the second half of the 18th century—mitigated the force of the gender-biased focus on reason characteristic of the early Enlightenment, but it proved just as repressive as the early notions of female virtue that advocated chastity, silence, and obedience. Women's voices were heard in public debates about religion, science, literature, and social justice throughout the 18th century, but political pressure for women's civil and political rights failed to emerge until the 19th century.

ANSWER: MATTHEW QUEST, "NO, THE ENLIGHTENMENT MARGINALIZED WOMEN'S VOICES"

The Enlightenment or Age of Reason took place from roughly the 1650s to the 1780s. It appears distinct for increasing rationalism and individualism, challenging feudal authority, and hierarchical religious traditions. There was much talk of reform, tolerance, science, and skepticism and a growing notion of self-government and liberty, "masterlessness," previously unknown in European political thought. But was there an Enlightenment for women?

Enlightenment could suggest condemnation of slavery, feudalism, and elite representative government or simply the increasing sovereignty of the progressive mind. Where Enlightenment scholarship desired to conquer superstition and nature, however, it was a meditation on what terms women might be cultivated from inferiority, subordinated, or kept "in their place." Reason was a critical measure but frequently it was state-driven propaganda for colonial projects. One message, for example, represented the world as a hydra—a constellation of monstrous creatures emerging from untamed nature that must be conquered. These "monsters" often were minimally paid laborers or the "wageless," particularly women. If Enlightenment was a philosophical project of reason and self-reliance, most often women were placed outside voluntary associations such as academies by elite and popular patriarchy. When this age is considered in the broader framework—not just of European History but also of Atlantic World History—it can be seen that although women were remarkably autonomous in previous periods, and survived and resisted subsequently, overall there is great repression and significant violence against women.

The Enlightenment in reality was most often a "loyal opposition" to the emerging modern nation-state that accepted patronage from ostensibly forward-looking aristocrats and monarchs. With rare exceptions, there was no Enlightenment or reason for women on these terms because they were policed, coerced, and divided into a hierarchy based on sex, race, and class. Feudal-capitalist regimes feared incipient proletarian insurgencies and women arriving on their own authority.

Women often were deemed emotional, mentally weak, lusty, disobedient, vain, and inferior to men. Women also were said to be unable to govern themselves and had to be placed under male control. Clashing with the purportedly rational Enlightened agenda, women were manufactured as being irrational and wild. New laws and state initiatives disciplined women's independent thought and made their bodies subordinate, especially for African-descended and Native American women but also for Europeans.

The denial of women's autonomy is best embodied in "the witch hunt," an intellectual and social activity which mostly predates the Enlightenment but which also helped consolidate how male enlightenment was founded. This overlapped with the pursuit of women who "scolded" with their own reason, and "whores" whose sexual freedom had to be condemned and curtailed. In Europe and North America during the Age of Reason, women who were accused of being scolds or nags were muzzled like dogs and paraded through the streets. Prostitutes were whipped, caged, and subjected to fake drownings, and capital punishment was established for women convicted of adultery. Woman also were gang raped, their children were stolen from them, and their bodies were ritually branded and burned.

Popular literature defined women as akin to Native American "savages." Just as demonizing indigenous peoples justified colonization, enslavement, and expropriation of their land and resources, the attacks on women created excuses for appropriation of their labor, whatever property they might own or inherit, and their reproductive freedom. The price of resisting this terror often was physical abuse and death. Woman's reproduction was appropriated both for social reproduction of labor in the new colonies but also as part of a scientific intellectual trend that encouraged population growth as the power of development over nature.

Before the search for global markets by colonization began, autonomous theologies, knowledge systems about woman's health and vaccinations, and mutual aid practices had been the foundation of a collectivist woman's power. The shame and silence associated with these attacks on women later shadowed women who were invented as "ladies" and distinguished by their "respectability." This violence was brought to the New World by those settling there. As the Atlantic World was made, the African enslaved woman, Indian colonized woman, and European indentured woman—having a common uprooted experience, and before modern white supremacy began to be codified—founded remarkable subversive dialogues and communities. These are embodied in Providence's Ann Hutchinson and Tituba—the black witch of the Salem, Massachusetts, Witch Trials—and also on plantations and port communities in New York, Virginia, Bristol, and Jamaica.

As both the image and the reality of the "independent woman" of a previous era were being smashed, women also were maintaining their own reason and sense of self-government, and a new model of the feminine gender surfaced. The ideal woman was a wife, passive, obedient, thrifty, always busy at work, and chaste. As women generally were "conquered," the historical images in this period transitioned from illustrating women as bestial and dangerous to reversing such previous claims. Women now were more moral than men, a "maternal instinct" was invented, and—like Rousseau's noble savage—now the feminine could humanize men in a peculiar fashion. Yet Rousseau, especially in his *Émile*, argued that women were not to be given a formal education to develop their intellects for public life.

European intellectuals—in the name of advancing reason—often appropriated "science" as an invented project of great male theorists. They often simply wrote down what mechanics, midwives, pastoralists, hunter-gatherers, and small farmers understood from practical experience. Independent women were placed on trial or were conquered as the embodiment of the irrational or the deviation within nature which had to be brought under control for this male intellectual power to be consolidated.

Still there were spaces where women resisted and crafted their own "enlightenment," following Ann Hutchinson and Tituba's historical moment. "Nanny," leader of the Maroons of Jamaica (1685–1755), and later more unsung midwives and medicine women of the Haitian Revolution (1791–1804), struck out against the colonialism by the English and French by using reason, science, and strategy, and poisoning horses, cattle, and the children of the slave masters. The slave poet Phyllis Wheatley (1753–1784)—who served a paternal family in New England—learned Latin, Greek, and ancient history and through her poetry proved that women of color could be civilized and embody reason so long as they were not transparently leading an epistemological revolt against how European males understood gender roles, nature, or science. Of course, in the shadow of both patriarchy and white supremacy, Wheatley did so by illustrating her capacity to think and write on her own.

Women in coffeehouses, taverns, and alehouses—whether proprietors or merchants of popular literature—often were scandalized as owing their success to prostitution rather than business know-how. The perception of coffeehouse women as associated with sexual immorality was not totally unfounded. It was not simply about what they chose to do with their bodies, however; their minds were in revolt against the patriarchal policing of public and private space.

The salons of France appear to be different. These were more upper-class gathering places in furnished rooms. More than strictly public places, they were for elite networking as much as intellectual discussion. Among these elite could be found Émilie Marquise du Châtelet—a woman known as a physicist, mathematician, translator, and philosopher who studied Newton closely and was friends with Voltaire. She is best understood as Voltaire's patron and protector. Why is she not remembered as his equal in intellectual affairs?

As she wrote at her desk—pregnant—she also was an affectionate and sensual lover. Châtelet wrote love letters to her paramour with her husband at a distance. Yet it was her unorthodox intellectual pursuits as a woman that annoyed her contemporaries and made her the subject of ridicule even more so than did her sex life. After her premature death, Voltaire incorporated her into his popularization of the Enlightenment, but it is unclear why her own intellectual reputation had to be saved from obscurity by later scholars. Châtelet—who had access to formal education like few women of her generation—questioned why women rarely produced a great philosophical or artistic work. She also wished to balance dedicated study and romantic love in her life. When governments condemned Voltaire, it was Émilie du Châtelet who used her social mobility to elevate his reputation and network him back into good graces.

Châtelet reveals something crucial about elite women in the Enlightenment. Their capacity to write and study and express themselves was not to pursue a living. Their intellectual work often came to prominence when widowed or separated from their husbands. Their prime role was to preside over salons. This revealed that women revered for their own intelligence and who are of economic means, still never quite escaped the private familial space of patriarchy and instead became the nurturers of male philosophers.

What Émilie du Châtelet has in common with maroon women, slave women, and midwives, is that during the Enlightenment, women's intellects were minimized, denied, and feared. Their gendered behavior and sexual autonomy were subject to gossip, ridicule, and coercion. No matter how well women knew nature and science, toiled and mastered technology, did the work of or defended men, their lives were conceived as a heresy and their caring work, supposedly valued, was discounted. The genius of women was marked by scars of bondage.

CLOSING

Manning employs a basically progressive narrative that sees the Enlightenment as a crucial stage in the long and incomplete process of the liberation of women in western society. Quest is more pessimistic about the process of modernization in general, and the role of the Enlightenment within it. Even those few women who were able to participate in the Enlightenment, such as du Châtelet (who Manning discusses as a positive example), were marginalized and belittled due to their gender.

DOING MORE

Bodek, Evelyn G., "Salonières and Bluestockings: Educated Obsolescence and Germinating Feminism," *Feminist Studies* 3, no. ¾ (1976): 185–199.

Caretta, Vincent, *Phyllis Wheatley: Biography of a Genius in Bondage* (Athens, GA: University of Georgia Press, 2011).

Cowan, Brian, *The Social Life of Coffee: The Emergence of the British Coffee Houses* (New Haven: Yale University Press, 2005).

Curtis-Wendlandt, Lisa, Paul R. Gibbard, and Karen Green (eds.), *Political Ideas of Enlightenment Women: Virtue and Citizenship* (Farnham, Surrey, U.K.; Burlington, VT: Ashgate, 2013).

Eze, Emmanuel, *Race and the Enlightenment: A Reader* (Cambridge: Wiley-Blackwell, 1997).

Federici, Sylvia, *Caliban and the Witch* (Brooklyn, NY: Autonomedia, 2004).

Goodman, Dena, *The Republic of Letters: A Cultural History of the French Enlightenment* (Ithaca, NY: Cornell University Press, 1994).

Harding, Sandra, "Feminism, Science, and Anti-Enlightenment Critiques," in *Feminism/Post-Modernism*, Linda J. Nicholson (ed.) (London: Routledge, 1990), 83–106.

Hesse, Carla A., *The Other Enlightenment: How French Women Became Modern* (Princeton, NJ: Princeton University Press, 2001).

Knott, Sarah, and Barbara Taylor (eds.), *Women, Gender, and Enlightenment* (New York: Palgrave MacMillan, 2007).

Linebaugh, Peter, and Marcus Rediker, *The Many Headed Hydra: Sailors, Slaves, Commoners and the Hidden History of the Revolutionary Atlantic* (Boston: Beacon Press, 2000).

Merchant, Carolyn, *The Death of Nature* (New York: Harper & Row, 1980).

O'Brien, Karen, *Women and Enlightenment in Eighteenth Century Britain* (Cambridge: Cambridge University Press, 2009).

Pateman, Carole, *The Sexual Contract* (Cambridge: Polity, 1988).

Pollak, Ellen (ed.), *A Cultural History of Women in the Age of Enlightenment* (London; New York: Bloomsbury, 2013).

Whelan, Frederick G., *Enlightenment Political Thought and Non-Western Societies* (New York: Routledge, 2009).

Judith P. Zinsser, *Émilie Du Châtelet: Daring Genius of the Enlightenment* (New York: Penguin, 2007).

WEB RESOURCES

Lilti, Antoine, "The Kingdom of Politesse: Salons and the Republic of Letters in Eighteenth-Century Paris," available at http://arcade.stanford.edu/rofl/kingdom-politesse-salons-and-republic-letters-eighteenth-century-paris (accessed August 11, 2015).

National Portrait Gallery, "Brilliant Women: Eighteenth Century Bluestockings," available at http://www.npg.org.uk/whatson/exhibitions/2008/brilliant-women/the-bluestockings-circle.php (accessed August 11, 2015).

QUESTION 2: WAS THE ENLIGHTENMENT SECULAR?

One idea very commonly associated with the Enlightenment is secularism. A dominant narrative of the development of modernity is the rise of a secular society, and the Enlightenment often is seen as the turning point that launched Western society irrevocably on the road to removing religion from the central place it had occupied for most of history. Many Enlightened writers, however, were religious believers, clerics, or defenders of the religious establishment in their countries. Given the overwhelming power of religion in 18th-century Europe, how secular was the Enlightenment?

Many of the leading figures in the Enlightenment, particularly in France, were strongly anticlerical, and highly distrustful of the power of the clergy and the established churches. Given the prominence of the passionately anti-Christian Voltaire in how we think about the Enlightenment, it is no surprise that the Enlightenment is so strongly associated with secularizations. Voltaire also was not even the most militantly anti-religious person in France—the circle around the Baron d'Holbach was explicitly atheist, and Voltaire believed in God. Outside of France, David Hume—although far too skeptical to be any sort of crusader—believed that the power of churches was deplorable, even though his friends included ministers in the established Church of Scotland.

Although they believed in religious toleration, however, many of the Enlightened were not supporters of secularization. John Locke, an influential champion of toleration, did not believe that atheists could be responsible members of society because they lacked fear of supernatural punishment. Some believed that Enlightenment thought, properly understood, would support and even help improve religion. This concept often was described as "reasonable religion."

The association of the Enlightenment with secularization and even atheism was strengthened by the French Revolution which, at its peak, included a radical "Dechristianizing" movement that claimed to be inspired by the Enlightenment ideal of reason. Christians and political conservatives horrified by the revolution's persecution of Christianity and religious people often condemned it as the fulfillment in practice of Enlightenment secularism. In the 19th century battles over the secularization of Western society—the establishment of civil marriage and of religious institutions not affiliated with a church, are but two—the banner of the Enlightenment frequently was waved by the champions of secularization, particularly in France. The late 20th and early 21st century rise of political Islam in the Islamic world, Christian conservativism in the United States, and the "new atheism" in the West have given new life to these battles and have made the Enlightenment a lively topic of polemic in popular culture again.

Some scholars, however, have questioned the traditional picture of a secularizing Enlightenment. Part of this is the growing emphasis on the plurality of the Enlightenment, in the fact that the Enlightenment could mean different things to different people in different places. Part of this scholarly pluralism has been the recognition of religious Enlightenments.

Shama Adams and George Klaeren take opposing positions on this issue. Although acknowledging the diversity of the Enlightenment, Adams focuses on how even relatively moderate Enlightened thinkers fostered secularization by challenging the hegemony of religion over intellectual life and subordinating religious concerns to those of the state and society as a whole. More radical thinkers also contributed to secularization by opposing religion directly. George A. Klaeren denies that the Enlightenment was secular, in part by moving the focus away from France to those large areas of the Catholic world where the clergy were not only not the principal foes of Enlightenment, they were its indispensable supporters.

ANSWER: SHAMA ADAMS, "YES, THE ENLIGHTENMENT MOVED EUROPE TOWARDS SECULARISM"

The Enlightenment is the period of European and Occidental world history generally understood to begin with the Scientific Revolution in the mid-17th century and culminate in the French Revolution of 1789. Scholars have long been divided as to whether the Enlightenment was secular or if the secular characteristics and impulses of the Enlightenment have been misunderstood or retrospectively overstated. As the Enlightenment was a period in which philosophers unapologetically called for the rethinking of privileged and outmoded understandings of society, history, politics, and religion, however, the collective ambitions and broader aims of the Enlightenment—that is, to advance the cause of reason—were unambiguously secular, regardless of whether their proponents intended this outcome. Therefore, when examined from the perspective of both its more conservative and its most radical philosophers, the Enlightenment most certainly was secular.

Beaering this in mind, it is fair to say that conventional understandings of the period usually occlude more than they illuminate, for despite its lofty and far-reaching consequences, the Enlightenment was not unified or monolithic. Significantly, although scholars of previous decades referred to the Enlightenment as a "project," this term now is being questioned, as it is reductive and does not reflect the breadth or scope of diverse and conflicting ideas which characterized the Enlightenment itself, and the study of the Enlightenment's varied and contested histories in the present. Thus, although it is tempting to speak of the Enlightenment as a singular and homogenous historical movement, nuanced studies of the period reveal that the age was composed of a Pan-European series of developments, each with its own internal debates and incongruencies. The lived experience and intellectual consequences of Enlightenment were not the same in all parts of Europe or across the Occident during the 250 to 300 years of upheaval and change that the Enlightenment initiated. Instead, there were, in effect, numerous simultaneous, independent though interconnected, Enlightenments throughout the emerging nation-states of Europe and elsewhere.

Characterized by unprecedented discoveries in science, and dramatic advances in the humanities and intellectual culture, the independent though interconnected Enlightenments were a period of tremendous social, cultural, and political change. The long 18th century in particular, especially in Western Europe, was an age in which philosophy in the broadest sense of the term (meaning all of knowledge) was extricated from the stranglehold of religious orthodoxy. Science, the increasingly humanist philosophies of the era, and bold proclamations about theology itself, such as Johann Gottfried Herder's declaration that the Bible was merely another "profane text," gave knowledge intellectual autonomy. With the ability to explain phenomena previously only understood in theological terms, the natural sciences contributed to a demystification and rationalization of knowledge which empowered and emboldened Enlightenment thinkers to critically examine ideas received, and to question the intellectual basis of their assumptions about the world. By questioning understandings of the self, society, and the cosmos, Enlightenment philosophers' self-conscious and confident quest to challenge privileged systems of knowledge and government heralded the advent of the modern, western world.

Central to this project of modernization was the gradual but concentrated and deliberate diminution of religion and religion's influence on social, civic, and individual life, by way of a process which can be described as "secularization." Like the notion of "the Enlightenment," the words "secular," "secularization," and "secularism" are complex and problematic terms, particularly within the context of the Enlightenment. There are several reasons for this complexity. First, as has been noted, the broad processes of the Enlightenment were Pan-European and not monolithic. Similarly, secularization occurred at different rates, and in varying degrees, across the diverse areas of a highly regionalized Europe. Further, the continent continued to experience great turmoil and witnessed much bloodshed from the confessional split between Catholicism and Protestantism in centuries prior, and there were ongoing internal disputes between conservatives and liberals of both faiths alike.

Owing to this turmoil and discord, it became the duty of the state to manage, restrict, and privatize religion. Indeed, as early as the 16th century, following the bloody institution of Protestantism as the official state religion of England, Queen Elizabeth I remarked that she did not want to make windows into people's souls. The history of a particular nation-state determined both the religious nature of that state, and how the state would manage religion. For example, post-revolutionary Republican France's political reconstruction was actively and explicitly secular, precisely because it was the institutions of both the monarchy and the church which had previously ruled and reigned over the country with such tyrannical excess. It also must be remembered that the official secularization processes of various European regions and states did not necessarily correspond with a tangible decline in religiosity of the average citizen or inhabitant of the state, or vice versa. That the architects of the new French Republic explicitly defined the state to be secular tells us little about the rate or degree of religious fervor among French citizens.

Despite the inherent difficulties of defining both the Enlightenment and what being secular meant in the Enlightenment context, a case can be made that the movement was indeed secular. At the very least, the period's most influential theorists as well as its social and political processes, tended towards secularism. Some historians—including a preeminent scholar of the Enlightenment, Jonathan Israel—have argued that the Enlightenment was comprised of at least two concurrent though often-conflicting streams or movements, one moderate or mainstream, the other radical and unapologetically against the status quo. Israel isolates and describes what he calls the "Radical Enlightenment," as a project which ran parallel with, though often in opposition to, the moderate "mainstream Enlightenment." The mainstream Enlightenment included philosophers such as Locke, Hobbes, and Voltaire. Although these thinkers did not automatically adopt progressive views, they sought to accommodate reason and faith, and advocated for new and contractual, social and political settlements. Their views, despite constituting the more conservative elements of the Enlightenment, did lend themselves towards a type of secularism, however limited or conciliatory.

Although the mainstream Enlightenment accepted the established, confessional mode of the state, for instance, and called for something less than universal intellectual freedom and social justice, it also instituted nominal concessions for religious minorities, the gradual acceptance of religious pluralism, and the development of civil law. Religion was beginning to be managed and regulated by the state, but still was not wholly separated from governance, or rejected outright. Therefore, the mainstream Enlightenment, however moderate, experimented with a "passive" sort of secularism, in which the state attempted to accommodate religion on its own terms and to its own benefit.

In contrast to this passive secularism, the Radical Enlightenment rejected outright the authority of the Church, and dismissed religion. Radical Enlightenment thinkers—including the philosophes d'Alembert and Condorcet—crafted nuanced and highly radical arguments about the legitimacy of religion and the role of the established Church in both the affairs of the state and the private life of the individual. As accomplished scientists and mathematicians in their own right, theirs can be regarded as an "active secularism," as they were heavily influenced by secular knowledge, and were advocates for its liberating properties. Condorcet wrote, "There does not exist any religious system, or supernatural extravagance, which is not founded on an ignorance of the laws of nature." (146)

A secular view of Enlightenment also is evident in the works of the philosopher who is today regarded as the most influential theorist of the Enlightenment, Immanuel Kant. Although Kant did not explicitly identify as an atheist, or as wanting to dismiss religion completely, his 1784 essay, "Answering the Question: What is Enlightenment?" ("Beantwortung der Frage: Was ist Aufklärung?") captures the progressive spirit of the age. The philosopher argues that the Enlightenment can be understood as our attempt to become intellectually autonomous, a process which Kant regards as inseparable and nearly synonymous with overcoming the intellectual limitations which religion engenders. In Kant's mind, religion was an archaic institution, and fervent religious belief was a sign and relic of humanity's intellectual infancy. He writes "Enlightenment is man's emergence from his self-incurred immaturity . . . all that is needed is freedom" (1–3). Kant also argues that the greatest freedom is that which develops from the "shrugging off" of religious and state paternalism. He explains that, "religious immaturity is the most pernicious and dishonourable variety of all." (17) Following on from this, Kant states that it is impossible to agree "even for a single lifetime" to a permanent "religious constitution" such as church doctrine, as this is tantamount to "renouncing Enlightenment." (67) Thus, the Enlightenment was a period of tremendous social change, and the movement was, by virtue of its commitment to the cause of advancing reason and human liberty, undoubtedly secular.

ANSWER: GEORGE A. KLAEREN, "NO, MUCH ENLIGHTENMENT THOUGHT WAS RELIGIOUS"

The Myth of Secularism

The Enlightenment was marked by challenges and changes in the intellectual and religious sphere—traditional ways of establishing knowledge and ascertaining truth were forced to negotiate with daily advances in scientific knowledge and revivals of old philosophical systems such as skepticism and empiricism. Historians have described the period as one of epistemic rupture, marked by a tension between old and new or, according to many historians, between traditional religious and monarchical institutions and "enlightenment ideology." Implicit in many of these analyses is an estrangement between

"Reason" and "Religion"—a religio-intellectual battle involving European society on multiple levels and in various forums, creating a general intellectual crisis. This equation between secularism and enlightenment ideology has become a dominant presupposition of Enlightenment studies, only recently challenged.

For several years, the assumption that secularism was a defining characteristic of the Enlightenment was seen in works that described the rise of modern "Paganism" or studies which described the liberation of civil society from the Catholic Church and from absolute monarchs. The well-known examples of Voltaire (1694–1778), Diderot (1713–1784), Baron d'Holbach (1723–1789), and other outspoken atheist or agnostic philosophes became emblematic for the entirety of Enlightenment thought, obscuring its diversity. As historians began to question the unity of one, singular "Enlightenment," and instead began to break it into several coterminous, overlapping ideological movements across Europe and her colonies, they likewise revisited the role that religion and religious figures played in creating, engaging, and adopting Enlightenment philosophies. It soon was realized that secularization and liberalism are incomplete frames of analysis for understanding the Enlightenment, and in many cases—for example, the Enlightenments of Spain or Italy—they are useless. The mutual exclusivity of Enlightenment and of religion posited by earlier historians must be rejected and the category of Enlightenments be broadened to include religious thought and activity by religious individuals if a more complete understanding is to be attained.

The Catholic Enlightenment and Spain

One of the most prominent counter-examples to an exclusively secular Enlightenment is the notion of a Catholic Enlightenment—or the intersection of Catholicism (culturally, intellectually, and socially) and enlightenment thought. For the most part, the Catholic Enlightenment was experienced as an attempt by Catholic thinkers to defend Catholic doctrine from atheist and materialist attacks and simultaneously incorporate many of the intellectual and social reforms of the broader Enlightenment movement. During the introduction of enlightenment thought into many countries—Spain, Portugal, Italy, and Ireland especially—classic enlightenment ideas, such as natural rights, freedom of expression, and increased individual equality were embraced without being seen as necessarily contrary to established religion.

In Spain and in Spanish America, for example, it was the clergy who had the time, necessary knowledge, contacts, and resources to read and understand Enlightenment works, disseminating these ideas further by responding to these publications. Many of the major figures of the Enlightenment across the Iberian Atlantic were religious individuals known for their work in the sciences, in medicine, or in philosophy. To these thinkers, the new philosophies and ideas of the 18th century were in no way contradictory to the Catholic framework. The Spanish Benedictine Benito Jerónimo Feijóo (1676–1764) confidently wrote in 1745, for example, that "theology and philosophy have their limits clearly distinguished, and that no Spaniard is ignorant of the fact that revealed doctrine has a right of superiority over that of human discourse, [a right] which all the natural sciences are lacking." Yet Feijóo was deeply invested in understanding the natural sciences and defending the work of contemporary physicians and scientists in Spain, as well as writing essays advocating for increased liberties for women.

Similarly, historians have shown that "traditional" institutions of learning, such as the University of Salamanca, were actually instrumental in disseminating new ideas in the 18th century. This was an experience shared in Portugal and Italy. The Marquis of Pombal in Portugal, Carlos III of Spain, Pope Benedict XIV, Holy Roman Emperor Joseph II, and Louis XVI of France all ruled over kingdoms which simultaneously adopted Enlightenment ideals and professed the Catholic faith. The Catholic Enlightenment in these countries worked to incorporate enlightenment ideas into the overarching and preexisting framework of Catholic theology. The result often was a distinct form of "reformed" Catholicism—Jansenism in France and in Spain, Josephinism in the Holy Roman Empire, Febronianism in Germany, and Pistorianism throughout the Italian peninsula. These reformed, enlightened Catholicisms often advocated national churches, emphasized the authority of bishops and councils over popes, and supported the vernacular publication of the Bible and increased responsibility of the individual within the community of believers.

The Broader Religious Enlightenment

Catholicism was not the only religious tradition to engage the Enlightenment. Recent scholarship has extended consideration of the intersection of religion and the Enlightenment to England, Scotland, the Netherlands, Germany, and the Americas, among other countries. Historians recently analyzed how enlightened forms of Calvinism, Anglicanism, Lutheranism, and Judaism, were important in the reception, development, and dissemination of essential elements of Enlightenment thought, including the partitioning of the church-state relationship, an emphasis on reason and natural law in religion, toleration, vernacular publication of religious texts, and the integration of the new sciences and philosophies. This challenges the idea of a static religious establishment. Instead of viewing religious institutions as purely reactionary or stubbornly refusing to adapt to the times, this new research shows how many religious thinkers actively engaged Enlightenment thought, pruning and discerning helpful from harmful ideas and incorporating them into their particular worldviews.

Importantly, this "religious Enlightenment" transcended sectarian and regional differences. Jews in Berlin, Catholics in Paris, and Protestants in London all included numerous individuals who saw no conflict between Enlightenment ideology and their religions, and sought to integrate the two. The most famous example of an integrated religious Enlightenment is probably that of the Scottish Enlightenment and the Reverend William Robertson (1721–1793). In Scotland, the promulgation of Enlightenment thought, the intellectual environment of the universities, and the Presbyterian Church of Scotland all were intimately connected. Robertson, for example, was both the moderator of the general assembly of the Church of Scotland (1766–1780), the principal of the University of Edinburgh (1762), and the founder of the Select Society of Edinburgh (1750)—an academic coterie that included the great skeptic David Hume, economist Adam Smith, and clergyman Robert Wallace (1697–1771).

Traditionally, the "radical" and secular enlightenment has been associated particularly with the 18th-century experience in France and England. Yet, even in these countries, examples of a non-secular, religious Enlightenment abound. Deism, for example, should be clearly seen as an attempted compromise between traditional religion and enlightenment philosophy. Deism was a religious philosophy that affirmed the existence of a God and of a religiously grounded morality, but prized human reason over divine revelation, eliminated the supernatural, and generally depreciated ritual and institutional religion. Deism was immensely popular with Enlightenment intellectuals in Britain and France, as well in the American colonies. Within the ranks of Deists, a wide spectrum of beliefs were espoused—Jean-Jacques Rousseau (1712–1778), for example, argued for the belief in a personal God, and Voltaire described God as a "watchmaker" who remained uninvolved in the affairs of nature. Some scholars argue that Deism was invented as a socially acceptable way of declaring skepticism or atheism, and debates continue today about the Deistic status of individuals such as Thomas Jefferson or Hume. It should not be forgotten, however, that Deism contained distinct religious claims, and thus represents a clear historical example of a religious, non-secular, Enlightenment.

Revising the Enlightenment

In short, although the Enlightenment was in many famous cases associated with irreligion or an embittered, outspoken atheism, by no means was the

Enlightenment a secular or a secularizing movement. There are numerous examples ranging from the individual experience to entire imperial cultures in which Enlightenment ideology was cultivated alongside traditional Christian religion. In such cases, faith was seen as "suprarational," the larger container of understanding which could accommodate any possible advances in science, philosophy, or social ideas. In many ways, the false dichotomy between religion and a secular interpretation of the Enlightenment is a repetition of the familiar refrain of the conflict thesis between faith and reason. In the words of Enlightenment historian David Sorkin, "the time has come to discard the still popular, if threadbare and outmoded notion of an exclusively secular Enlightenment . . . to let go of this false specter and to recognize that the Enlightenment was a spectrum of opinion that included a distinctly religious Enlightenment." Once discarded, scholars are free to more accurately address the questions of how 18th-century individuals thought and what they thought about, rather than endlessly posturing for a defensible label to describe these ways of knowing. Once disabused (though remaining sentient) of the necessity of imposed categories such as "Enlightenment," "Religious Enlightenment," and "Counter-Enlightenment," actual discursive analysis—the real work of the student of history—can occur.

CLOSING

There is plenty of evidence on both sides of the debate on the secularity of the Enlightenment. Adams focuses on the realm of ideas and policies, viewing the Enlightenment in the long term of the development of western secularism from the Protestant Reformation to the rise of the secular state. Klaeren disrupts the focus of traditional Enlightenment scholarship on a few, mostly French big names, to consider the Enlightenment in Mediterranean Catholic countries such as Spain and Italy. His view is more narrowly rooted in the 18th century than is Adams', and less concerned with fitting the Enlightenment into a "big picture" of the development of secularization.

DOING MORE

Barnett, S. J., *The Enlightenment and Religion: The Myths of Modernity* (Manchester: Manchester University Press, 2003).
Bradley, James E., and Dale K. Van Kley (eds.), *Religion and Politics in Enlightenment Europe* (Notre Dame: University of Notre Dame Press, 2001).
De Condorcet, Antoine-Nicholas, *Outlines of an Historical View of the Progress of the Human Mind*, trans. by Anonymous (Chicago: Langer and Ulrich, 2009).
Hill, Jonathan, *Faith in the Age of Reason* (Oxford: Lion Hudson Plc., 2004).

Kant, Immanuel, *An Answer to the Question: What is Enlightenment?* Trans. H. B. Nisbet (London: Penguin, 1991).

Lehner, Ulrich L., and Michael Printy (eds.), *A Companion to the Catholic Enlightenment in Europe* (Leiden: Brill, 2010).

Lehner, Ulrich L., "What is 'Catholic Enlightenment'?" *History Compass* 8/2 (2010), 166–178.

Sheehan, Jonathan, "Enlightenment, Religion, and the Enigma of Secularization: A Review Essay," *American Historical Review* 180, No. 4 (October 2003), 1061–1080.

Sorkin, David, *The Religious Enlightenment: Protestants, Jews, and Catholics from London to Vienna* (Princeton: Princeton University Press, 2011).

WEB RESOURCES

British Museum Virtual Tour. Enlightenment, Religion, and Ritual. https://www.britishmuseum.org/explore/online_tours/britain/enlightenment_religion/enlightenment_religion.aspx (accessed August 11, 2015).

Hudson, Wayne, "The Enlightenment Critique of Religion," *American eJournal of Theology.* http://aejt.com.au/__data/assets/pdf_file/0007/395503/AEJT_5.2_Hudson.pdf (accessed August 11, 2015).

Sorkin, David, "Godless Liberals: The Myth of the Secular Enlightenment," Religion Dispatches (University of Southern California, Annenberg), April 2, 2010, http://religiondispatches.org/godless-liberals-the-myth-of-the-secular-enlightenment/ (accessed August 11, 2015).

QUESTION 3: WAS THE ENLIGHTENMENT DEMOCRATIC?

A characteristic of the modern world is democracy, the idea that power comes from the choices of ordinary people. Not every modern regime is democratic, but most claim the title. Few questions in the history of the Enlightenment are more controversial than whether it can be claimed as democratic. The ideals of the American and French Revolutions, which many claim as the origin of modern democracy, derived from the Enlightenment, but so did some anti-democratic ideas. Even the Revolutions' claim to democracy can be questioned as the American Revolution was compatible with slavery, and the French Revolution led to the Terror and the military dictatorship of Napoleon Bonaparte. To what degree were these failures actually failures of the Enlightenment?

The Enlightenment emerged in an undemocratic world. Europe and its colonies were dominated by privileged elites whose monopoly over political decision making was endorsed by most political theorists. A few states—notably Great Britain and the Dutch Republic—had the idea that voters could influence or even choose the government, but most—including such leading Enlightenment states as France and Prussia—viewed power as coming from God or the king rather than from the people. Even in "constitutional" states such as Britain, voting power was restricted to a small minority of property-owning men, rather than being perceived as the right of the individual citizen. "Democracy" was a pejorative term, often associated with mob rule. The democracies of the ancient world (where the term originated) including Athens and to a lesser degree the Roman Republic, were widely viewed as failures. The Enlightenment's foremost student of constitutions and political orders, the Baron de Montesquieu, was at best ambivalent about democracy, although he did believe it superior to the worst form of government, despotism.

The Enlightenment challenged the "top-down" theory of political authority, but without necessarily replacing it with democracy. Some feared the people, often viewed as superstitious, short-sighted, and greedy rather than living up to the ideals of a democratic citizenry. Others, such as Voltaire and Montesquieu, valued the decisiveness of monarchical government and believed that Enlightened kings and ministers offered the best hope for instituting Enlightenment reforms. Jean-Jacques Rousseau, a proud citizen of the nondemocratic republic of Geneva, sometimes supported democracy in theory and was influential during the more radical phases of the French Revolution.

The application of Enlightenment ideas in the great revolutions of the 18th century—the American and French—was uneven and not always democratic. American revolutionaries, inspired by Enlightenment ideals, overthrew monarchy and established a constitutional republic, but one that kept slavery and restricted the franchise in some states to propertied males. Still the idea of human rights and a government responsible to the people, often phrased in Enlightenment language, was enshrined in the American founding documents, however uneven their application in practice. The French Revolution also proclaimed the "rights of man" and had a very wide franchise for men at some points in its development. The "Terror," however, the purging of tens of thousands of French people identified as "enemies" of the republic, brought democracy into further disrepute. Opponents of the revolution, such as the Anglo-Irish politician Edmund Burke, did not hesitate to blame the Enlightenment for what they saw as the violence and horror of the overthrow of the established monarchical order in the name of democracy. The ultimate rise to power of the military dictator Napoleon Bonaparte further discredited the connection of Enlightenment ideas and democracy, as Napoleon adopted those elements of the Enlightenment that "Enlightened despots" such as Frederick II of Prussia already had adopted—efficiency and administrative order—but strongly opposed democracy.

The alarm that American elites felt at the French Revolution also led to a conservative reaction directed at both democratic and Enlightenment values with the passage of the Alien and Sedition Acts in 1798. Revolutionary Enlightenment-influenced democracy reemerged, however, with the Latin American Revolutions of the early 19th century and the European revolutions of the mid-19th century.

Michael Hill and Alexander Maxwell take opposing positions on the issue. Hill argues for the importance of Enlightenment ideas—human rights and the capacity for self-government—on subsequent political developments. Maxwell points out that Enlightenment ideals can inform a number of political positions, and that authorities that were in no way democratic, ranging from kings in Europe to slave owners in the Americas, could view themselves as supporters and even practitioners of the Enlightenment. The political legacy of the Enlightenment is totalitarian as much as it is democratic.

ANSWER: MICHAEL HILL, "YES, THE ENLIGHTENMENT LAID THE FOUNDATION FOR MODERN DEMOCRACY"

Enlightenment assumptions about human nature and human rights provided the foundation for modern democracy. The idea that all men possessed a moral sense and were capable of self-government underlay the political theory of republics established in the Americas and Europe beginning in the late 18th century. Conceptions of reason and equality at the heart of Enlightenment thought have fueled the expansion of civil and political rights to the present.

Reason and equality were the dual essences of Enlightenment thought. During the Scientific Revolution, Europeans had applied reason to observations of the natural world. From this process they developed a conception of the universe as governed by natural laws, such as Sir Isaac Newton's laws of motion. In the Enlightenment, Europeans and Americans came to believe that similar laws applied to human societies. Just as Newton had discovered laws of the universe, the Enlightenment scholars worked to uncover natural laws governing human behavior, economies, and politics. If they could learn how societies functioned, they reasoned, they hoped to reform institutions and governments to improve life for all humankind.

Above all, the philosophes sought to create more equal societies by eliminating the privileges of social elites and empowering ordinary men of reason and talent to direct society. Early modern Europe and the Americas were hierarchical and unequal societies. Contemporaries conceived of society as a divinely inspired system in which individuals belonged simultaneously to multiple groups, each with unique rights and responsibilities. For example,

French nobles were exempt from certain taxes and some commoners were obligated to provide free labor to noble landlords.

Influenced by the English philosopher John Locke (*An Essay Concerning Human Understanding*, 1690), Enlightenment thinkers came to believe that all people were essentially equal. Locke argued that all people were born with the same mental faculties, and that each individual differed from others only by his subsequent life experiences. In other words a nobleman and a peasant were born with the same human potential; the different social privileges they exercised as adults derived merely from the social status in which they grew up rather than any innate difference between them. And regardless of their life experiences, Enlightenment writers argued, all people shared a common moral sense. All people—whether merchants, artisans, peasants, or nobles—were capable of using reason to judge right and wrong.

This shared moral sense underlay the conviction that representative governments were practicable and just. As the historian Gordon Wood notes of revolutionary America, colonial leaders believed "a certain moral capacity in the populace as a whole" was the foundation of self-government in the United States (*The Radicalism of the American Revolution*, 234). Put simply, if all people were equally capable of judging right from wrong, all were qualified to participate in government. Enlightenment thinkers in America and Europe thus advocated reforms regarded as hallmarks of democracy today. In general they argued that governments derived from popular sovereignty—that is, the people are the source of governing authority. They called for representative governments in which qualified people would elect representatives to do the work of governing. Citizens were those people who possessed civil and political rights, including the right to vote. Empowered by freedoms of speech, the press, and other rights, citizens exercised their common moral sense to judge and direct their government.

Between 1776 and 1821, the people of the United States, France, and Latin America launched revolutions partly inspired by Enlightenment ideals of equality. In Britain's American colonies, Thomas Jefferson proclaimed in the Declaration of Independence (1776) that "all men are created equal" and possessed "unalienable Rights" to life, liberty, and the pursuit of happiness. Because all government rested upon the "consent of the governed," he argued, Britain's infringement of their rights justified the colonists' bid for independence (U.S. Declaration of Independence, 1776). Across the Atlantic, leaders of the French Revolution worked to eliminate inequality in France. In *What is the Third Estate?* (1789), the Abbé Sieyés complained that a tiny minority of French nobles and clerics dominated French society and government at the expense of better qualified commoners. On August 4, 1789, revolutionary leaders declared civic equality and abolished the feudal system that guaranteed social privileges to the nobility: "Every citizen, whatever their origins are, can hold any ecclesiastic, civilian, or military job" (4 August Decrees). In tearing down the privileges of the nobility, the decree helped level French society. These principles were codified in the "Declaration of the Rights of Man and Citizen" (1789), a foundational document of the French Revolution, which affirmed that "all men are born and remain free and equal in rights; social distinctions may be based solely upon general usefulness."

Having asserted equality, the revolutionaries enacted democratic reforms. Prior to independence, the American colonists had reserved political rights to men of property. Only adult white males who owned land or paid taxes could vote or hold office. All other people—women, slaves, Native Americans, most free blacks, and others—lacked political rights. After the American Revolution, however, Enlightenment notions of equality inexorably expanded the narrow franchise. Although the United States Constitution (1787) did not explicitly assert a right to vote for Americans, the framers assumed that members of the House of Representatives would be chosen "by the People of the several states" in "Elections . . . prescribed in each State by the Legislature [itself an elected body]." In 1791, the Bill of Rights guaranteed a bundle of rights to all Americans citizens such as the freedoms of speech and of assembly. Thus, although less than 60% of white men could vote before the revolution, by 1792 the proportion of white male voters was as much as 80%.

In France, the National Assembly transformed an absolute monarchy into a constitutional government that at first extended the vote to a minority of male citizens. The Constitution of 1791 defined citizens as either "active" or "passive." As in the early United States, owning land or paying taxes qualified active citizens to participate in government; poorer people were classified as passive citizens and were denied political rights. But as the revolution radicalized in 1792–1794, access to the ballot box grew. Inspired by Jean-Jacques Rousseau, whose influential title, *The Social Contract* (1762), argued for government based on the "general will" of all its subjects, the French revolutionaries proclaimed a republic and elected a new legislature by universal adult male suffrage in 1792. They ratified the Constitution of 1793, which defined citizenship extraordinarily broadly to include all Frenchmen older than age 21. Following Rousseau, the Constitution of 1793 defined the law as "the free and solemn expression of the general will" so that "each citizen has an equal right to participate in the formation of the law" through the election of representatives. Likewise between 1812 and 1814 the Constitution of Cádiz granted suffrage to all adult men (excluding those of African descent) in Spain's vast American colonies.

Although the United States, France, and Spain extended suffrage to include more adult male voters in the late 18th century, those who remained without political rights have voiced Enlightenment ideas of reason and equality to demand the vote to the present day. In the 19th-century American men who lacked property continued to seek the vote, arguing that denying them betrayed the Declaration of Independence; by 1855 only 6 states of 31 retained a property requirement or required taxation for white men to vote. In 1848, delegates to the Woman's Rights Convention at Seneca Falls, New York, issued a "Declaration of Sentiments" (1848) that sought civil equality for women because women were "man's equal . . . intended to be so by the Creator." Demanding their "inalienable right to the elective franchise," the delegates echoed the Declaration of Independence. Civil rights leaders of the 20th century called for equality for African Americans in Enlightenment terms and referred to America's Enlightenment era founding documents. In his "I Have a Dream" speech (1963), Dr. Martin Luther King, Jr., described the Declaration of Independence and U.S. Constitution as promises "that all men . . . black men as well as white men, would be guaranteed the unalienable rights of life, liberty, and the pursuit of happiness." Such promises included the right to vote; as King argued, "[W]e cannot be satisfied as long as the Negro . . . cannot vote." Likewise, the French constitution (1958) declares its "attachment to the Rights of Man and the principles of national sovereignty as defined by the Declaration of 1789" and declares universal adult suffrage: "All French citizens of either sex who have reached their majority . . . may vote as provided for by statute."

Between 1776 and 1821, Enlightenment ideas of reason and equality inspired revolutions in the United States, France, and Latin America that created representative governments. Although Enlightenment texts justified decidedly nondemocratic actions such as the "Reign of Terror" (1793–1794) in revolutionary France, and although the new nations enfranchised far fewer people than is considered proper today, intellectual and political conditions derived from the Enlightenment would facilitate further expansion of political and civil rights in the 19th and 20th centuries.

ANSWER: ALEXANDER MAXWELL, "NO, THE ENLIGHTENMENT EXHIBITED MANY ANTIDEMOCRATIC IDEAS AND PRACTICES"

Several scholars locate the origins of democracy in the Enlightenment. Sociologist Milan Zafirovski, for example, argued in his recent book *The Enlightenment and its Effects on Modern Society* that "the Enlightenment is the primary foundation and point of origin of modern democratic societies and their fundamental values and institutions." (2) Such celebratory interpretations of the Enlightenment tell only part of the story: the Enlightenment also inspired absolute monarchy, tyranny, and oppression. This section seeks to explain how Enlightenment thinking could give rise to the mutually incompatible political philosophies of autocracy and democracy, but focuses on explaining the undemocratic "dark side" of the Enlightenment.

Although no single definition of "the Enlightenment" can fully capture the multifaceted diversity of what many scholars prefer to discuss as plural "Enlightenments," Immanuel Kant nevertheless provided a good initial answer to the question: What Is Enlightenment?

> Enlightenment is man's emergence from his self-incurred immaturity. Immaturity is the inability to use one's own understanding without the guidance of another. This immaturity is self-incurred if its cause is not lack of understanding, but lack of resolution and courage to use it without the guidance of another. The motto of enlightenment is therefore Sapere aude! Have courage to use your own understanding! (*Political Writings* 54)

A wide variety of political philosophies can rest on this broad foundation.

During the Enlightenment itself, political thinkers courageously applied their own understanding to the leading issues of the day. Enlightenment thinking reflected an era of increasingly rapid social change: New technologies enabled new forms of economic production, which in turn generated new professions and even new social classes. Unprecedented social conflicts required novel solutions: the previously unquestioned reliance on age-old traditions had become inappropriate. Kant, and Enlightenment thinkers generally, thus discounted the accumulated experience of their ancestors, trusting instead in unaided human reason to find the right path.

Although some enlightenment thinkers famously rejected feudal hierarchies and proclaimed the equality of citizens, Kant himself accepted monarchy, hierarchy, and social inequality. He urged independent thought primarily to undermine the authority of unquestioned traditions. In certain circumstances, he explicitly endorsed blind obedience:

> it would be very harmful if an officer receiving an order from his superiors were to quibble openly, while on duty, about the appropriateness or usefulness of the order in question. He must simply obey. (*Political Writings*, 56)

Indeed, Kant's famous essay on independent thought ended with an obsequious tribute to the Prussian King Frederick the Great, who, according to Kant, could rule according to the principle of "argue as much as you like and about whatever you like, but obey!" (*Political Writings*, 56).

Although Frederick the Great, friend of Voltaire, vividly illustrates the quintessentially Enlightenment phenomenon of "enlightened despotism,"

Frederick was only one of several monarchs invoking Enlightenment ideals in support of their own power. The Enlightenment's attack on tradition appealed to ambitious monarchs seeking to replace traditional constraints on their power with royal absolutism. Austrian Emperor Joseph II (1741–1790), no less an enlightened despot than his better-remembered Prussian counterpart, refused to be crowned King of Hungary, despite his right to the title, because the coronation oath would have obliged him to respect the privileges of the Hungarian nobility. Joseph II also trampled Hungarian sensibilities by imposing German as Hungary's administrative language, all in the name of bureaucratic rationality. Perhaps his most characteristic edict, however, forbade wooden coffins and required bodies be buried in linen sacks. Joseph II complained that his subjects "go to great lengths to ensure their bodies will decay slowly after death, and thus remain stinking carrion for as long as possible. So I no longer care how they want to be buried" (Braunbehrens, 415–16). Grieving relatives understandably experienced their monarch's indifference as tyrannical.

Enlightened despotism and enlightenment democracy both emerged from similar intellectual traditions. Political theorists John Locke (1632–1704) and Jean-Jacques Rousseau (1712–1778) argued for representative government on the basis of contract theory, yet Thomas Hobbes (1588–1679), the founder of contract theory, had outspokenly defended absolute monarchy. Hobbes reasoned that absolute monarchy under a single ruler, even a despotic ruler, served the enlightened self-interest of ordinary citizens. His 1651 *Leviathan* argued not only that subjects lacked the right of rebellion, but even the right to "speak evil" of monarchs, even when those monarchs acted "in pursuit of their passions . . . which is a breach of trust and a law of nature" (Hobbes, 220).

The Enlightenment also led to diverging ideas about equality. The democratic enlightenment's resolute opposition to social hierarchy inspired the memorable revolutionary watchword, "egalité." Whatever sense aristocratic privileges might have made in the middle ages, the nobility of the late 18th century struck many contemporaries as a parasitic social class. Several enlightenment thinkers, however, sought not to destroy social hierarchy, but to strengthen it through reform. Justus Möser (1720–1794), a government official in the small prince-bishopric of Osnabrück, admitted that "the good-for-nothing who claims his grandfather's rank along with his walking stick and sword" contributed less to the state than an artisan or master craftsman; but he urged a new social hierarchy which would reward those citizens for their actual contributions. He specifically wanted to impose an obligatory ranked uniform, much like a military uniform, complete with yellow cockades of shame which would be used as punishments. Wealthy taxpayers could obtain the right to wear highly ranked uniforms for cash, which Möser described as "financial acts which lead to honor." Similar schemes for ranked civilian uniforms appeared in Poland, Austria, and Spain; Sweden's enlightened despot Gustav III actually imposed such a uniform on his court (Maxwell, 80–95).

Enlightened absolutism often found inspiration in the military, seeking to apply order and regimentation of the army to civilian life as a whole. Russian emperor Alexander I (1777–1825), unsentimental about the customs of village life, memorably tried to impose rationality and discipline to peasant labor by organizing military colonies. Existing villages were destroyed and then rebuilt according to a standard plan, a process which often took more than a year, leaving some inhabitants homeless over the Russian winter. Children older than 7 years attended military schools, and therefore were subject to army discipline. The educational and agricultural achievements in the military settlements proved impressive, yet historian Richard Pipes concluded that peasants responded with "bitter resentment" because "the severity they now experienced as not the sporadic cruelty of a landlord but the more persistent and penetrating severity of discipline and efficiency" (Pipes, 207, 218).

Although absolute monarchs attempted to govern the state's inhabitants like military conscripts, Enlightenment thinkers in Britain and its colonies devised other forms of rationality and social control. The infamous Panopticon of Jeremy Bentham (1748–1832), originally designed to reform prisoners who would be "taught to love labour" (Bentham, I, 105), eventually struck its creator as an appropriate basis for organizing factories and schools. Bentham sought to destroy privacy, hoping ultimately to extend "the range of inspection over every moment of a boy's time." He believed constant surveillance would improve discipline and thus create happiness, "[C]all them soldiers, call them monks, call them machines, so they were but happy ones, I should not care." He frankly admitted that he would grant to schoolmasters power "much exceeding any thing that is hitherto been signified by despotic" (Bentham, II, 125, 128).

Bentham's ideas influenced the labor conditions in early factories and, most horrifically, on slave plantations. Detailed work logs, according to historian Justin Roberts' recent study of Atlantic slavery, reflected "new management systems geared toward extracting more work from enslaved workers." Roberts sees "the dark side of the Enlightenment" in the "ruthless rationalism . . . pragmatism and expediency" which created "exhausting work regimes in which planters strove to reduce the workers into depersonalized and interchangeable units of production" (Roberts, 6). Perhaps the Enlightenment experienced by enslaved Africans on Caribbean sugar plantations was the most tyrannical of all Enlightenments.

The undemocratic Enlightenment, whether espoused by crowned monarchs or merely by thinkers overconfident in their capacity to direct the lives of others, dreamed of a society characterized by discipline and obedience to the social hierarchy. Enlightened monarchs of the 18th century lacked technology necessary to create the sort of totalitarian nightmare George Orwell memorably imagined in his novel *1984*, but although the means were lacking, the will to impose them was not. The word "totalitarian" appeared only in the 1920s, but the undemocratic enlightenment frankly was totalitarian in aspiration. Modern democratic government as seen in Western Europe, North America, and Australasia, does have roots in Enlightenment thinking, yet the tyrannical techniques of government perfected by Stalin also can claim an Enlightenment genealogy. Although we can celebrate the democratic heritage of the Enlightenment, we should not lose sight of the Enlightenment's capacity for despotism and tyranny.

CLOSING

Hill and Maxwell differ not only in their conclusions but in their methods of argument. Hill takes a long view, discussing how Enlightenment ideals did not immediately lead to the creation of modern democracies, but contributed to the emergence of democracy over the following centuries. Maxwell focuses more on practices, and the compatibility of Enlightenment values with a variety of political and social regimes, including authoritarian and even totalitarian ones. Hill focuses on the long road from the Enlightenment to modern democracy; Maxwell points out that this is merely one among many roads that start from or pass through the Enlightenment.

DOING MORE

Braunbehrens, Volkmar, *Mozart in Vienna*, translated by Timothy Bell (New York: Weidenfeld, 1990).

Hobbes, Thomas, *Leviathan*, revised edition (Peterborough: Broadview, 2010).

Kant, Immanuel, *Political Writings*, edited by H. S. Reiss (Cambridge: Cambridge University Press, 1991).

Maxwell, Alexander, *Patriots against Fashion* (London: Palgrave, 2014).

Pipes, Richard, "The Russian Military Colonies, 1810–1831," *Journal of Modern History*, vol. 22, no. 3 (September 1950).

Roberts, Justin, *Slavery and the Enlightenment in the British Atlantic, 1750–1807* (Cambridge: Cambridge University Press, 2013).

Rousseau, Jean-Jacques, *The Social Contract and other Later Political Writings*, edited and translated by Victor Gourevitch (Cambridge and New York: Cambridge University Press, 1997).

Wood, Gordon S., *The Radicalism of the American Revolution* (New York: Vintage Books, 1993).

Zafirovski, Milan. *The Enlightenment and its Effects on Modern Society* (New York: Springer, 2011).

WEB RESOURCES

Bentham, Jeremy, *Panopticon, or, the Inspection-House* (Dublin, T. Payne, 1791). Google Books. https://books.google.com/books/about/Panopticon_Or_the_Inspection_House.html?id=Ec4TAAAAQAAJ&hl=en (accessed August 11, 2015).

Ralston, Shane J. "American Enlightenment Thought," *Internet Encyclopedia of Philosophy* http://www.iep.utm.edu/amer-enl/ (accessed August 11, 2015).

Selected Annotated Bibliography

REFERENCE BOOKS

Burns, William E., *Science in the Enlightenment: An Encyclopedia* (Santa Barbara: ABC-Clio, 2003). Covers western science from approximately 1700 to 1820.

Kors, Alan Charles (ed.), *Encyclopedia of the Enlightenment* (Oxford and New York: Oxford University Press, 2003). Four-volume work sums up scholarship on the Enlightenment as of the early 21st century.

Wilson, Ellen Judy, and Peter Hans Reill, *Encyclopedia of the Enlightenment*, revised ed. (New York: Facts on File, 2004). The Enlightenment with a great deal of its 18th-century context.

ANTHOLOGIES AND DOCUMENT COLLECTIONS

Eze, Emanuel Chukwudi, *Race and the Enlightenment: A Reader* (Malden: Blackwell, 1997). Short reader focusing on racial thought and racism in the Enlightenment.

Hyland, Paul (ed.), with Olga Gomez and Francesca Greensides, *The Enlightenment: A Sourcebook and Reader* (London and New York: Routledge, 2003). Combines thematically organized excerpts from major Enlightenment writers with some major 20th-century scholarly interpretations.

Jacob, Margaret C. (ed.), *The Enlightenment: A Brief History with Documents* (Boston: Bedford/St. Martins, 2000). A narrative history accompanied by documents and excerpts, with some unusual choices.

Kramnick, Isaac (ed.), *The Portable Enlightenment Reader* (New York: Penguin, 1995). Massive, thematically organized collection of Enlightenment writings designed to give a broad overview.

OVERVIEWS AND CLASSIC INTERPRETATIONS

Becker, Carl L., *The Heavenly City of the Eighteenth-Century Philosophers* (New Haven: Yale University Press, 1932). Controversial treatment from a leading early 20th-century historian shows the philosophes as having many similarities to the medieval Catholic philosophers they despised.

Cassirer, Ernst, *The Philosophy of the Enlightenment*, translated by Fritz C. A. Koelln and James P. Pettegrove (Princeton: Princeton University Press, 1951). Philosophically oriented study by a leading 20th-century German philosopher and historian of ideas.

Edelstein, Dan, *The Enlightenment: A Genealogy* (Chicago: University of Chicago Press, 2010). Discusses the cultural construction of the idea of "Enlightenment" in the 18th century, argues against the idea of plural Enlightenments in favor of a Francocentric approach.

Ferrone, Vicenzo, *The Enlightenment: History of an Idea*, translated by Elisabetta Tarantino (Princeton: Princeton University Press, 2015). A leading scholar of the Italian Enlightenment emphasizes the importance of the critical spirit of the Enlightenment.

Gay, Peter, *The Enlightenment: An Interpretation* 2 vols. (New York: Alfred A. Knopf, 1969). A survey focusing on big names and big ideas from a self-professed champion of the Enlightenment. Emphasizes the liberating quality of Enlightenment thought and action.

Hampson, Norman, *The Enlightenment* (Harmondsworth and New York: Penguin, 1976). Traces the historical development of the Enlightenment from early optimism to late 18th-century pessimism.

Hazard, Paul, *The Crisis of the European Mind, 1680–1715*, translated by J. Lewis May (New York: New York Review Books, 2013). Classic study emphasizing the importance of the early Enlightenment.

Himmelfarb, Gertrude, *The Roads to Modernity: The British, French, and American Enlightenments* (New York: Knopf, 2004). Contrasts the moderate, and successful, English-speaking Enlightenments with what Himmelfarb views as the radical and disastrous French Enlightenment.

Im Hof, Ulrich, *The Enlightenment*, translated from the German by William E. Yuill (Oxford: Blackwell, 1997). Wide-ranging study putting the European Enlightenment in its social, political, and intellectual contexts.

Israel, Jonathan, *Democratic Enlightenment: Philosophy, Revolution and Human Rights, 1750–1790* (Oxford: Oxford University Press, 2013).

Israel, Jonathan, *Enlightenment Contested: Philosophy, Modernity and the Emancipation of Man, 1670—1752* (Oxford and New York: Oxford University Press, 2006).

Israel, Jonathan, *Radical Enlightenment: Philosophy and the Making of Modernity, 1650–1750* (Oxford and New York: Oxford University Press, 2001).

Israel, Jonathan, *A Revolution of the Mind: Radical Enlightenment and the Intellectual Origins of Modern Democracy* (Princeton: Princeton University Press, 2010). Jonathan Israel's project of putting a materialist and atheist Radical Enlightenment inspired by Baruch Spinoza at the center of thinking about the

Enlightenment, and marginalizing the "moderate Enlightenment" represented by Voltaire, among others, has been both massively influential and extremely controversial in recent Enlightenment studies.

Jacob, Margaret C., *The Radical Enlightenment: Pantheists, Freemasons, and Republicans* (London and Boston: Allen and Unwin, 1981). Focuses on the early 18th century subculture of political and religious radicals, mostly in England and the Dutch Republic.

Munck, Thomas, *The Enlightenment: A Comparative Social History* (New York: Oxford, 2000). A "bottom-up" view of the Enlightenment rather than the traditional "top-down" approach, focusing on the role of Enlightenment in the lives of ordinary people in Europe's great cities.

Outram, Dorinda, *The Enlightenment* (Cambridge: Cambridge University Press, 1995). Synthesis incorporating scholarship on the Enlightenment and gender and the Enlightenment and non-European peoples.

Pagden, Anthony, *The Enlightenment: And Why It Still Matters* (New York: Random House, 2013). Emphasizes the influence and contemporary relevance of the Enlightenment.

Porter, Roy, and Mikulas Teich (eds.), *The Enlightenment in National Context* (Cambridge: Cambridge University Press, 1981). A collection of essays by leading scholars on the Enlightenment in various nations, including lesser-known Enlightenments such as the Swiss Enlightenment.

Zafirovski, Milan, *The Enlightenment and its Effects on Modern Society* (New York: Springer, 2011). Sociologist discusses the impact of Enlightenment ideals on the further development of the West.

SCIENCE

Fara, Patricia, *Fatal Attraction: Magnetic Mysteries of the Enlightenment* (Cambridge: Icon Books, 2005). Not just the science of magnetism, but the role it played in Enlightenment culture.

Hankins, Thomas L., *Science and the Enlightenment* (Cambridge: Cambridge University Press, 1985). Standard history of 18th-century science and the influence of the Enlightenment.

Jacob, Margaret, *Scientific Culture and the Making of the Industrial West* (New York and Oxford: Oxford University Press, 1997). Connects the Newtonian Enlightenment in Britain with the Industrial Revolution and the making of the modern world.

McClellan, James E., III, *Science Reorganized: Scientific Societies in the Eighteenth Century* (New York: Columbia University Press, 1985). A study of the globe-spanning world of Enlightenment scientific societies.

RELIGION

Elmarsafy, Ziad, *The Enlightenment Qur'an: The Politics of Translation and the Construction of Islam* (Oxford: Oneworld, 2009). Examines Enlightenment attitudes towards Islam through the lens of translations and studies of the Qur'an.

Sheehan, Jonathan, *The Enlightenment Bible: Translation, Scholarship, Culture* (Princeton and Oxford: Princeton University Press, 2005). Focuses on England and Protestant Germany to examine how the Bible became "secularized" in the 18th century.

Sorkin, David, *The Religious Enlightenment: Protestants, Jews, and Catholics from London to Vienna* (Princeton: Princeton University Press, 2011). Argues that the anti-religious nature of the Enlightenment has been greatly exaggerated, and there was a series of distinct religious enlightenments.

THE ENLIGHTENMENT IN AMERICA

Landsman, Ned C., *From Colonials to Provincials: American Thought and Culture 1680–1760* (New York: Twayne Publishers, 1997). A broad history of intellectual life in the British colonies of America in the early Enlightenment.

Staloff, Darren, *Hamilton, Adams, Jefferson: The Politics of Enlightenment and the American Founding* (New York: Hill and Wang, 2005). The influence of Enlightenment ideas on the American founding, through studies of three very different Enlightened Americans.

Wood, Gordon S., *The Radicalism of the American Revolution* (New York: Vintage, 1993). The influence of culture and ideas on the American revolutionaries.

THE ENLIGHTENMENT IN BRITAIN

Buchan, James, *Crowded with Genius: The Scottish Enlightenment: Edinburgh's Moment of the Mind* (New York: Harper Collins, 2003). A pleasantly written combination of the social and intellectual history of the city.

Porter, Roy, *The Creation of the Modern World: The Untold Story of the British Enlightenment* (New York and London: W. W. Norton, 2000). A voluminous work covering a multitude of English and Scottish thinkers and arguing for Britain's equal importance with France in the history of the Enlightenment.

Porter, Roy, *Flesh in the Age of Reason: The Modern Foundations of Body and Soul* (New York and London: W. W. Norton, 2003). A massive study of the body in 18th-century Britain, encompassing both the Enlightenment and reactions to it.

Stewart, Larry, *The Rise of Public Science: Rhetoric, Technology, and Natural Philosophy in Newtonian Britain, 1660–1750* (Cambridge: Cambridge University Press, 1992). The impact of Newtonianism on Enlightenment Britain.

THE ENLIGHTENMENT IN FRANCE

Cranston, Maurice, *Philosophers and Pamphleteers: Political Theorists of the Enlightenment* (Oxford: Oxford University Press, 1986). Despite its general title, focuses exclusively on the "big names" of the French Enlightenment, including Montesquieu, Voltaire, and Rousseau.

Darnton, Robert, *The Business of Enlightenment: A Publishing History of the Encyclo-pédie, 1775–1800* (Cambridge, MA: Belknap Press of Harvard University Press, 1979). Massive, groundbreaking study of the production and distribution of the *Encyclopédie*.

Darnton, Robert, *The Literary Underground of the Old Regime* (Cambridge, MA: Harvard University Press, 1982). Tracks the numerous pamphleteers and por-nographers who made up the underbelly of French Enlightenment culture.

Darnton, Robert, *Mesmerism and the End of the Enlightenment in France* (Cambridge, Massachusetts and London, England: Harvard University Press, 1968). Argues that, by the late 18th century, Enlightenment in France was being swept away by a tide of irrationalism.

Gay, Peter, *The Party of Humanity: Essays in the French Enlightenment* (New York: Knopf, 1964). Traditional intellectual history, with an emphasis on Voltaire and Rousseau.

McManners, John, *Death and the Enlightenment: Changing Attitudes to Death among Christians and Unbelievers in Eighteenth-Century France* (Oxford: Oxford University Press, 1981). Considers the impact of the Enlightenment on French cul-ture by examining how 18th-century French people faced death.

Roche, Daniel, *France in the Enlightenment*, translated by Arthur Goldhammer (Cambridge, MA: Harvard University Press, 2000). History of France from the death of Louis XIV in 1715 to the dawn of the French Revolution in 1789, foregrounding the Enlightenment.

Steinbrugge, Lieselott, *The Moral Sex: Woman's Nature in the French Enlightenment*, translated by Pamela Selwyn (New York: Oxford University Press, 1995). Finds the root of modern conceptions of women's nature in the Enlightenment.

THE ENLIGHTENMENT IN GERMANY

Behrens, C. B. A., *Society, Government, and the Enlightenment: The Experiences of Eighteenth-Century France and Prussia* (London: Thames and Hudson, 1985). Comparative study emphasizes the impact of the Enlightenment on Prussian governance.

Brunschwig, Henri, *Enlightenment and Romanticism in Eighteenth-Century Prussia*, translated by Frank Jellinek (Chicago and London: University of Chicago Press, 1974). The Prussian Enlightenment and the transition to Romanticism in their social and political contexts.

Reed, T. J., *Light in Germany: Scenes from an Unknown Enlightenment* (Chicago: University of Chicago Press, 2015). A champion of the German Enlightenment as-serts its richness and value.

THE ENLIGHTENMENT IN ITALY

Cochrane, Eric, *Tradition and Enlightenment in the Tuscan Academies 1690–1800* (Chicago: University of Chicago Press, 1961). A study of the impact of the

Enlightenment on the Della Crusca Academy in Florence, with implications for Italian elite culture as a whole.

Ferrone, Vincenzo, *The Intellectual Roots of the Italian Enlightenment: Newtonian Science, Religion, and Politics in the Early Eighteenth Century*, translated by Sue Brotherton (Atlantic Highlands: Humanities Press, 1995).

Venturi, Franco, *Italy and the Enlightenment: Studies in a Cosmopolitan Century*, translated by Susan Corsi (London: Longman, 1972). Classic study helped put the Italian Enlightenment on the map in Anglophone scholarship.

THE JEWISH ENLIGHTENMENT

Feiner, Shmuel, *The Jewish Enlightenment*, translated by Chaya Naor (Philadelphia: University of Pennsylvania Press, 2011). Treats the Jewish Enlightenment in its European context.

Ruderman, David B., *Jewish Enlightenment in a New Key: Anglo-Jewry's Construction of Modern Jewish Thought* (Princeton and Oxford: Princeton University Press, 2000). Ruderman argues convincingly that the Anglo-Jewish contribution to the Jewish Enlightenment has been undervalued in comparison with the German.

SOCIAL HISTORY

Goldgar, Anne, *Impolite Learning: Conduct and Community in the Republic of Letters 1680–1750* (New Haven: Yale University Press, 1995). Traces the development of an international community of scholars in the early decades of the Enlightenment.

Jacob, Margaret C., *Living the Enlightenment: Freemasonry and Politics in Eighteenth-Century Europe* (New York: Oxford University Press, 1991). Argues for the importance of Masonic lodges in spreading Enlightened ideas.

WEBSITES

Electronic Enlightenment, http://www.e-enlightenment.com/index.html (accessed August 11, 2015). Subscription service offering a networked set of Enlightenment letters and supporting materials.

The French Book Trade in Enlightenment Europe, http://fbtee.uws.edu.au/main/ (accessed August 11, 2015). Expanding site with a database tracking the circulation of French-language books across 18th-century Europe and video tutorials on how to use it.

The Thomas Jefferson Papers at the Library of Congress, http://memory.loc.gov/ammem/mtjhtml/mtjhome.html (accessed August 11, 2015). A huge collection of transcriptions of Jefferson manuscripts covering every phase of his life.

Tout Voltaire, https://artfl-project.uchicago.edu/tout-voltaire (accessed August 20, 2015). Searchable database of Voltaire's writing, excluding the correspondence available at the Electronic Enlightenment.

Index

About the Author and Contributors

WILLIAM E. BURNS is a historian who lives in the Washington, DC, area. His interests include the Enlightenment, British history, the early modern world, and the history of science. Some of his recent books include *Science and Technology in Colonial America* (2005); *Knowledge and Power: Science in World History* (2011); and *The Scientific Revolution in Global Perspective* (2015).

SHAMA ADAMS is a PhD candidate at Curtin University in Perth, Western Australia. She holds a BA and a BSocSc (Honours I), and her MA thesis explored notions of Enlightenment and constructions of art historical narratives in Sir John Soane's Museum in London. Shama's doctoral thesis focuses on the historiography of the concept of progress, and its centrality to both the Enlightenment, and the development of modern understandings of history. Shama is a current editor of the *International Journal of Humanities and Cultural Studies*. She also has worked as an editor for the Australian Edition of the United Nation's Public Policy and Society Youth Journal, *Perspectives*; Penn State University's "ICIK E-News"; Curtin University's *Graduate Humanities Journal*; and Leiden University's *Journal of the LUCAS Graduate Conference*. Shama has presented her research at numerous graduate and professional conferences, most recently in Leiden, Oxford, Melbourne, Ghent, and Sydney. Shama currently is working on completing her dissertation, and writing several articles for peer-reviewed publication.

MICHAEL HILL received his PhD in history from Georgetown University. His current work explores English conceptions of tropical climates in the

Atlantic world. He has taught at Georgetown University and the University of Mary Washington.

GEORGE A. KLAEREN is a doctoral student in the department of history at the University of Kansas. His thesis, "Encountering the Enlightenment: New Science, Religion, and Catholic Epistemologies across the Iberian Atlantic, 1680–1815," examines the way that traditional modes of thinking intersected with the new philosophies of the enlightenment in the Spanish empire. He is particularly interested at the history of the dialogue between religion, science, and magic and is currently working on the history of the philosophy of science in 18th-century Spain.

MARTIN J. MANNING is a research librarian in the Bureau of International Information Programs, U.S. Department of State, Washington, DC, on the American Spaces Team. Manning also is archivist of the Public Diplomacy Historical Collection, a position he also held with the bureau's predecessor, the United States Information Agency, from 1978–1999. His areas of research and expertise include popular culture, world's fairs, propaganda, New England culture, and library history. He has a BS from Boston College and an MSLS from Catholic University of America. He is a frequent contributor to ABC-CLIO publications, and is co-editor of *Media and Propaganda in Wartime America*, with Clarence Wyatt (2010).

ALEXANDER MAXWELL studied at the University of California-Davis, Georg-August University in Goettingen, and the Central European University in Budapest, before completing his PhD in history at the University of Wisconsin–Madison. He taught history at the University of Swansea, Wales, and the University of Nevada–Reno before taking his present position at Victoria University of Wellington in New Zealand. His first book, *Choosing Slovakia*, appeared in 2009. He translated an important Pan-Slav tract from English to German; it was published in 2009, with a lengthy introduction. Maxwell edited *The East-West Discourse* and a festschrift for Miroslav Hroch. He has published widely on nationalism theory, the history of Slovakia and Hungary, and history pedagogy. His most recent book, *Patriots against Fashion*, appeared in 2014.

MATTHEW QUEST received his PhD in American Studies from Brown University. He has taught American History, World History, Atlantic World History, and Africana Studies courses most recently for Georgia State University. Quest wrote his doctoral dissertation and has published many articles on C. L. R. James, best known as the author of *The Black Jacobins*, the classic history of the Haitian Revolution.